Péigenz

Translator : Je-wa Jeong
Editor : Je-wa Jeong / Soung Lee
Production Artist : Soung Lee
US Cover Design : Franco Errico
Production Manager : Jay Chung
Art Director : Yuki Chung
Marketing : Nicole Curry
President : Robert Kuo

English version production by
ComicsOne Corp. and Infinity Studios
www.infinitystudioz.com

Peigenz Volume 1 © 2000
by Park, Sung Woo
All Rights Reserved.
Original Korean edition
published 2000 by
Samyang Publishing
Co., Ltd. Seoul.

This English translation
rights arranged with Samyoung
Publishing Co., Ltd. through
Shin Won Agency Co. in Korea

Publisher
ComicsOne Corporation
48531 Warm Springs Blvd., Suite 408
Freemont, CA 94539

First Edition : July 2004
ISDN 1-58899-004-4

Volume
1

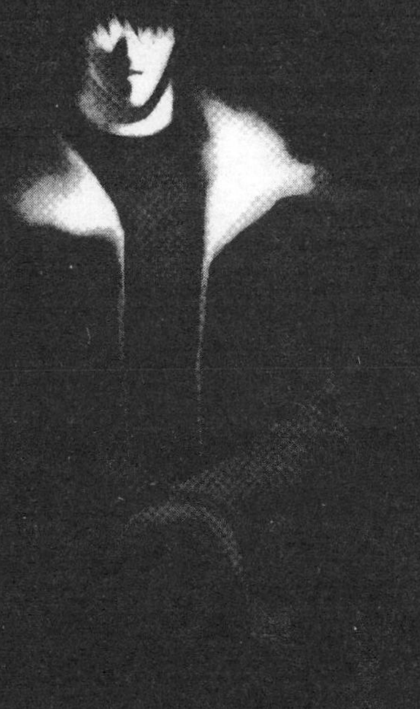

[Péigenz]

CONTENTS

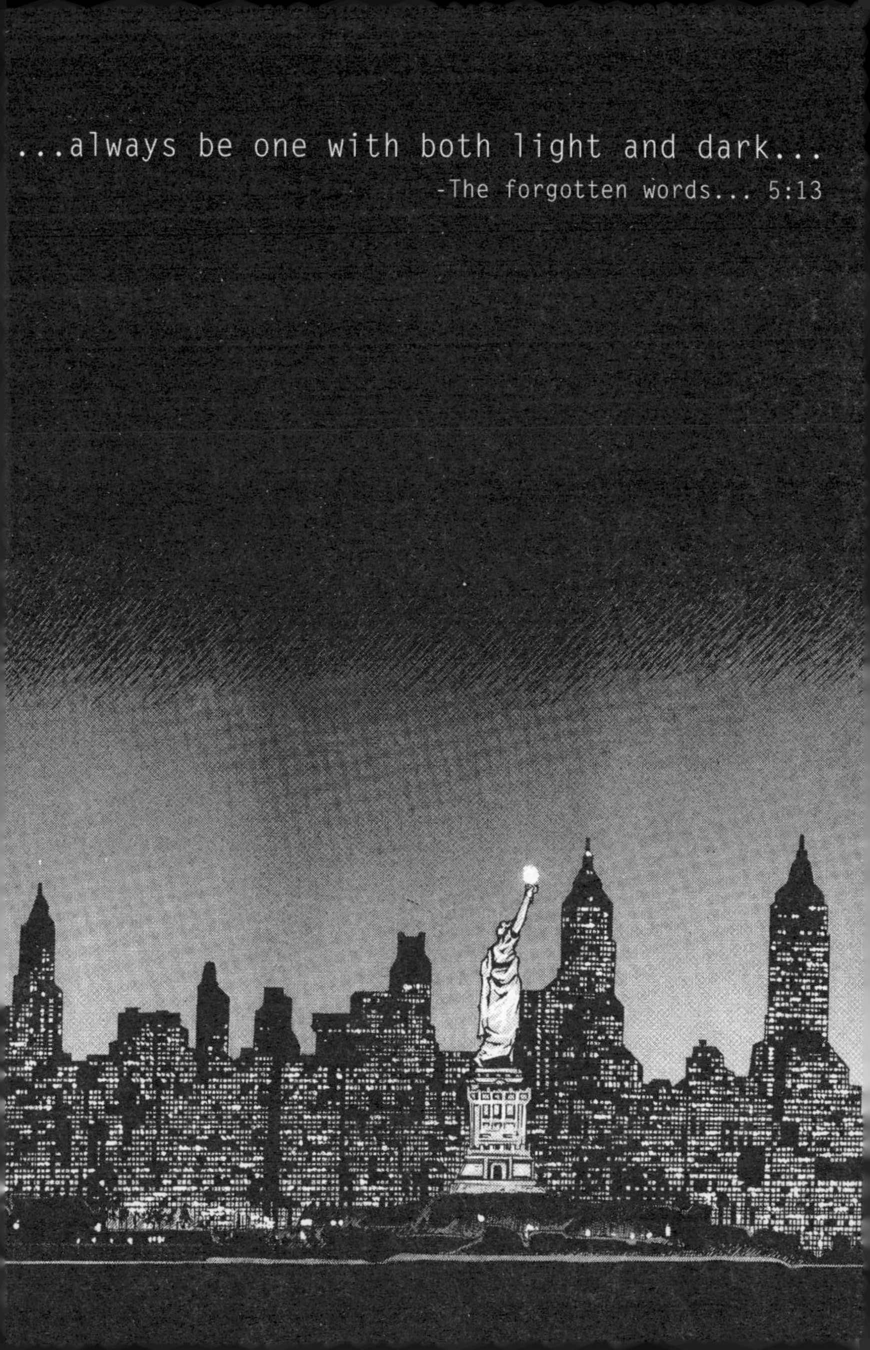
...always be one with both light and dark...
-The forgotten words... 5:13

revelation 0 : Foreigner

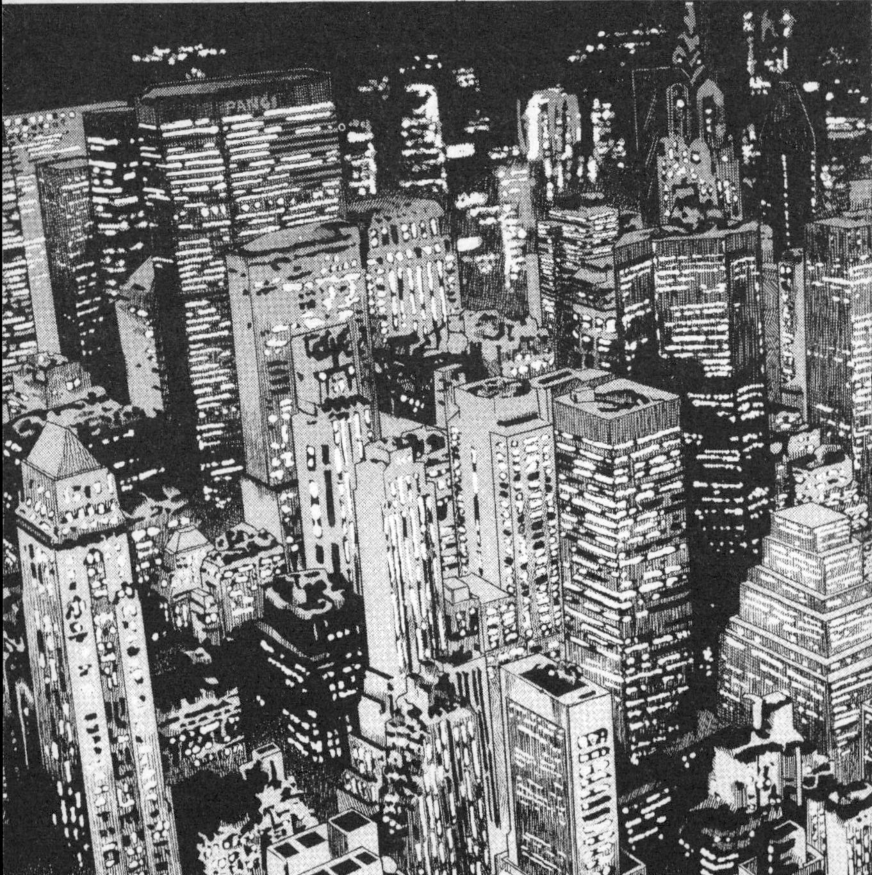

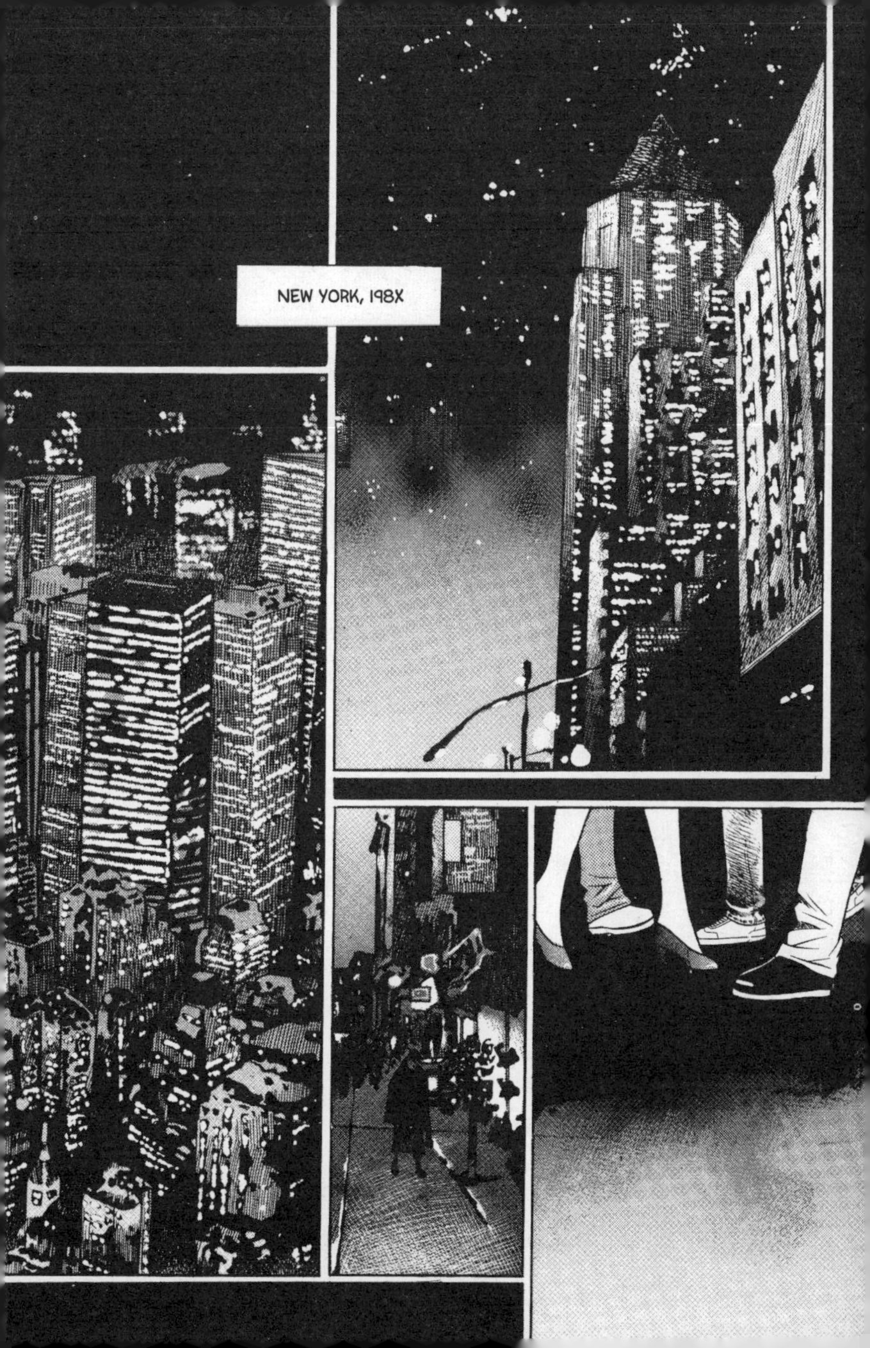
NEW YORK, 198X

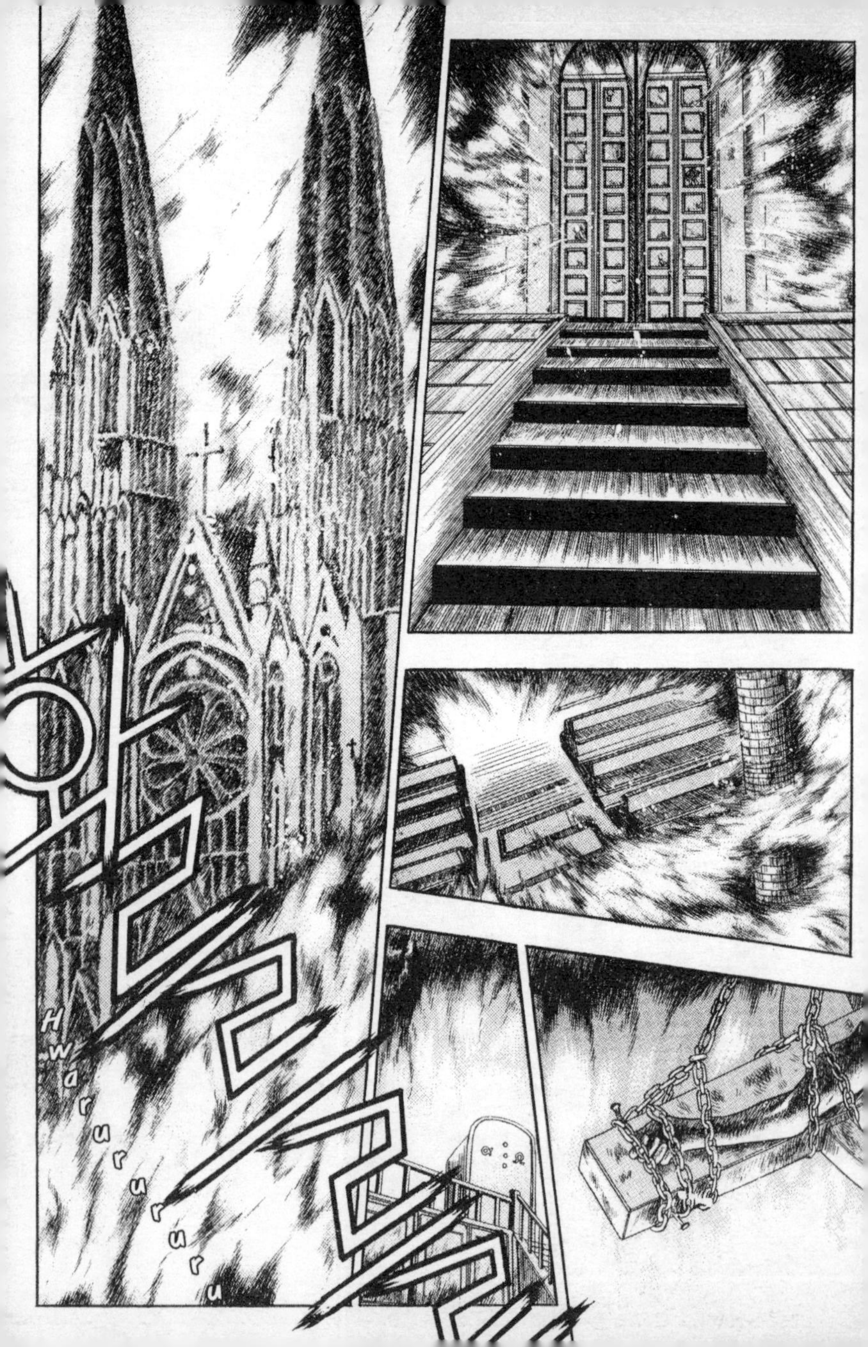
Hwarurururu

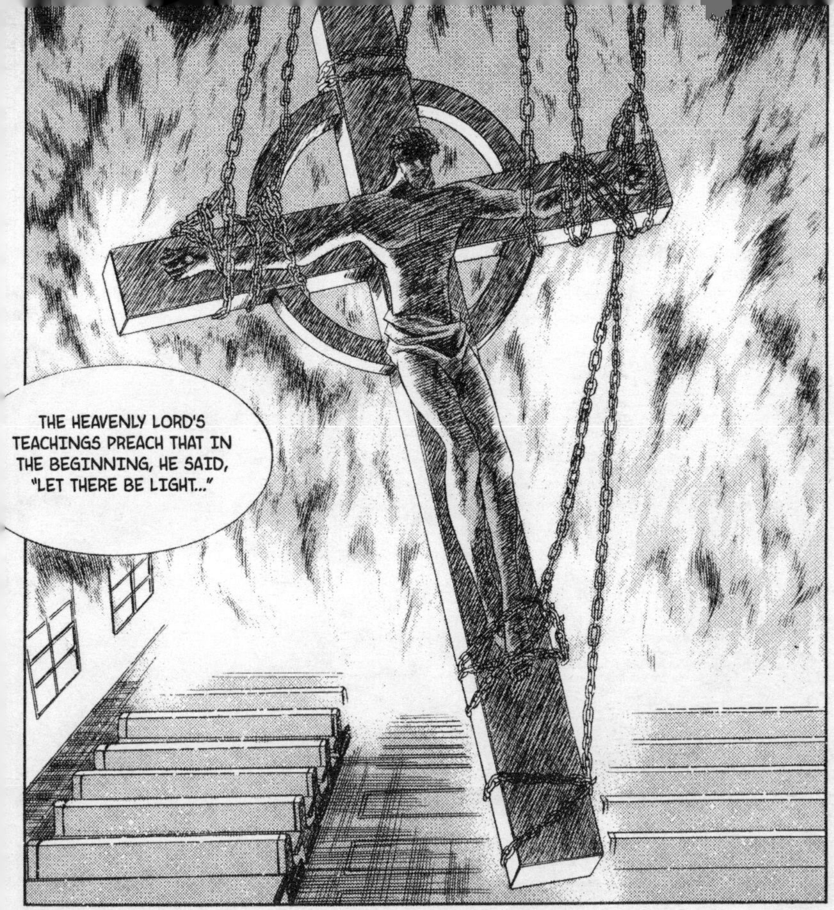
THE HEAVENLY LORD'S TEACHINGS PREACH THAT IN THE BEGINNING, HE SAID, "LET THERE BE LIGHT..."
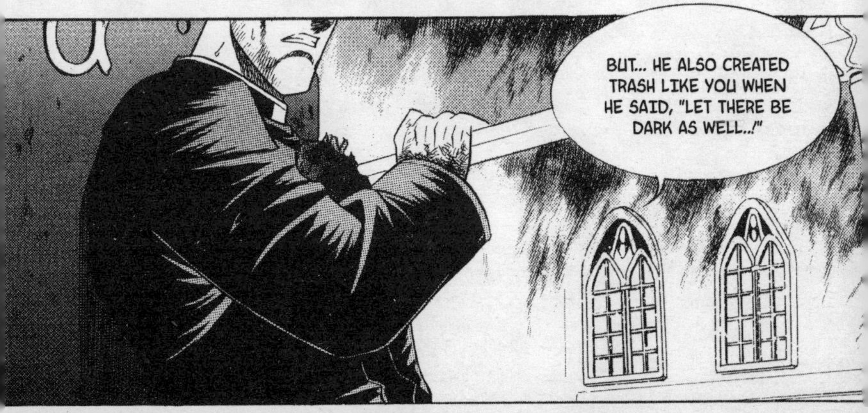
BUT... HE ALSO CREATED TRASH LIKE YOU WHEN HE SAID, "LET THERE BE DARK AS WELL..!"

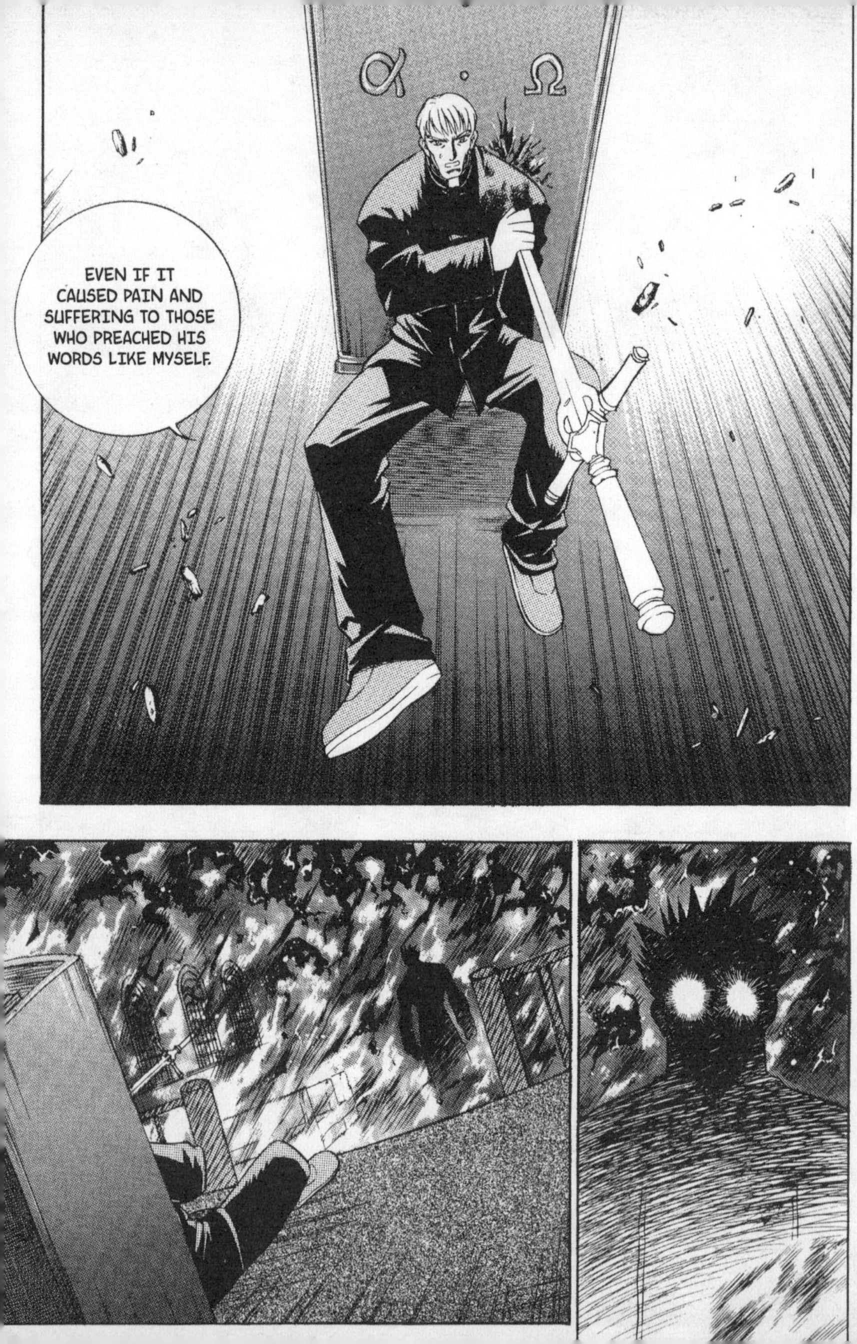
EVEN IF IT CAUSED PAIN AND SUFFERING TO THOSE WHO PREACHED HIS WORDS LIKE MYSELF.

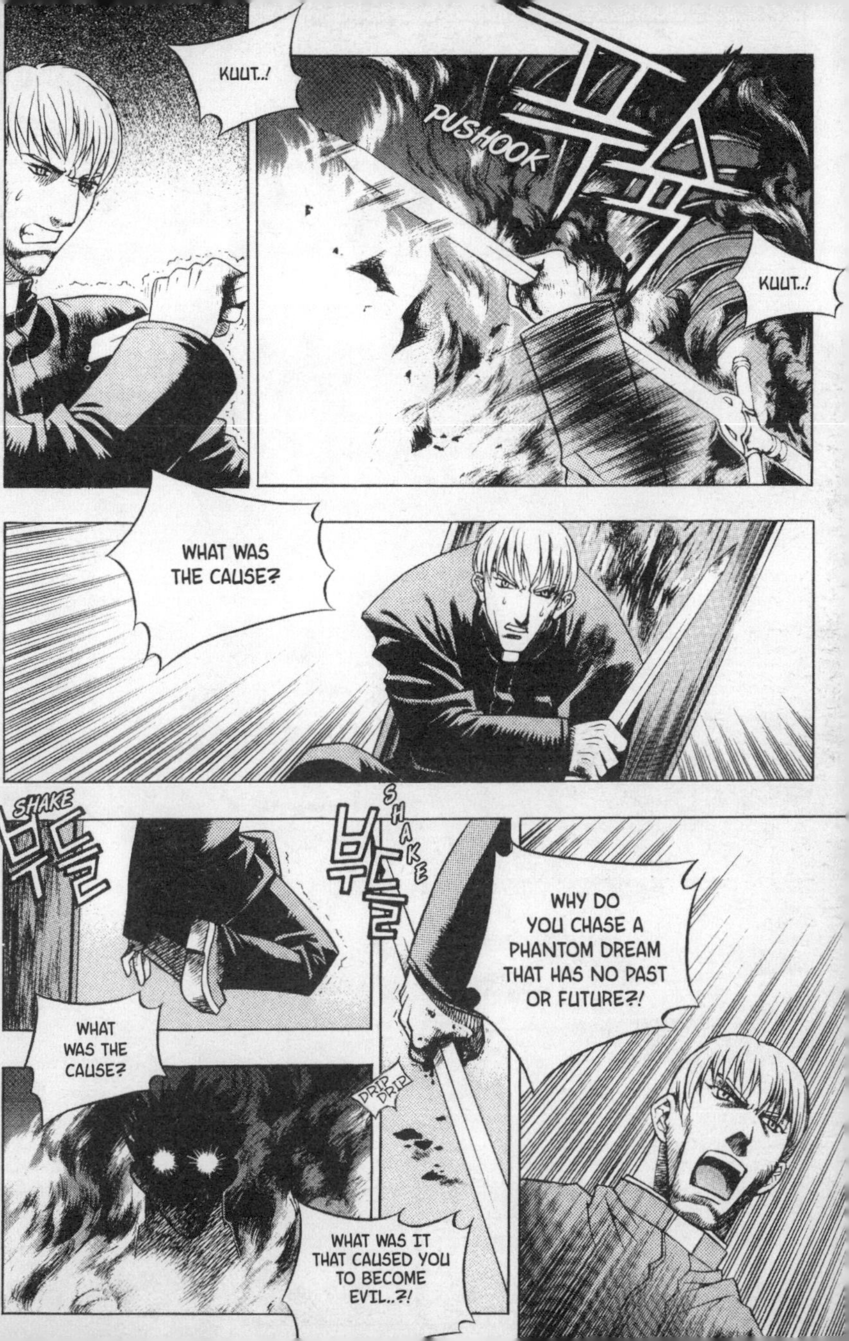
KUUT..!
PUSHOOK
KUUT..!
WHAT WAS THE CAUSE?
SHAKE
WHAT WAS THE CAUSE?
WHAT WAS IT THAT CAUSED YOU TO BECOME EVIL..?!
SHAKE
DRIP DRIP
WHY DO YOU CHASE A PHANTOM DREAM THAT HAS NO PAST OR FUTURE?!

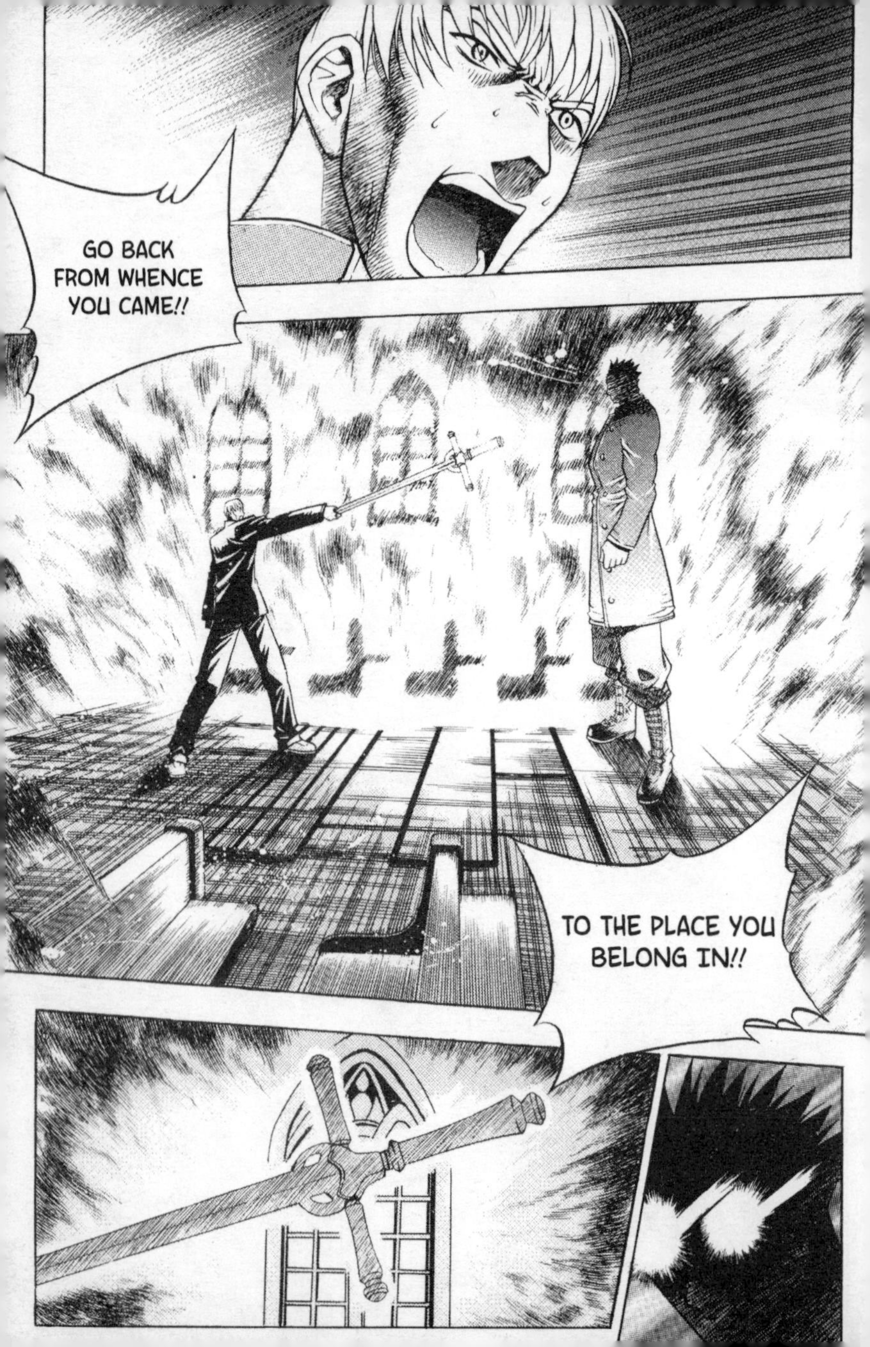
GO BACK FROM WHENCE YOU CAME!!
TO THE PLACE YOU BELONG IN!!

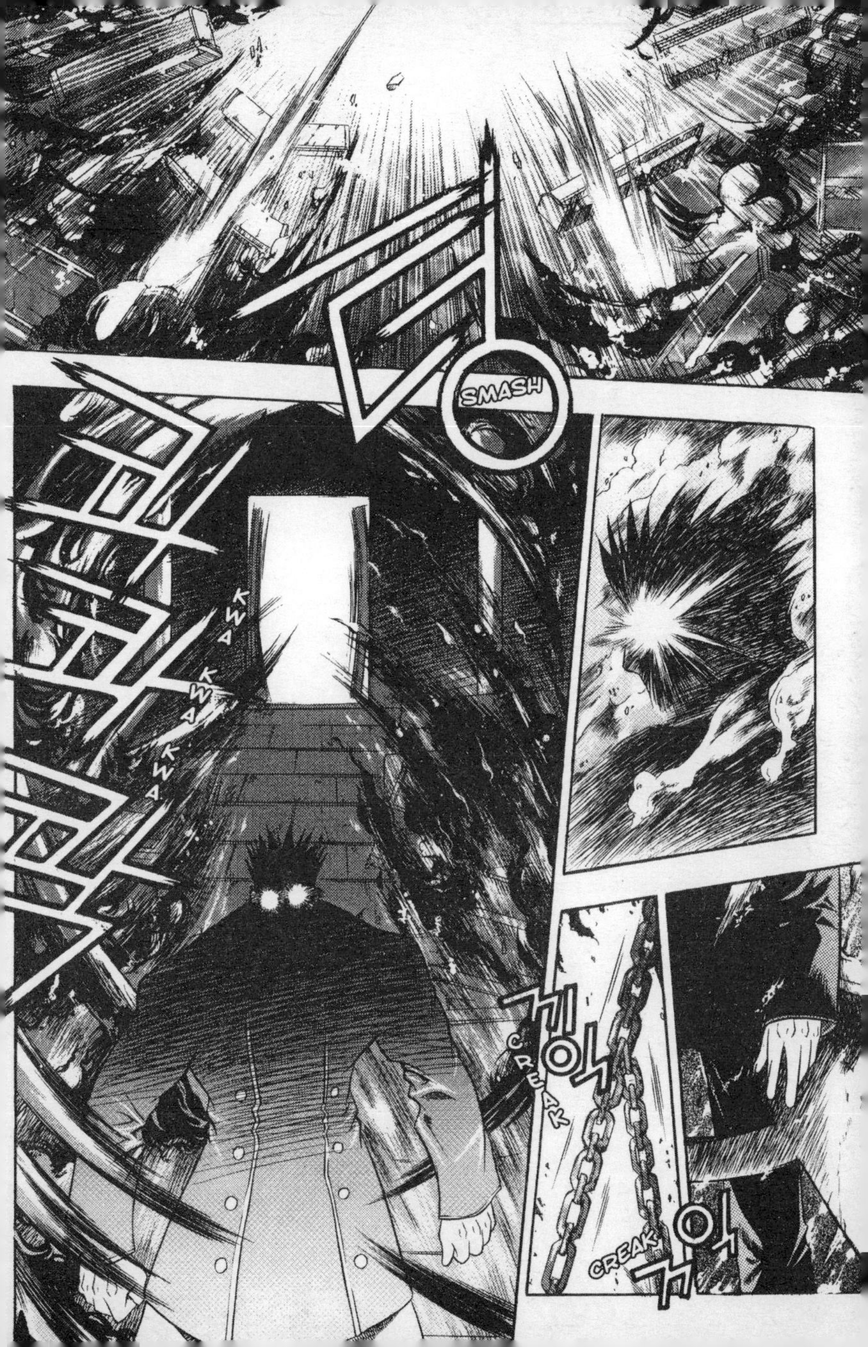
SMASH
KWA KWA KWA
CREAK
CREAK

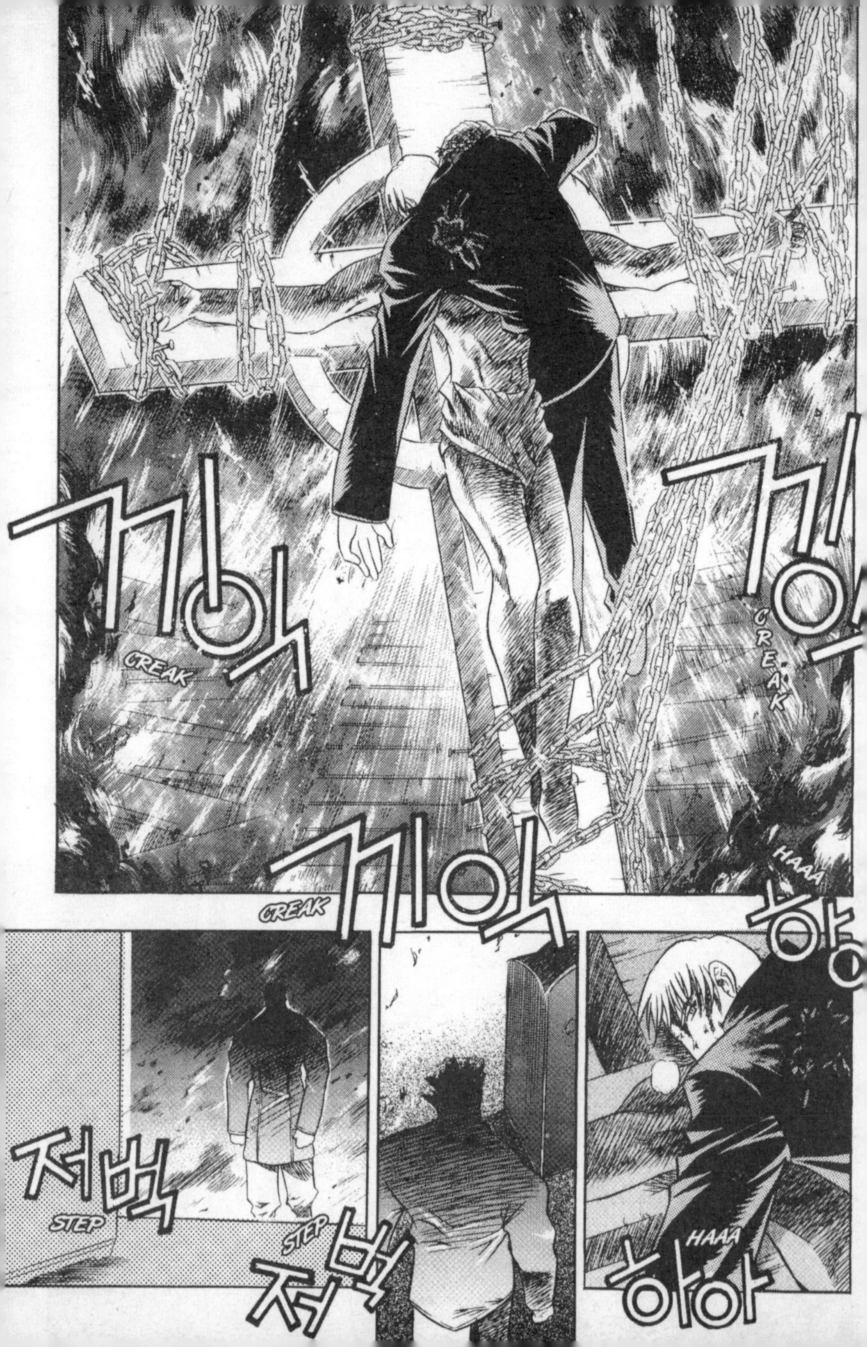
끼이익
CREAK
끼익
CREAK
CREAK
끼이익
HAAA
하아
저벅
STEP
STEP
저벅
HAAA
하아

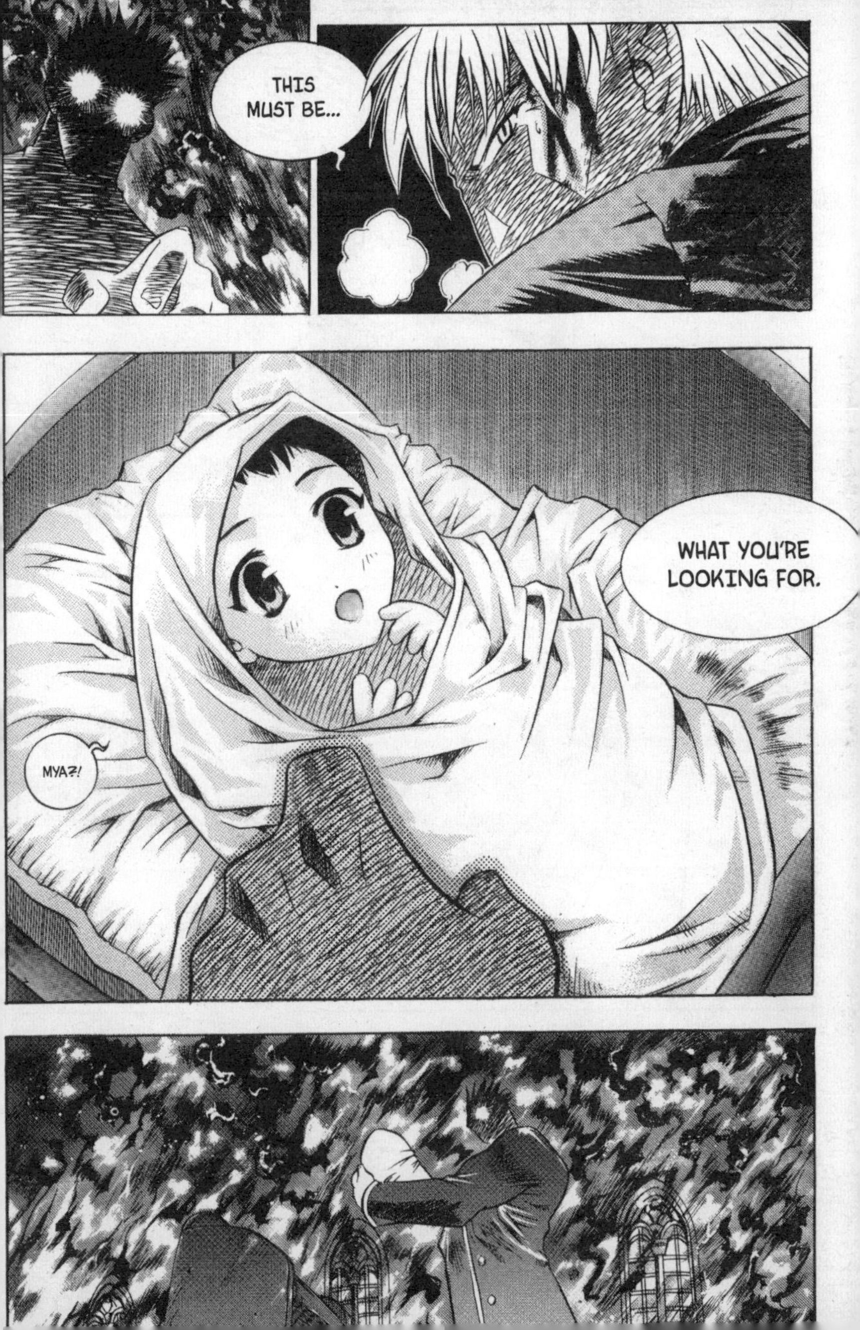
THIS MUST BE...
WHAT YOU'RE LOOKING FOR.
MYA?!

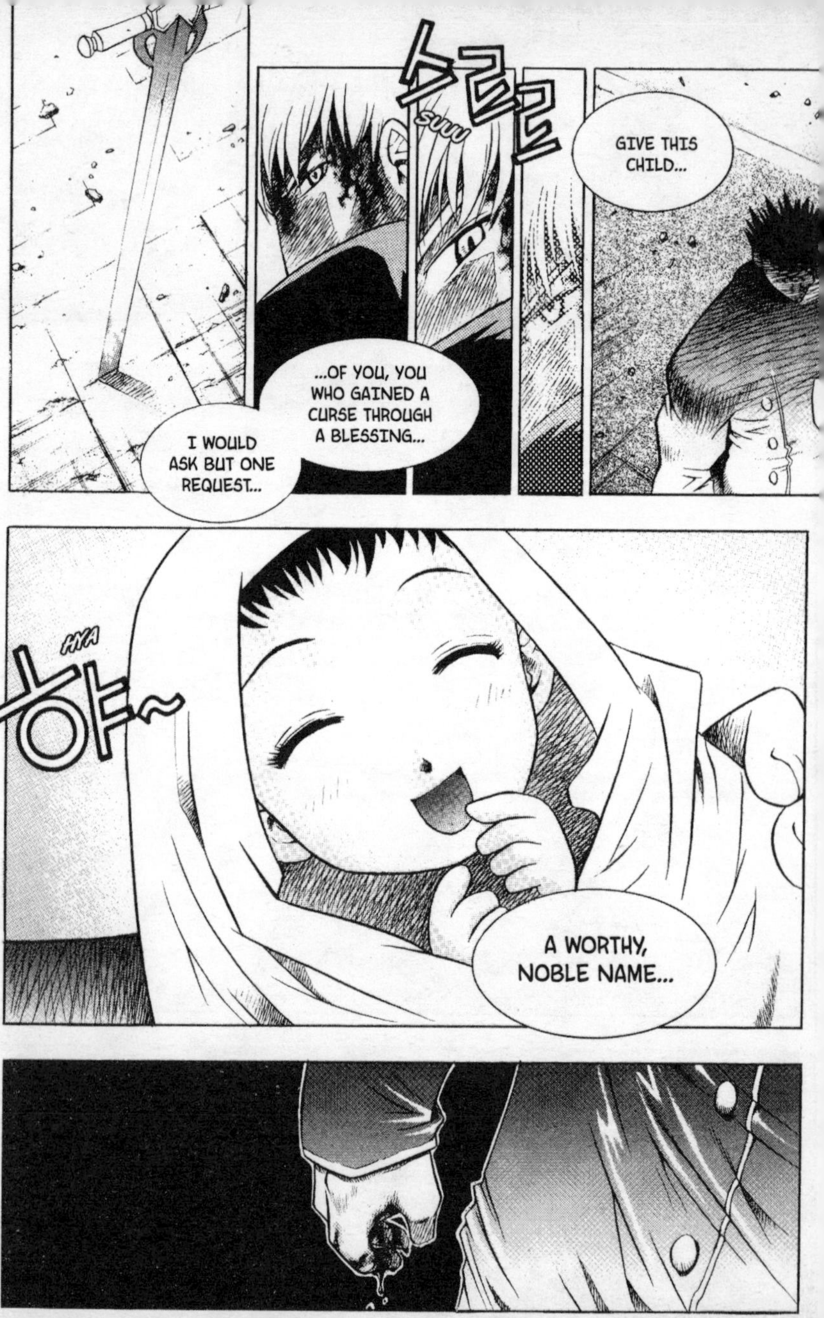

I WOULD ASK BUT ONE REQUEST...
...OF YOU, YOU WHO GAINED A CURSE THROUGH A BLESSING...
스르르
SUUU
GIVE THIS CHILD...
햐~
HYA
A WORTHY, NOBLE NAME...

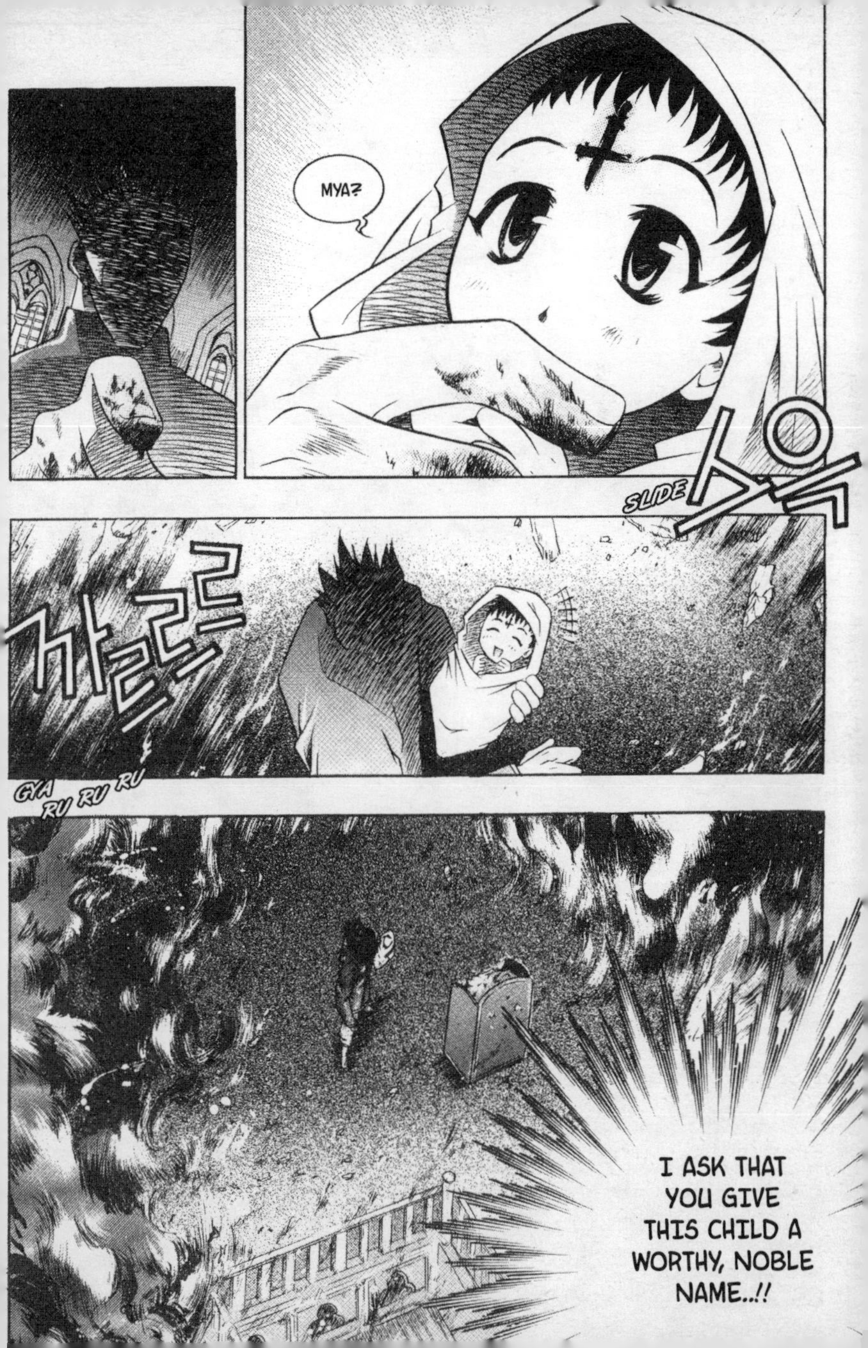
MYA?
SLIDE
GYA RU RU RU
I ASK THAT YOU GIVE THIS CHILD A WORTHY, NOBLE NAME..!!

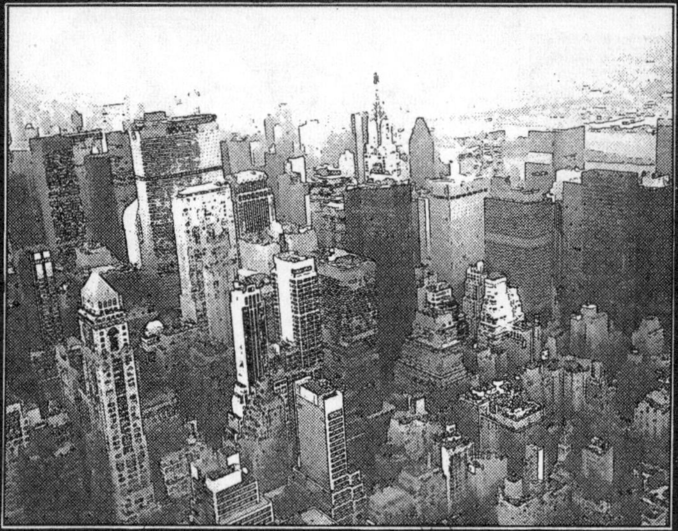

On July 7th of 2001,
a new city was born.

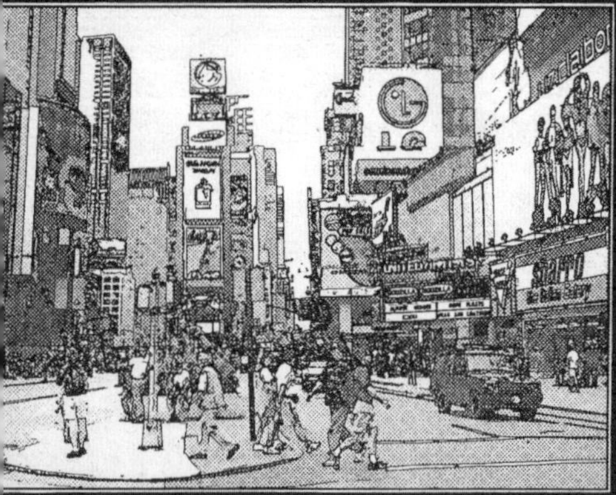

The poor and social outcasts from all across the U.S. were cast into this city along with immigrants from third world countries.

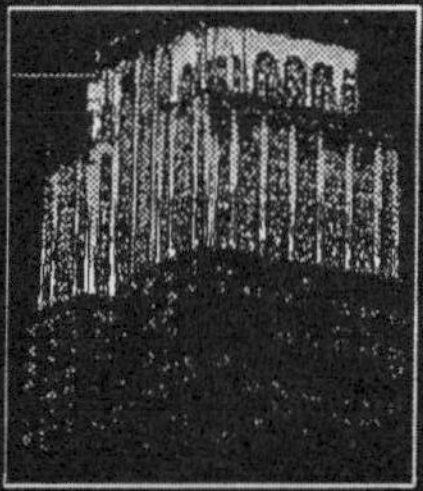

As a result of the population size, the demand for goods made the city the 2nd largest market economy in the U.S. Large corporations and black markets sprang up to meet all sorts of demands...

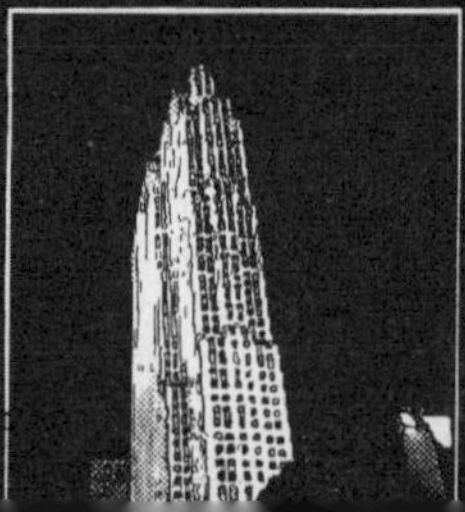

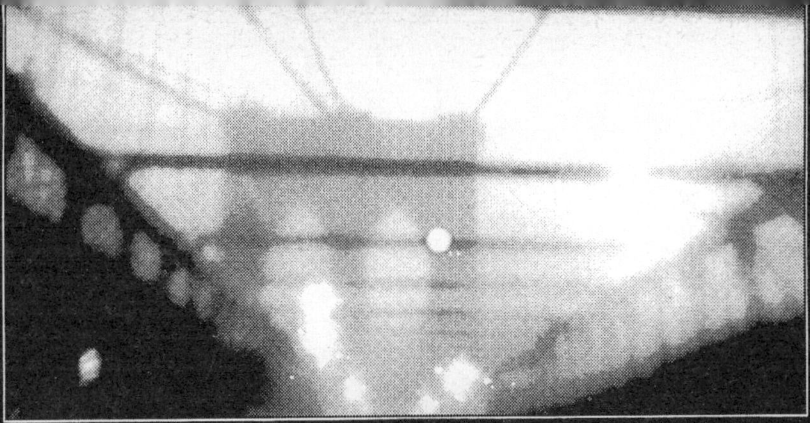

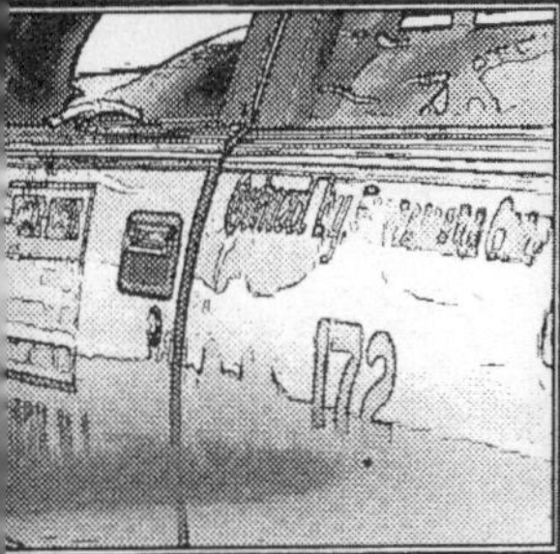

However, any city in the U.S. with a large population of the poverty stricken and criminals...

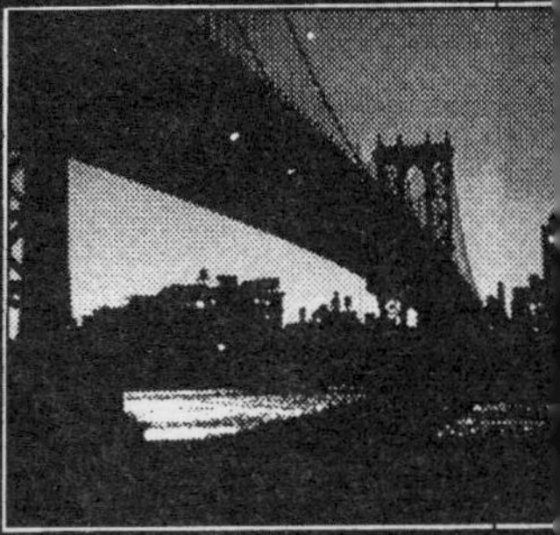

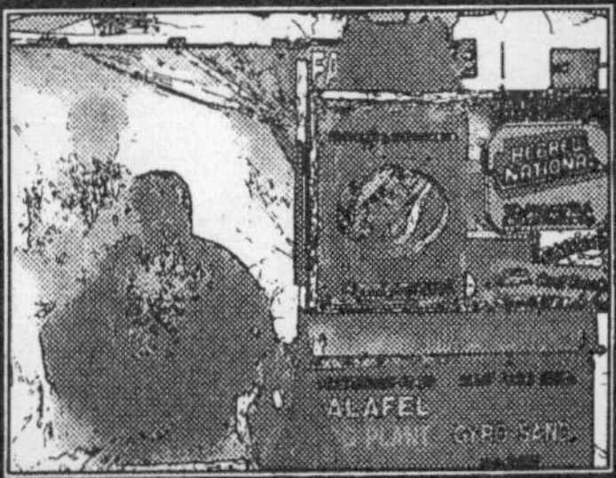

...is considered nothing but a problematic headache and was treated like a waste dump.

Those who unfortunately had to live here...

...called this N.O.A. City (Necropolis of America).

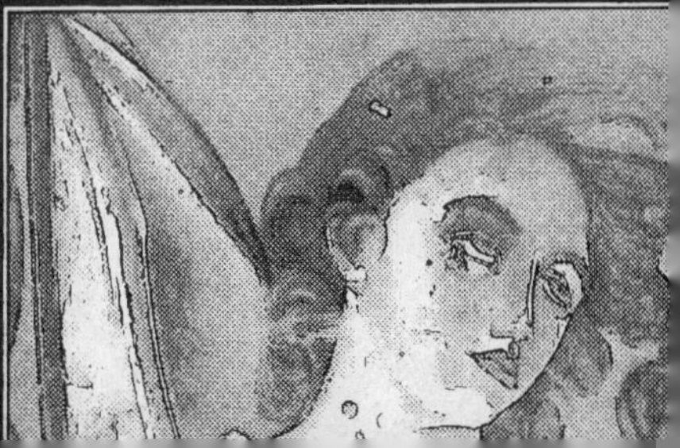

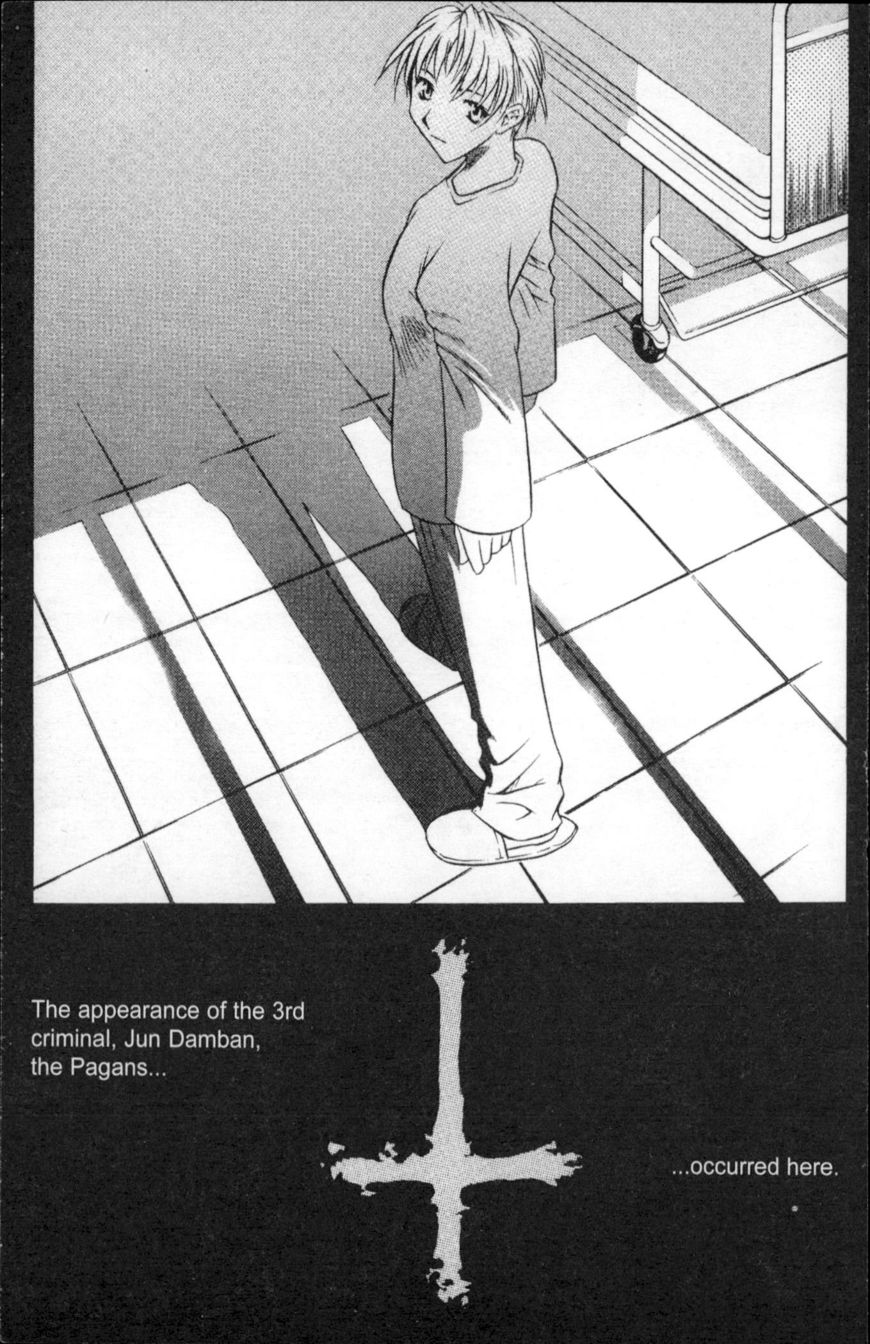
The appearance of the 3rd criminal, Jun Damban, the Pagans...
...occurred here.

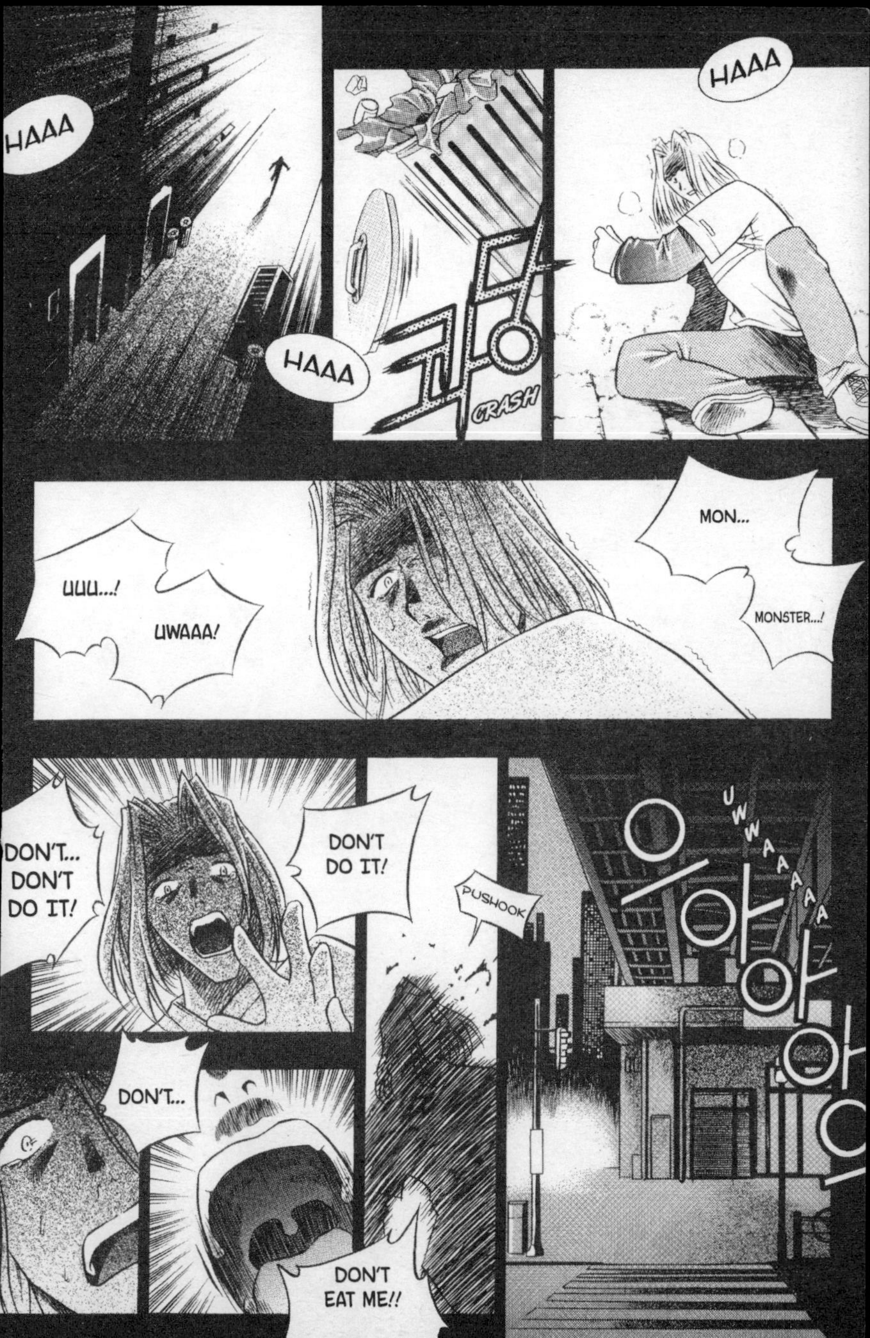
HAAA
HAAA
CRASH
HAAA
UUU...!
UWAAA!
MON...
MONSTER...!
DON'T... DON'T DO IT!
DON'T DO IT!
DON'T...
DON'T EAT ME!!
PUSHOOK
UWWAAAAAA

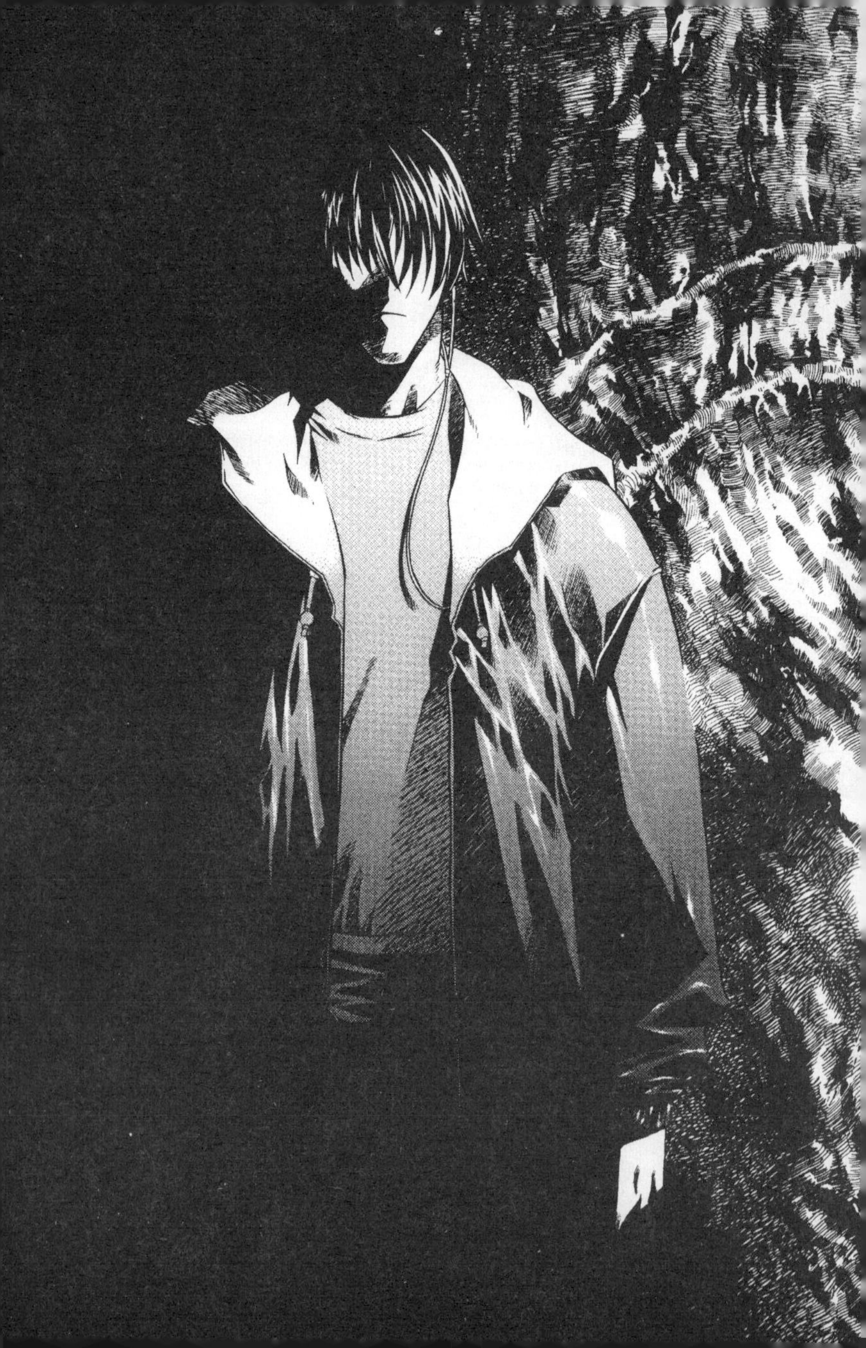

revelation 1 : J-α

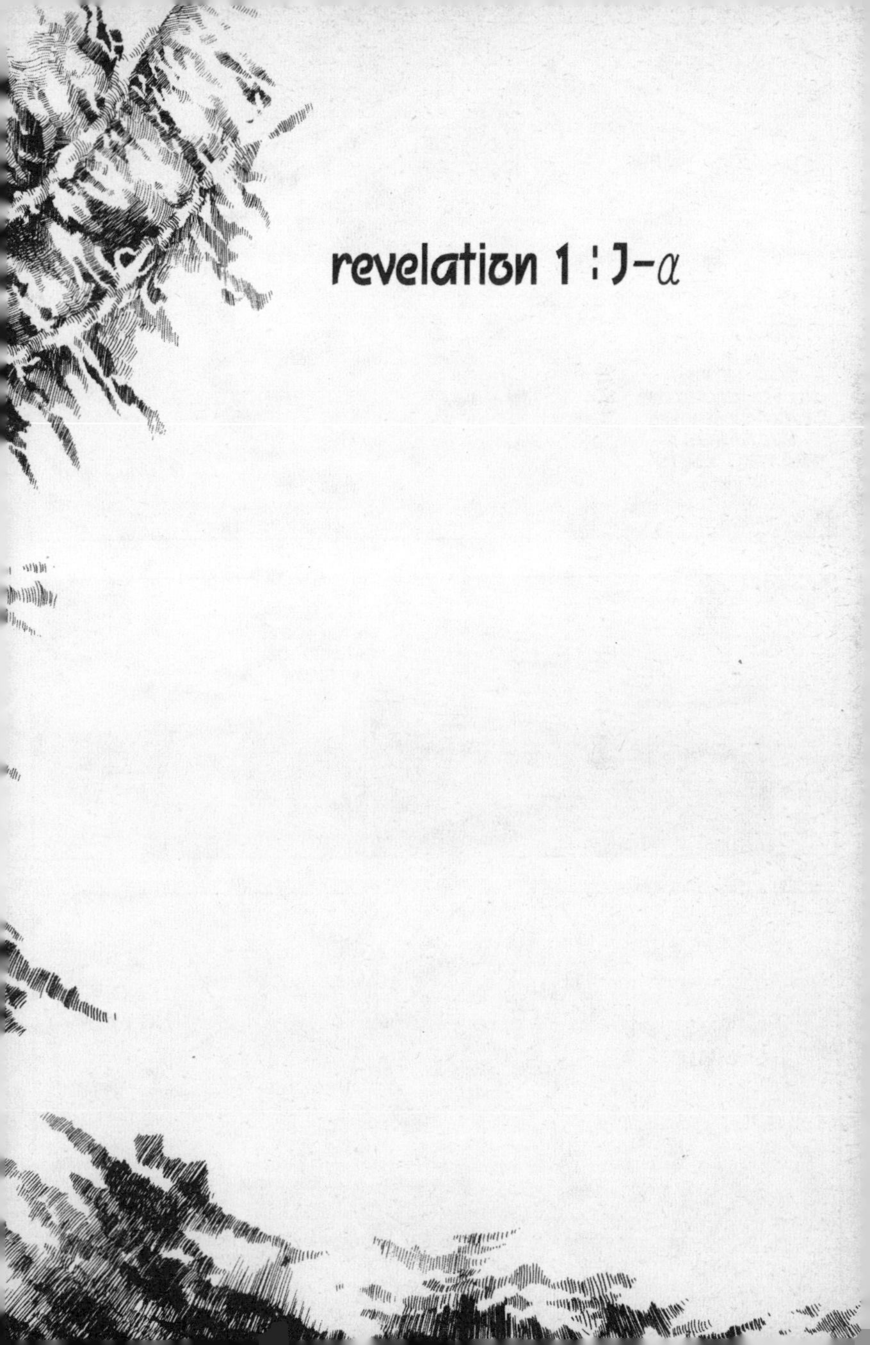

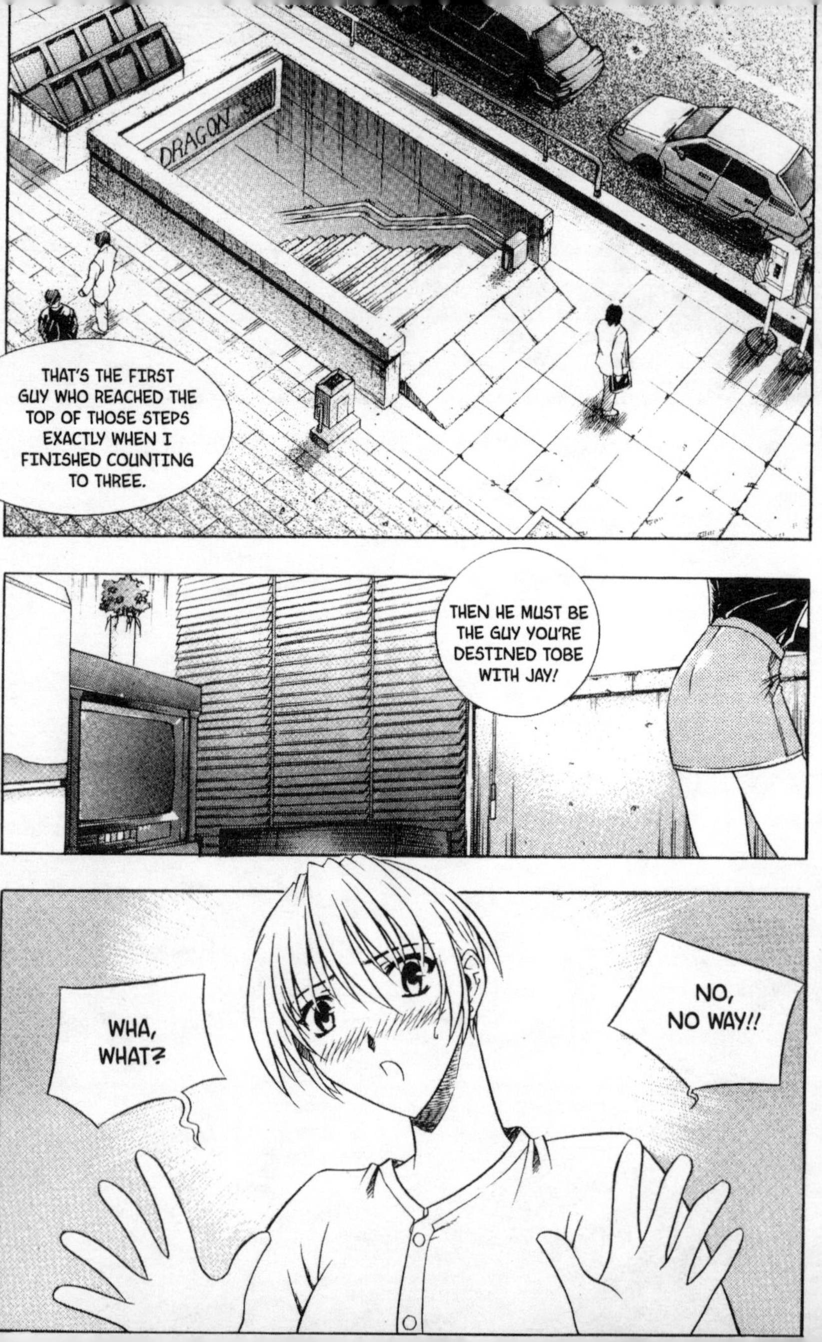
DRAGON
THAT'S THE FIRST GUY WHO REACHED THE TOP OF THOSE STEPS EXACTLY WHEN I FINISHED COUNTING TO THREE.
THEN HE MUST BE THE GUY YOU'RE DESTINED TOBE WITH JAY!
WHA, WHAT?
NO, NO WAY!!

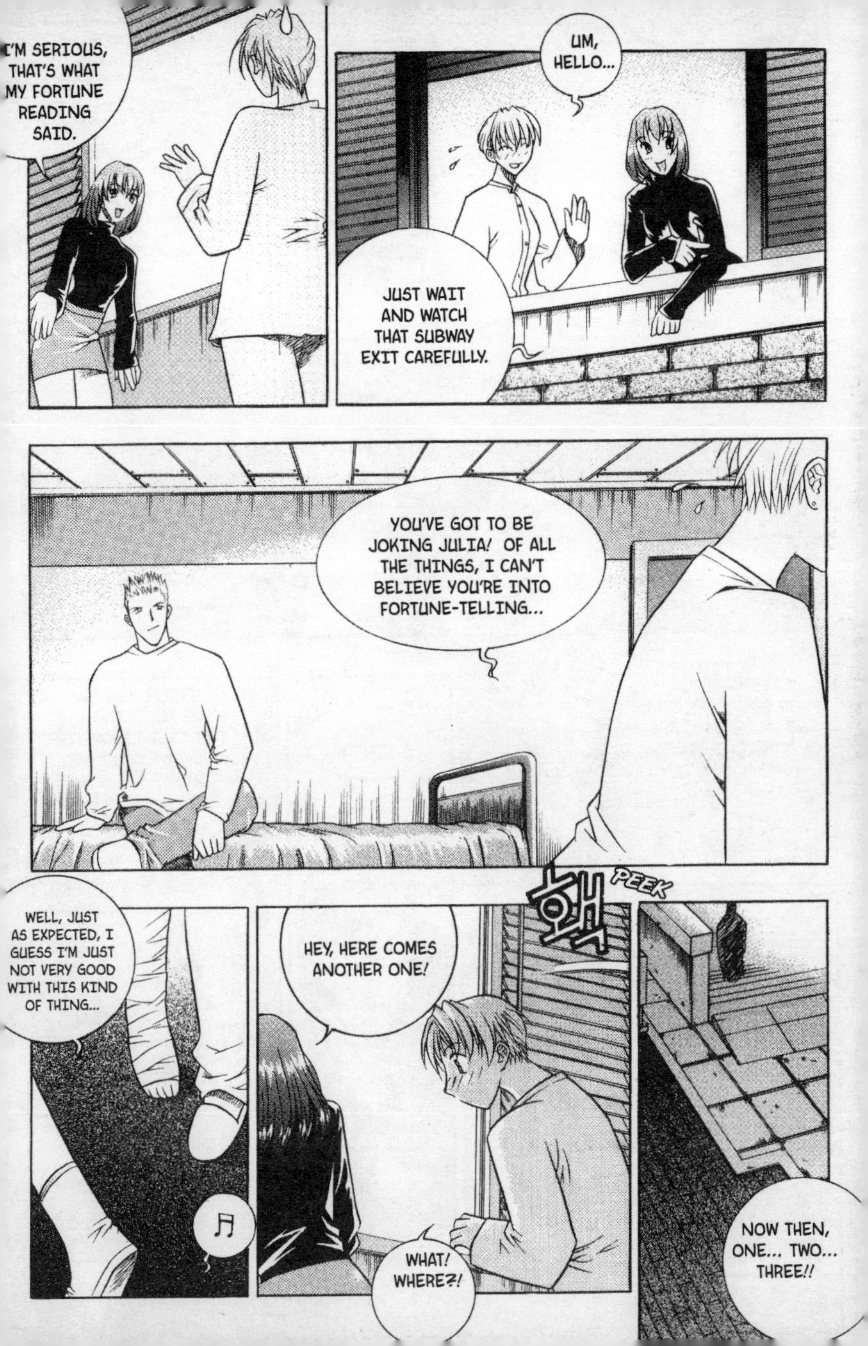
I'M SERIOUS, THAT'S WHAT MY FORTUNE READING SAID.
UM, HELLO...
JUST WAIT AND WATCH THAT SUBWAY EXIT CAREFULLY.
YOU'VE GOT TO BE JOKING JULIA! OF ALL THE THINGS, I CAN'T BELIEVE YOU'RE INTO FORTUNE-TELLING...
WELL, JUST AS EXPECTED, I GUESS I'M JUST NOT VERY GOOD WITH THIS KIND OF THING...
HEY, HERE COMES ANOTHER ONE!
PEEK
WHAT! WHERE?!
NOW THEN, ONE... TWO... THREE!!

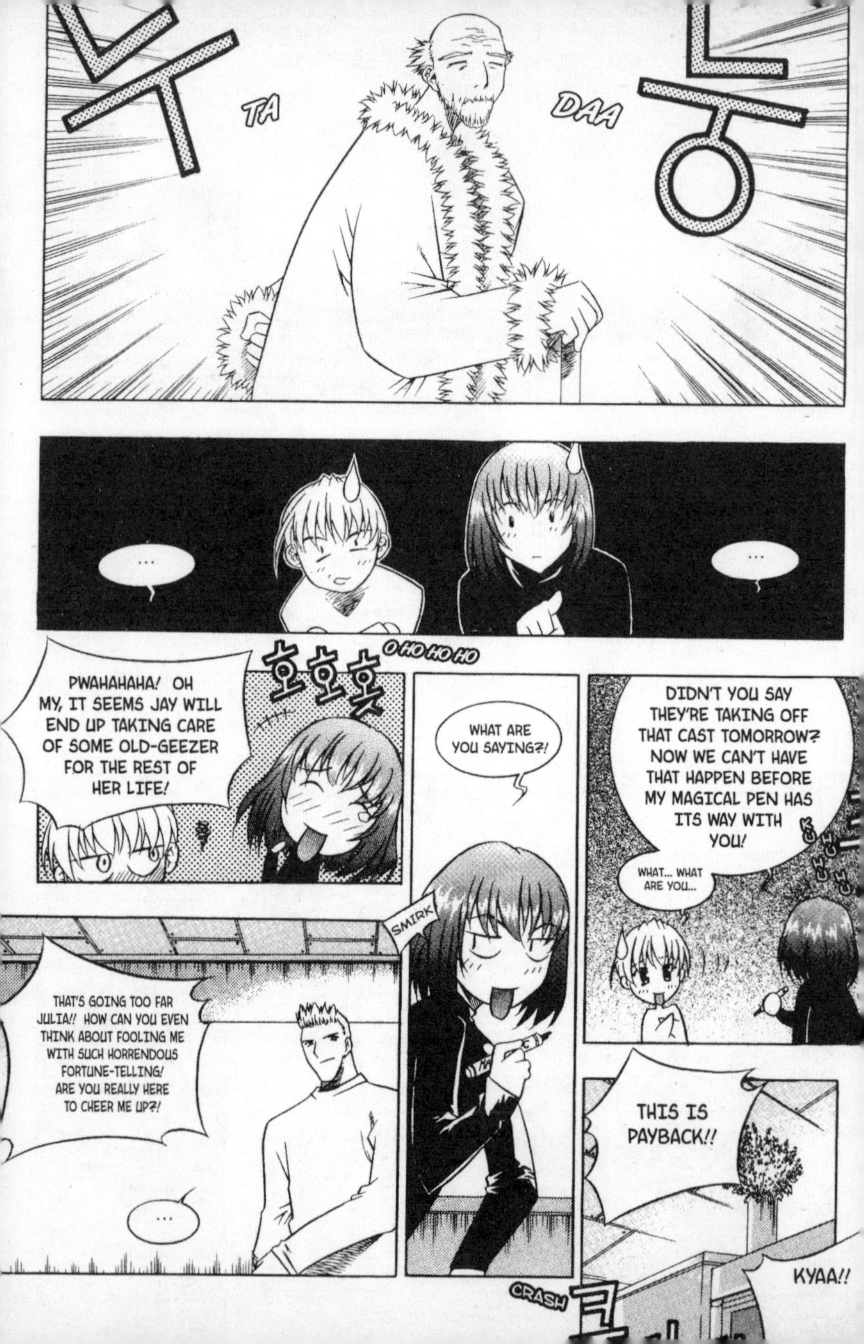
TA
DAA
...
...
PWAHAHAHA! OH MY, IT SEEMS JAY WILL END UP TAKING CARE OF SOME OLD-GEEZER FOR THE REST OF HER LIFE!
O HO HO HO
WHAT ARE YOU SAYING?!
SMIRK
DIDN'T YOU SAY THEY'RE TAKING OFF THAT CAST TOMORROW? NOW WE CAN'T HAVE THAT HAPPEN BEFORE MY MAGICAL PEN HAS ITS WAY WITH YOU!
WHAT... WHAT ARE YOU...
THAT'S GOING TOO FAR JULIA!! HOW CAN YOU EVEN THINK ABOUT FOOLING ME WITH SUCH HORRENDOUS FORTUNE-TELLING! ARE YOU REALLY HERE TO CHEER ME UP?!
...
THIS IS PAYBACK!!
CRASH
KYAA!!

MIKE GET YOUR BUTT OVER HERE AND LEND A HAND.

WHY DON'T YOU JUST LEAVE IT AT THAT JULIA. WE'LL BE LATE TO PRACTICE.

HUH? IT'S THAT TIME ALREADY?

I GUESS COACH WILL GET MAD IF WE'RE LATE!

Mike ♥ Julia

YOU'D BETTER GET BACK ON YOUR FEET QUICK JAY! IT'S NO FUN RUNNING THE 100M DASH WITHOUT A WORTHY RIVAL, GOT THAT?

YEAH.

WE'RE LATE, LET'S HURRY MIKE!

...WE'LL SEE YOU AT THE TRACK JAY.

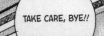

TAKE CARE, BYE!!

YEAH...
TAKE CARE...

...

SLAM

Mike ♥ Julia

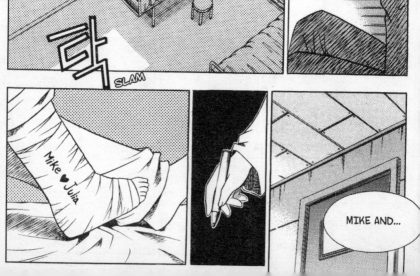

MIKE AND...

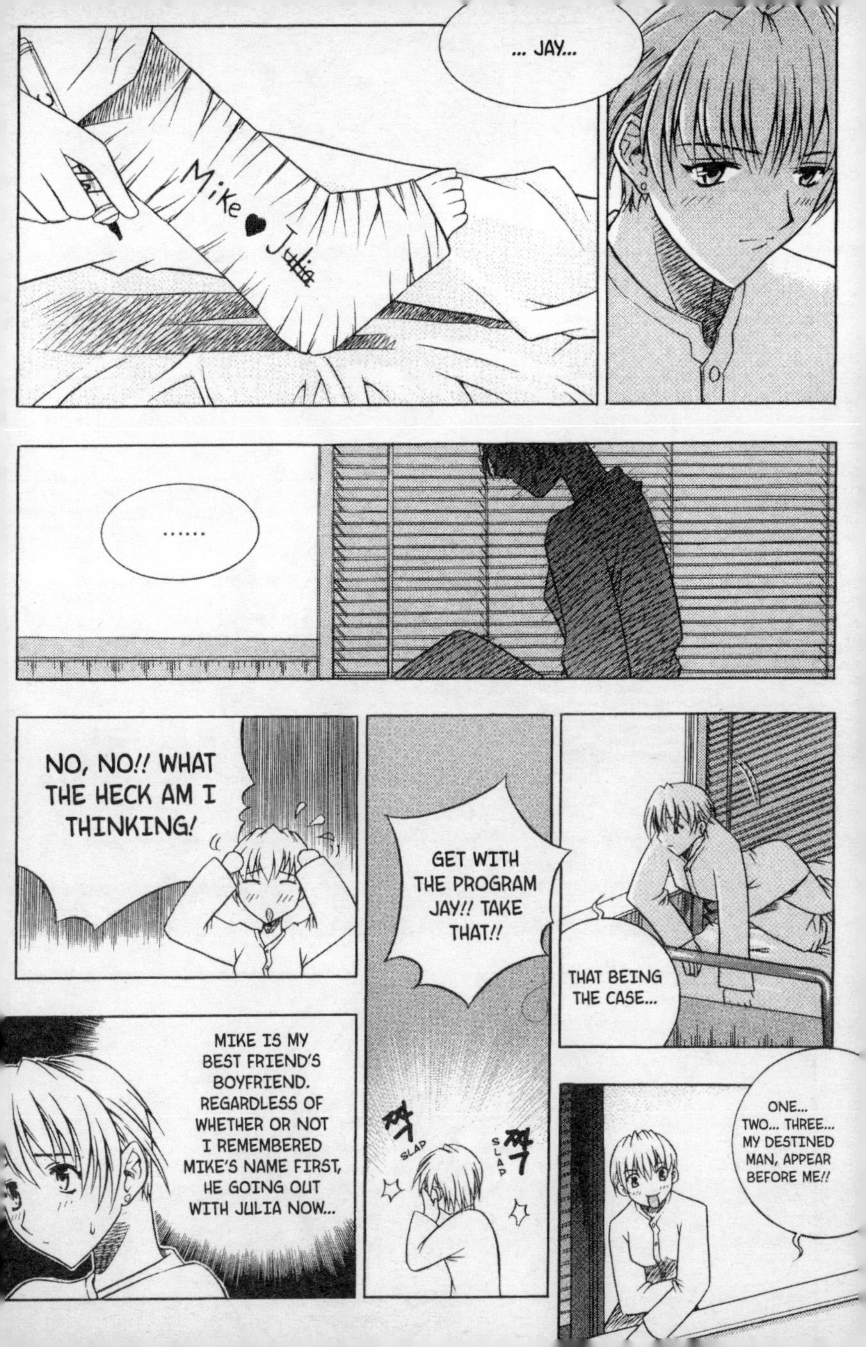
Mike ♥ Julia
... JAY...
......
NO, NO!! WHAT THE HECK AM I THINKING!
MIKE IS MY BEST FRIEND'S BOYFRIEND. REGARDLESS OF WHETHER OR NOT I REMEMBERED MIKE'S NAME FIRST, HE GOING OUT WITH JULIA NOW...
GET WITH THE PROGRAM JAY!! TAKE THAT!!
짝 SLAP
짝 SLAP
THAT BEING THE CASE...
ONE... TWO... THREE... MY DESTINED MAN, APPEAR BEFORE ME!!

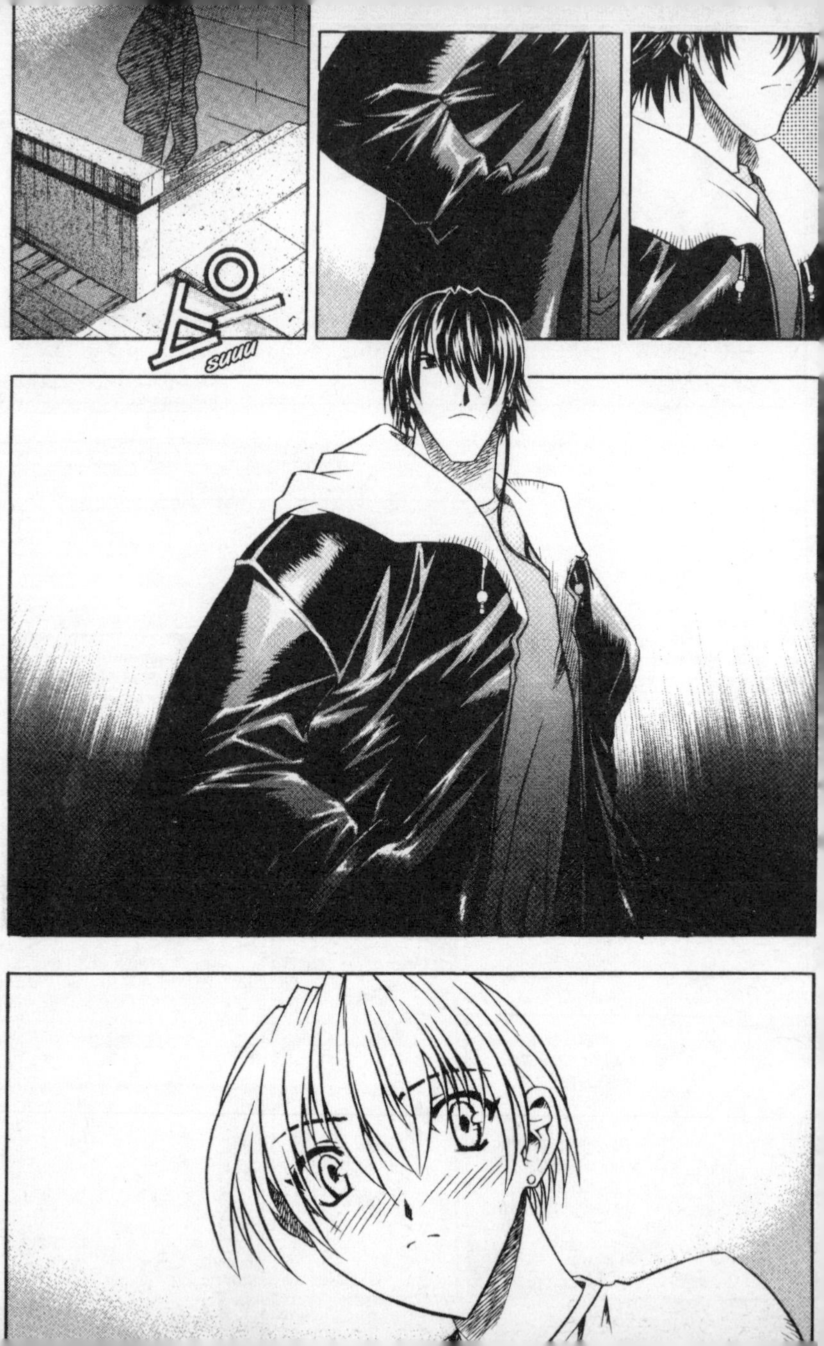
suuu

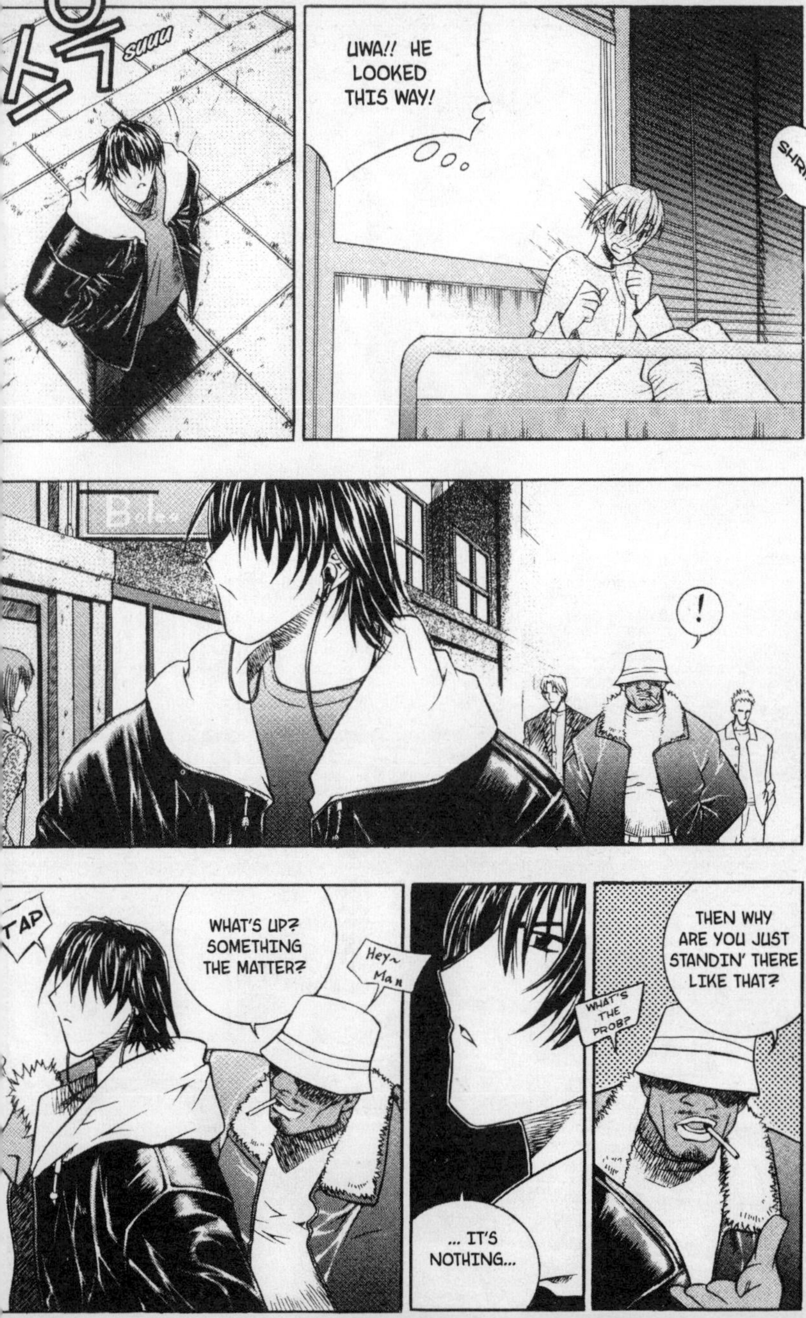
suuu
UWA!! HE LOOKED THIS WAY!
SHRINK
!
TAP
WHAT'S UP? SOMETHING THE MATTER?
Hey~ Man
WHAT'S THE PROB?
... IT'S NOTHING...
THEN WHY ARE YOU JUST STANDIN' THERE LIKE THAT?

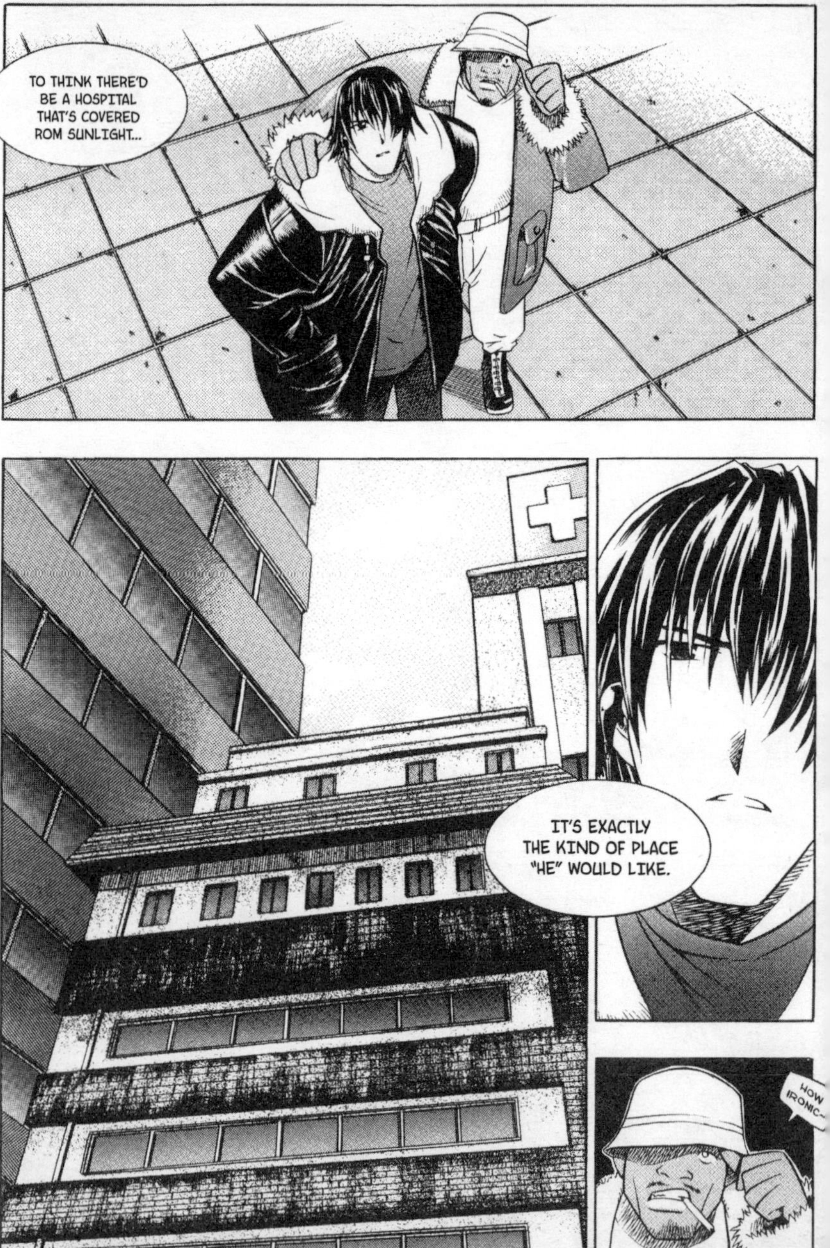
TO THINK THERE'D BE A HOSPITAL THAT'S COVERED ROM SUNLIGHT...
IT'S EXACTLY THE KIND OF PLACE "HE" WOULD LIKE.
HOW IRONIC—

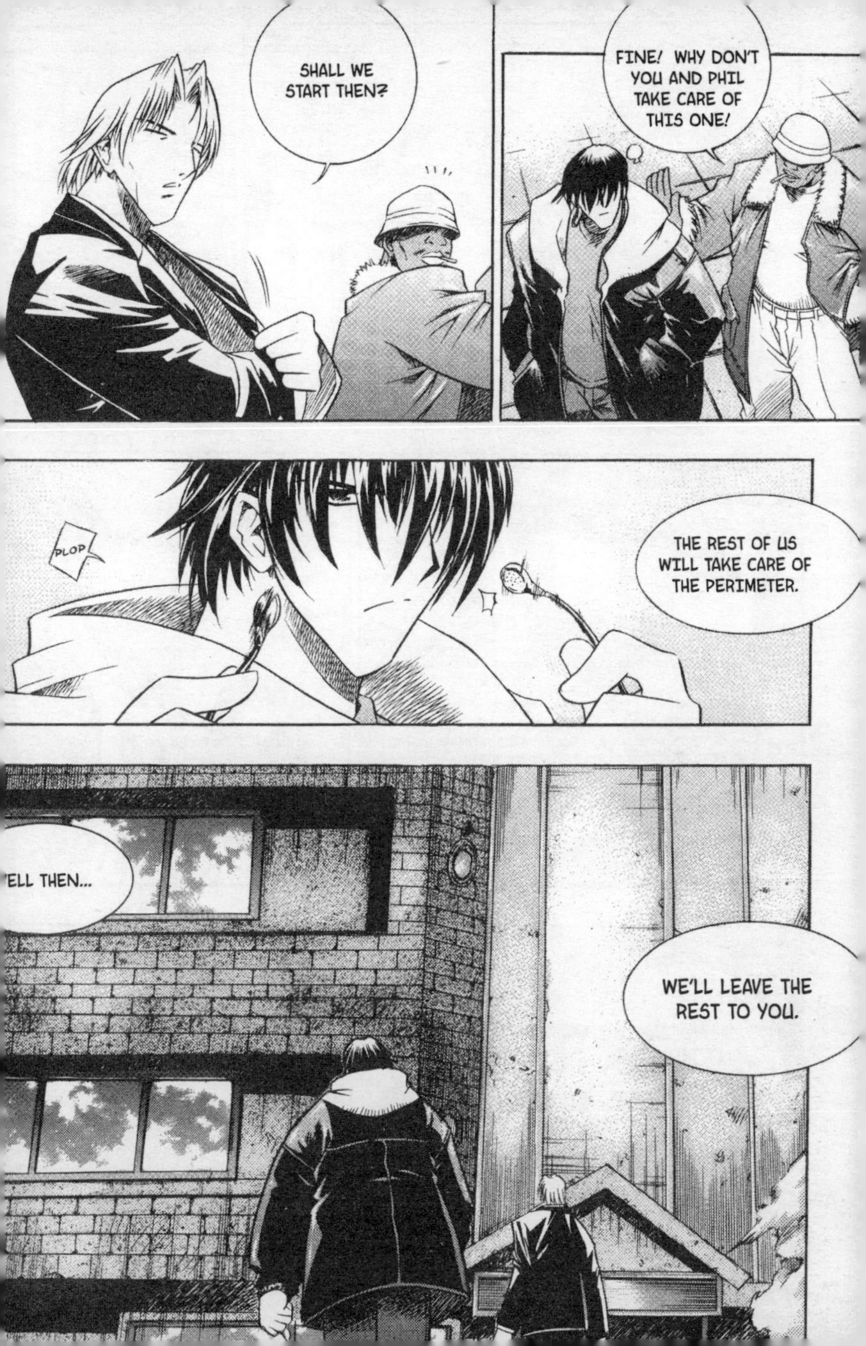
SHALL WE START THEN?
FINE! WHY DON'T YOU AND PHIL TAKE CARE OF THIS ONE!
PLOP
THE REST OF US WILL TAKE CARE OF THE PERIMETER.
ELL THEN...
WE'LL LEAVE THE REST TO YOU.

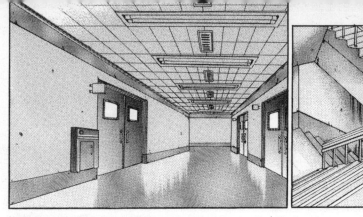

HEY MIKE, I HEARD THAT ONCE A PERSON HEALS FROM A LEG INJURY, THEIR LEGS WILL BECOME EVEN STRONGER THAN BEFORE.

SPARK

IN THAT CASE, JAY WILL BE ABLE TO RUN EVEN FASTER, RIGHT?

I GUE

IN ANY CASE, ISN'T THIS PLACE A BIT TOO DARK FOR A HOSPITAL?

!

HUH?

IT'D BE NICE IF THEY TURNED ON SOME LIGHTS...

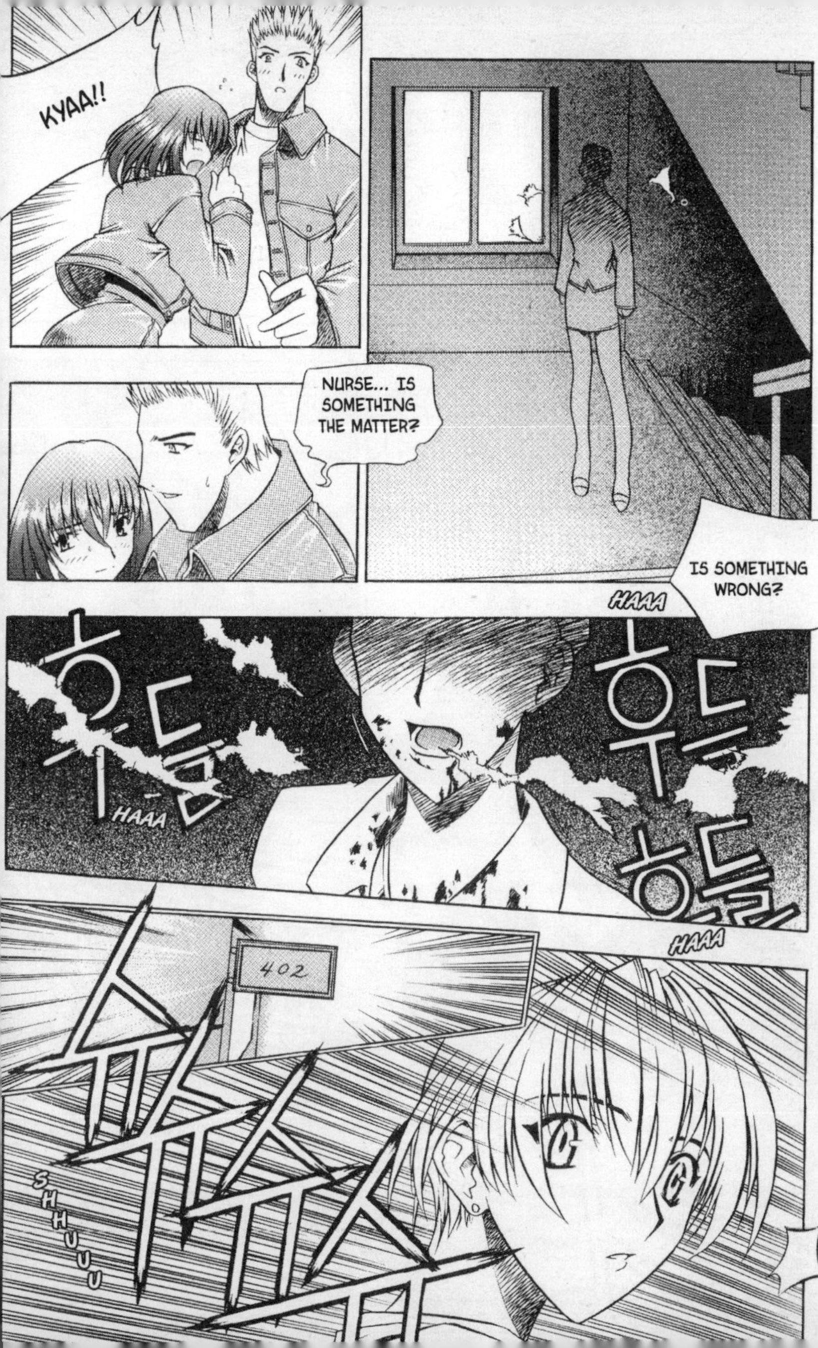
KYAA!!
NURSE... IS SOMETHING THE MATTER?
IS SOMETHING WRONG?
HAAA
HAAA
HAAA
402
SHHUUU

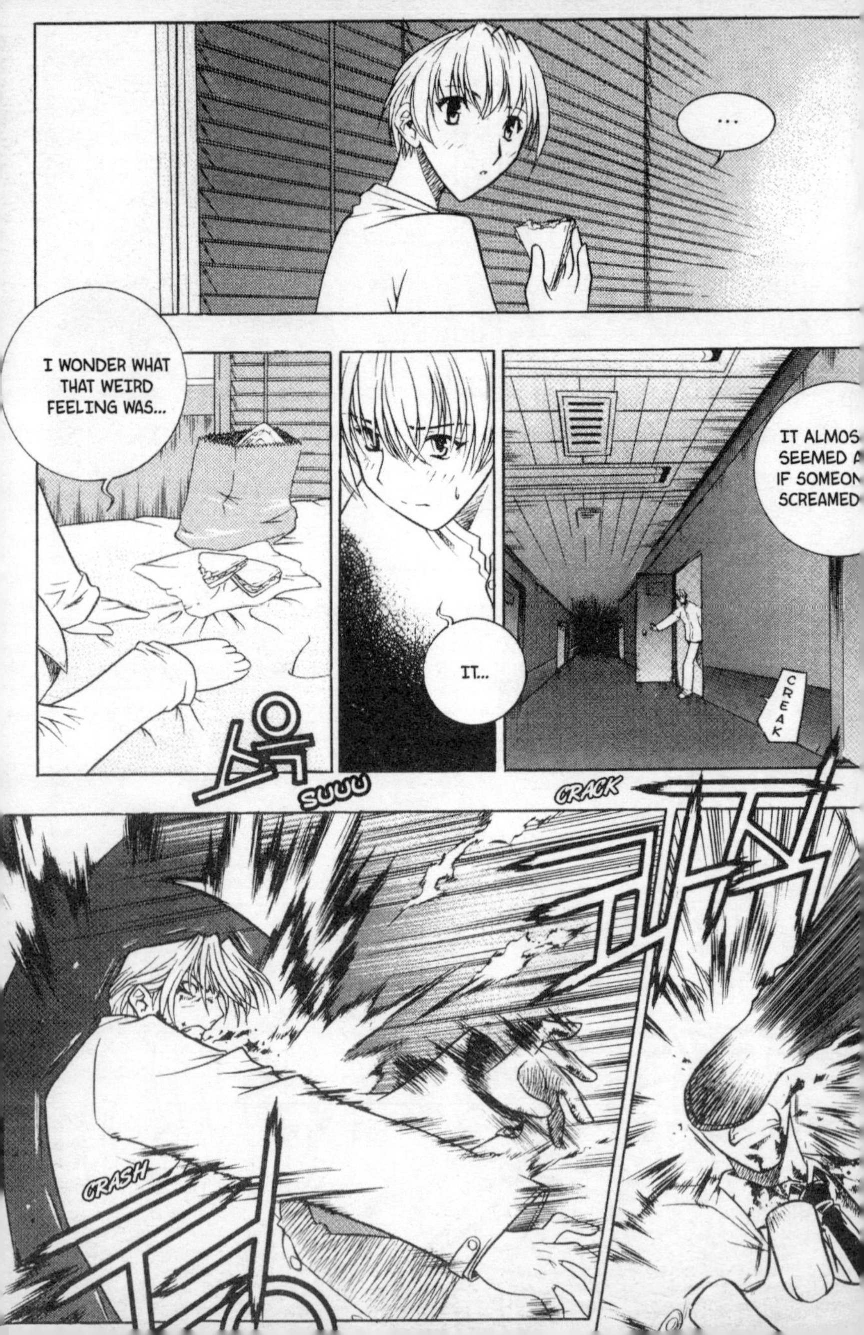
...
I WONDER WHAT THAT WEIRD FEELING WAS...
SUUU
IT...
IT ALMOS SEEMED A IF SOMEON SCREAMED
CREAK
CRACK
CRASH

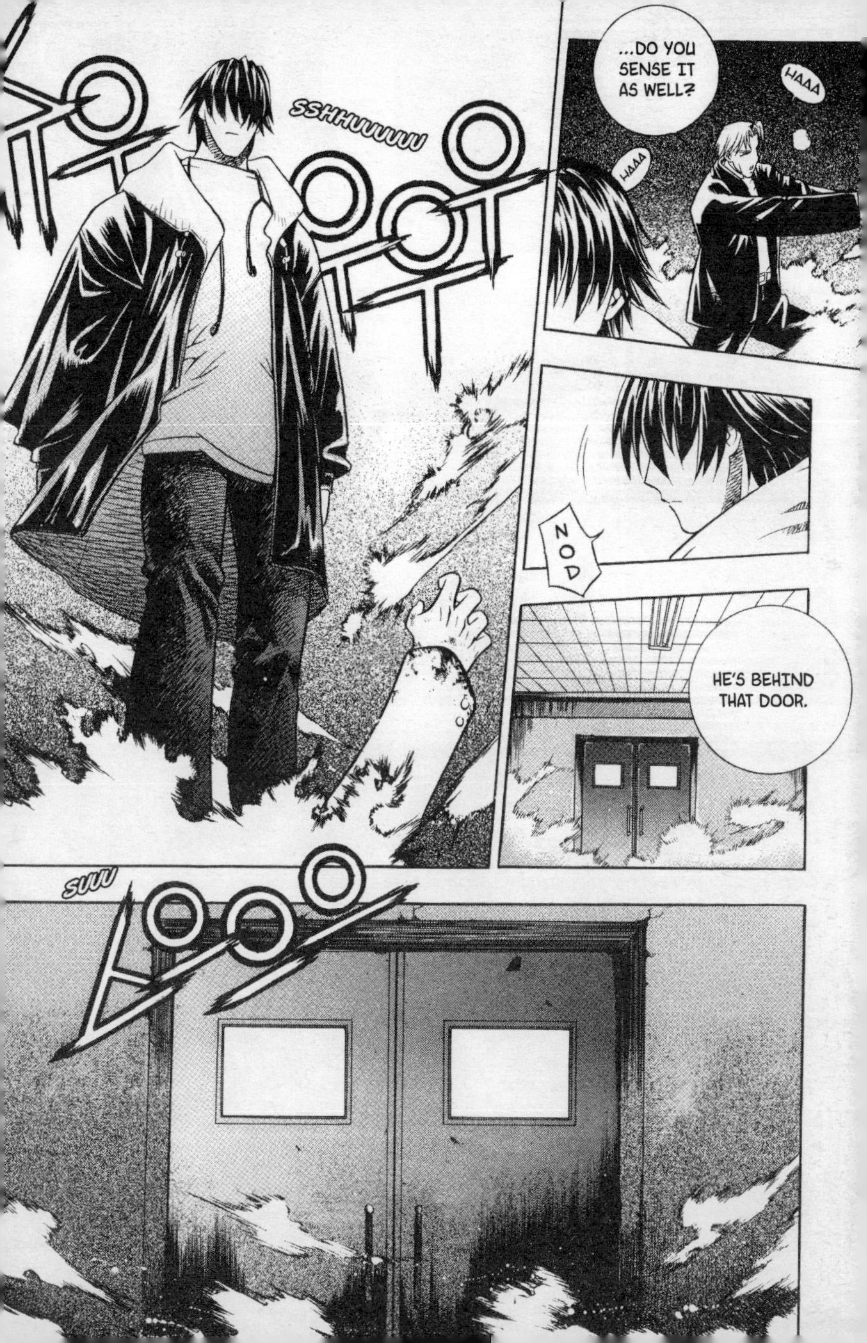
SSHHUUUUUU
...DO YOU SENSE IT AS WELL?
HAAA
HAAA
NOD
HE'S BEHIND THAT DOOR.
SUUU

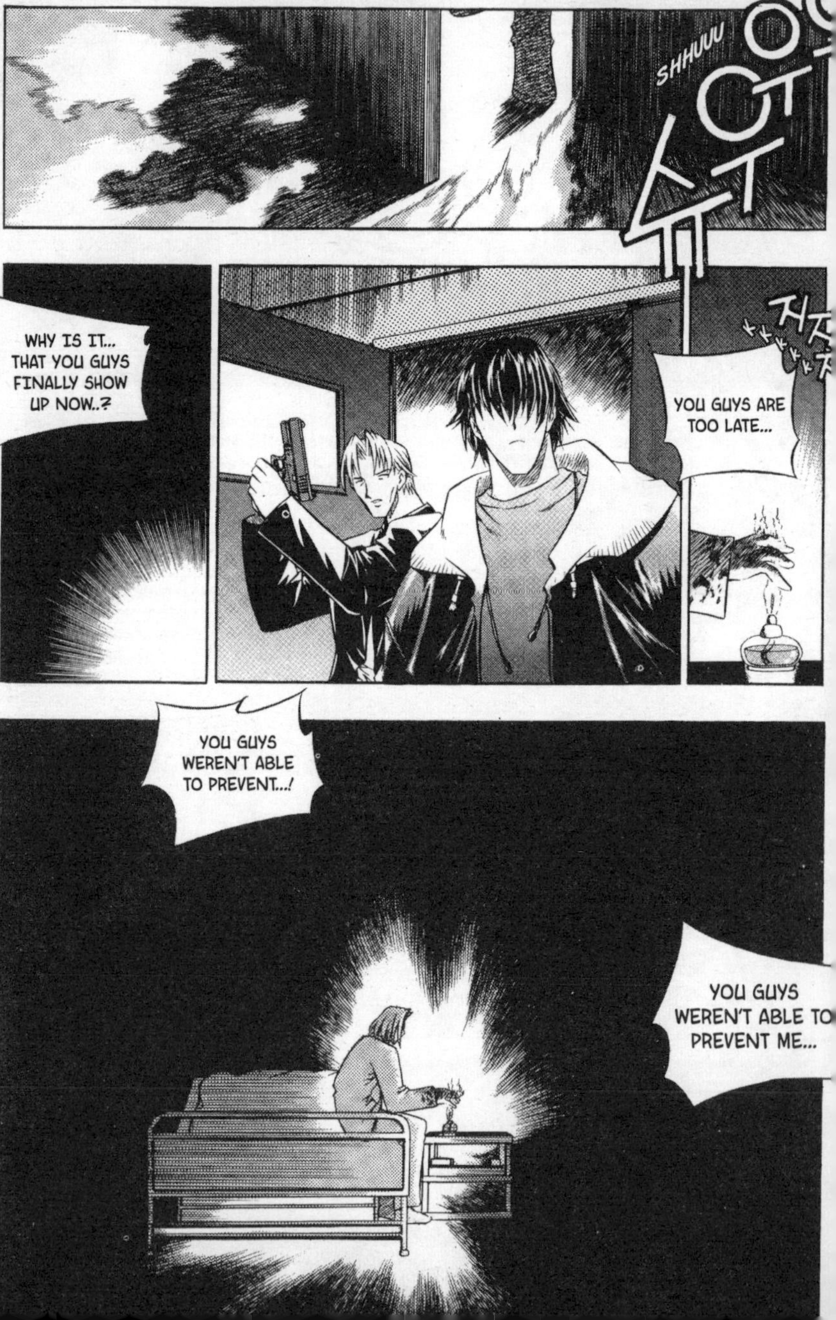
SHHUUU
WHY IS IT... THAT YOU GUYS FINALLY SHOW UP NOW..?
YOU GUYS ARE TOO LATE...
YOU GUYS WEREN'T ABLE TO PREVENT...!
YOU GUYS WEREN'T ABLE TO PREVENT ME...

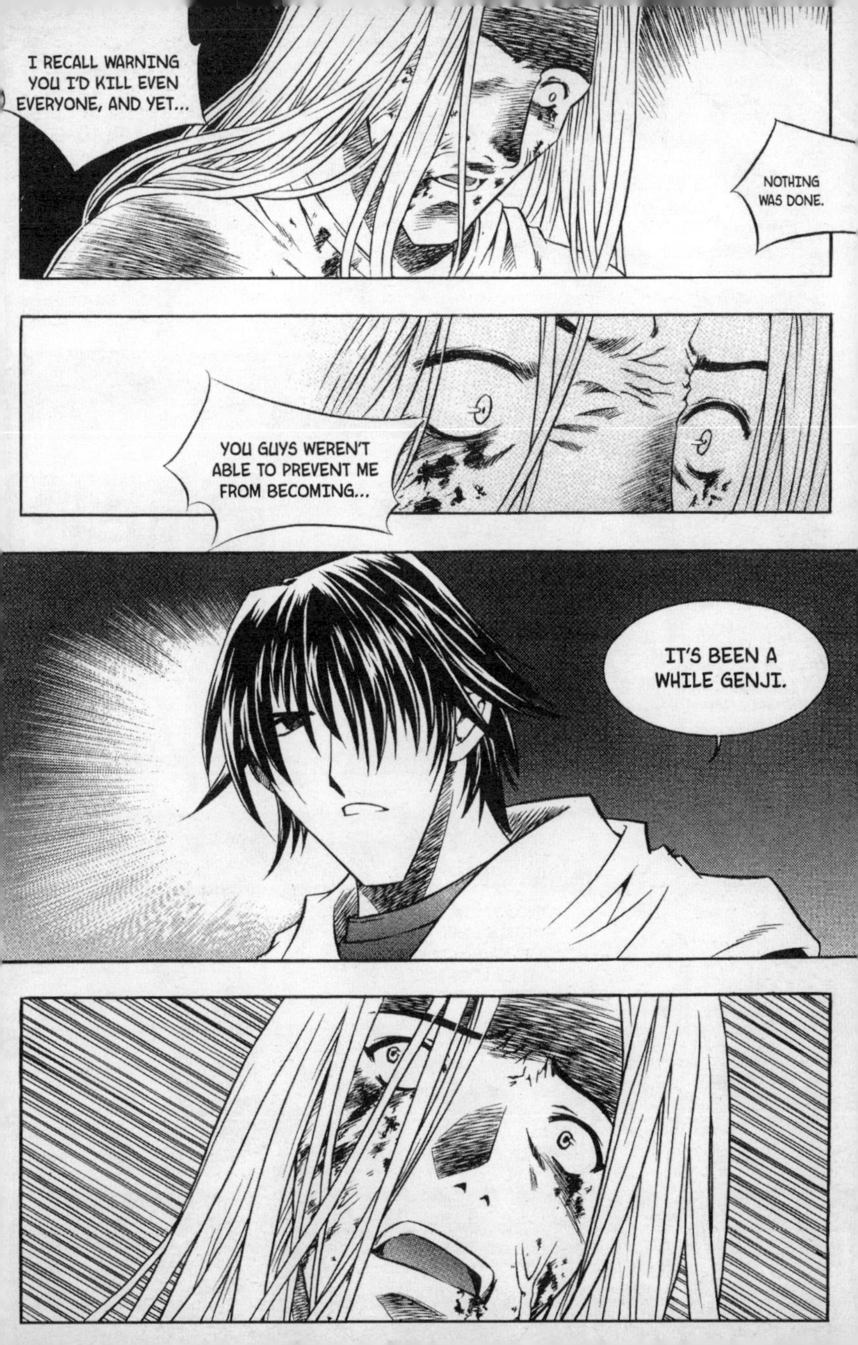
I RECALL WARNING YOU I'D KILL EVEN EVERYONE, AND YET...
NOTHING WAS DONE.
YOU GUYS WEREN'T ABLE TO PREVENT ME FROM BECOMING...
IT'S BEEN A WHILE GENJI.

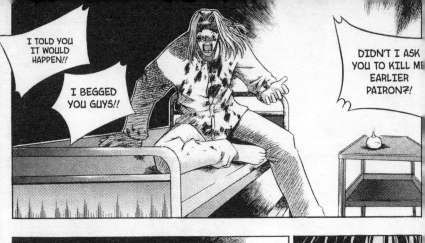

I TOLD YOU IT WOULD HAPPEN!!

I BEGGED YOU GUYS!!

DIDN'T I ASK YOU TO KILL ME EARLIER PAIRON?!

IS HE THE ONE? THE ONE THAT KEEPS ASKING FOR YOU..?

CLICK

DO YOU KNOW WHAT IT FEELS LIKE TO FEEL NAUSEATED JUST BY LOOKING AT ONE'S OWN REFLECTION IN THE MIRROR?!

SOMETHIN INSIDE M IS MAKIN ME GO CRAZ AND I DON EVEN KNO WHAT THAT MYSELF...

WHENEVER I FEEL THIS WAY, I START LOSING IT! I START FEELING LIKE KILLING SOMEONE!!

STUMBLE

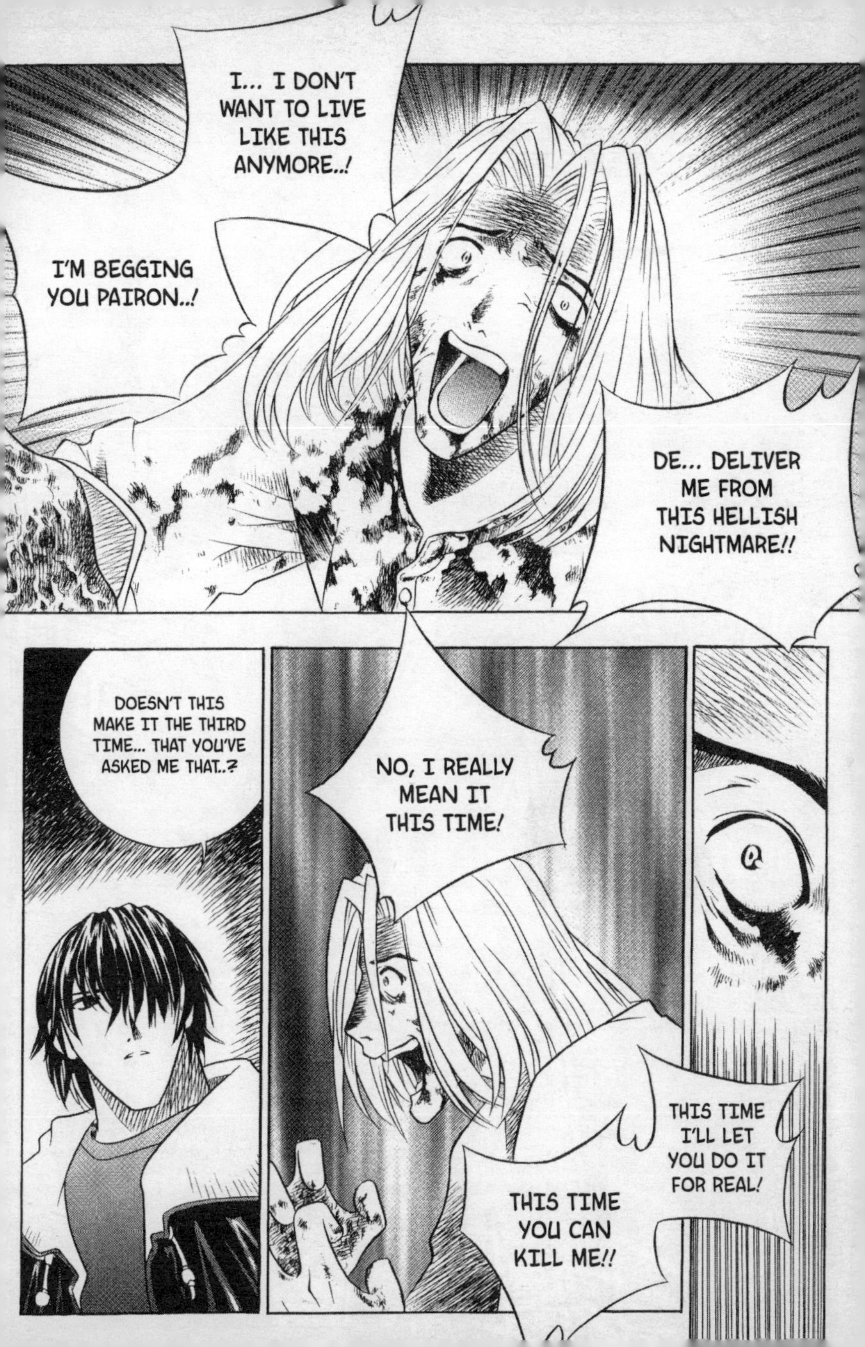
I... I DON'T WANT TO LIVE LIKE THIS ANYMORE..!
I'M BEGGING YOU PAIRON..!
DE... DELIVER ME FROM THIS HELLISH NIGHTMARE!!
DOESN'T THIS MAKE IT THE THIRD TIME... THAT YOU'VE ASKED ME THAT..?
NO, I REALLY MEAN IT THIS TIME!
THIS TIME YOU CAN KILL ME!!
THIS TIME I'LL LET YOU DO IT FOR REAL!

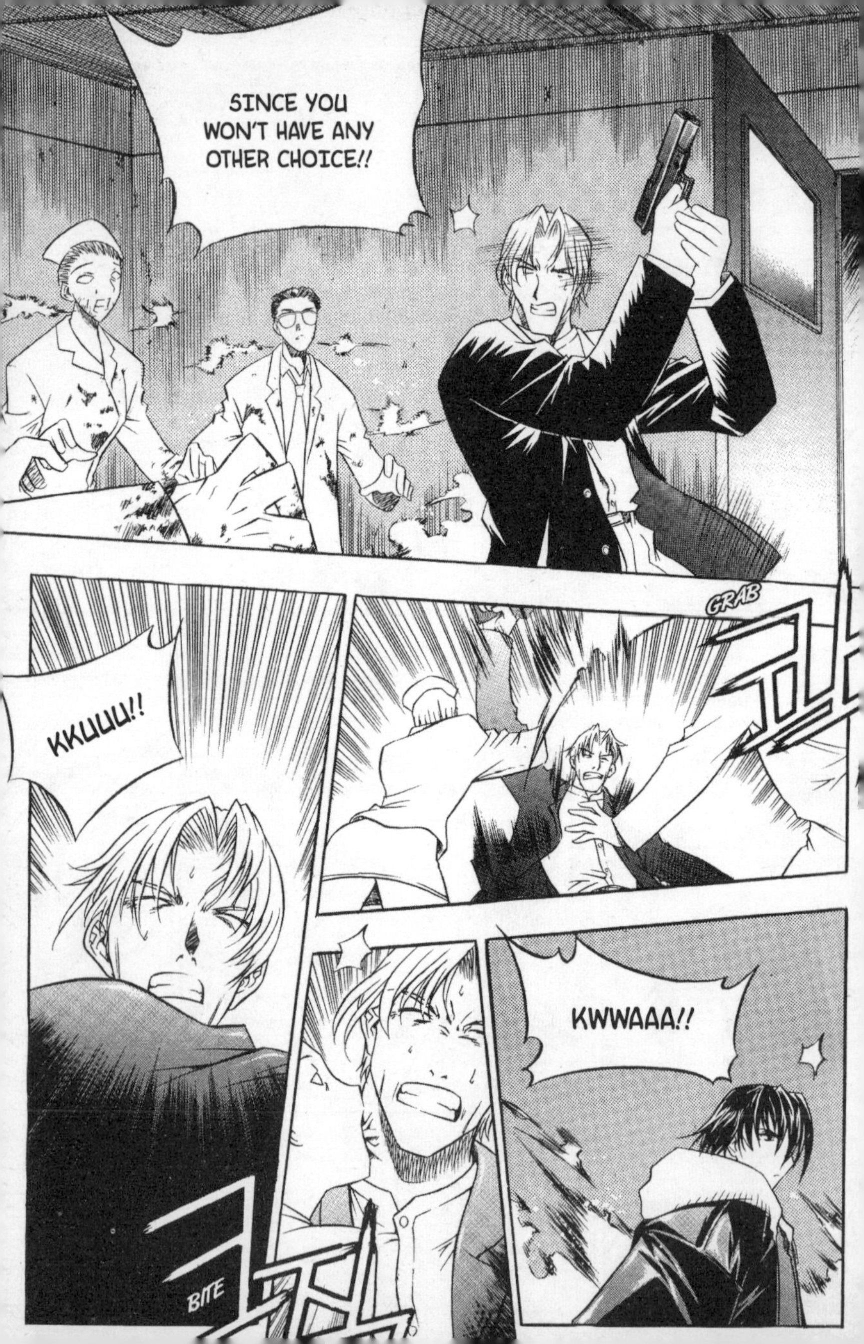
SINCE YOU WON'T HAVE ANY OTHER CHOICE!!
KKUUU!!
GRAB
KWWAAA!!
BITE

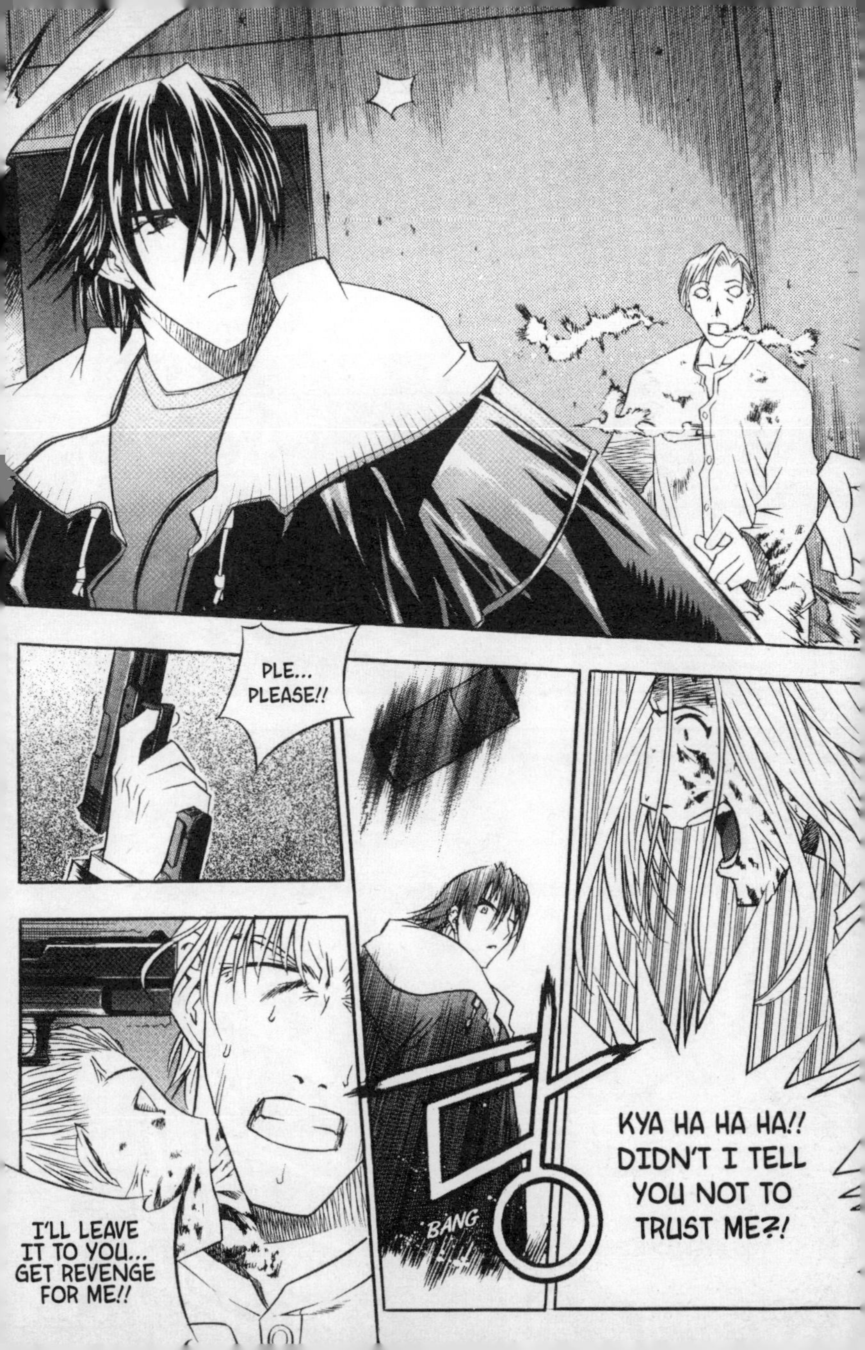
PLE... PLEASE!!
I'LL LEAVE IT TO YOU... GET REVENGE FOR ME!!
BANG
KYA HA HA HA!! DIDN'T I TELL YOU NOT TO TRUST ME?!

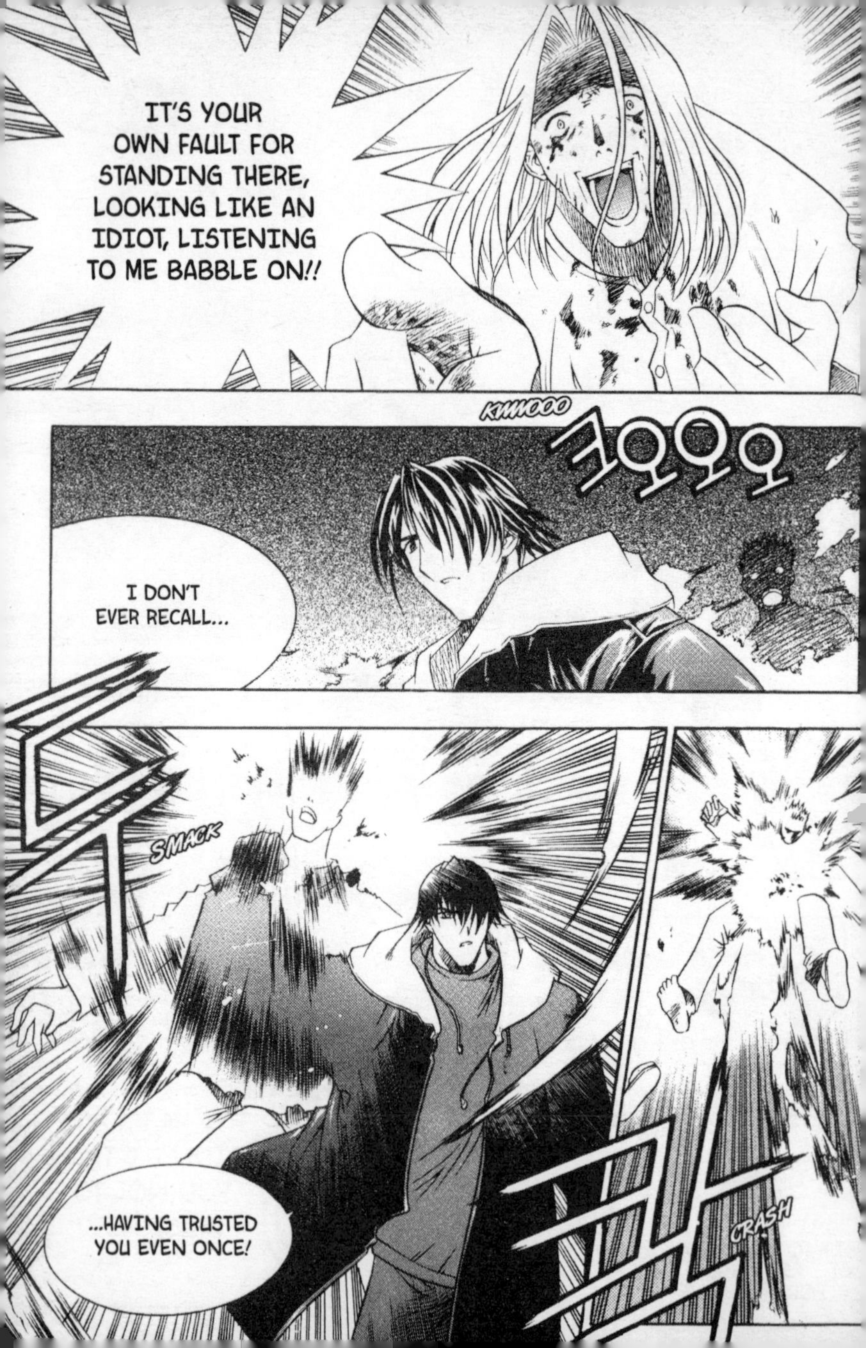
IT'S YOUR OWN FAULT FOR STANDING THERE, LOOKING LIKE AN IDIOT, LISTENING TO ME BABBLE ON!!
KWOOO
I DON'T EVER RECALL...
SMACK
...HAVING TRUSTED YOU EVEN ONCE!
CRASH

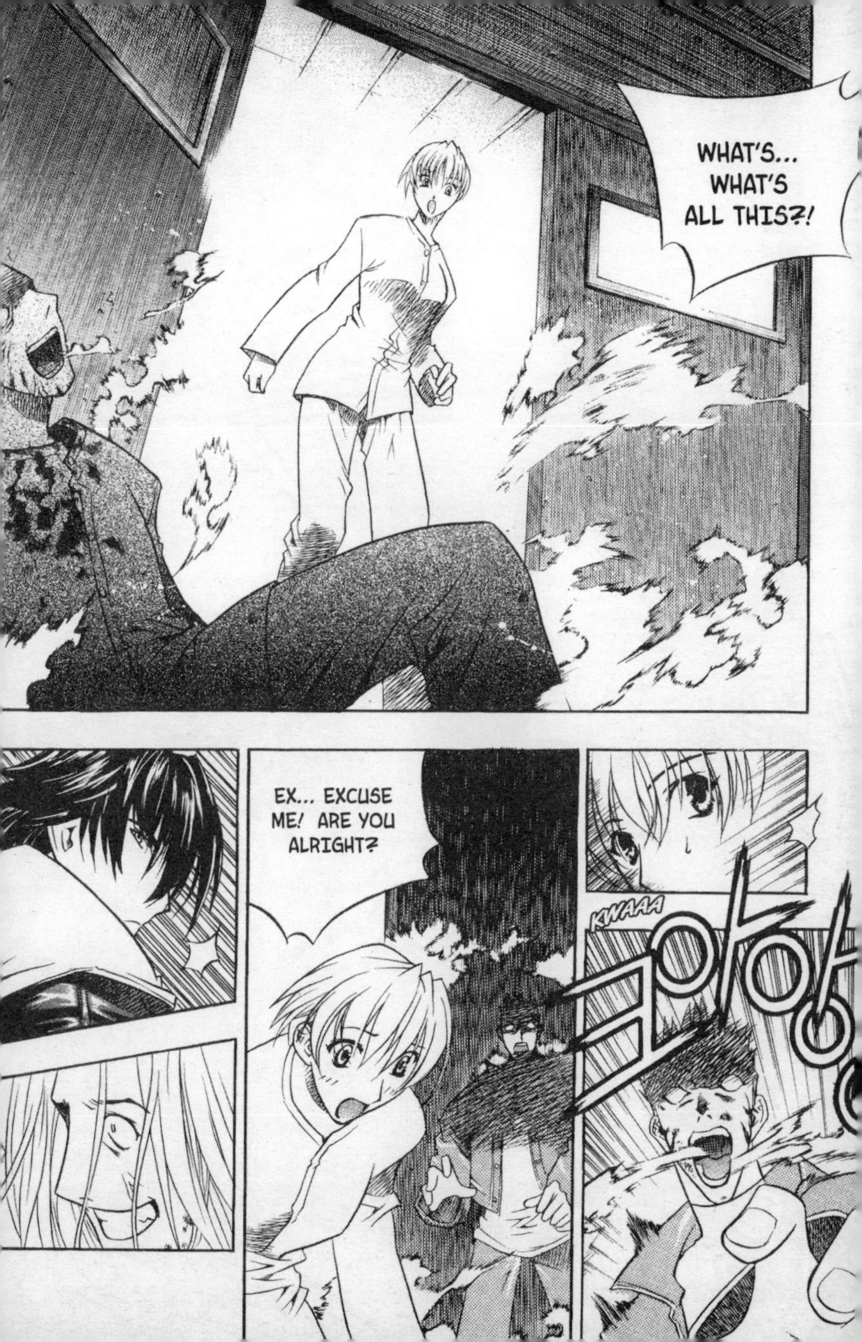
WHAT'S... WHAT'S ALL THIS?!
EX... EXCUSE ME! ARE YOU ALRIGHT?
KWAAA

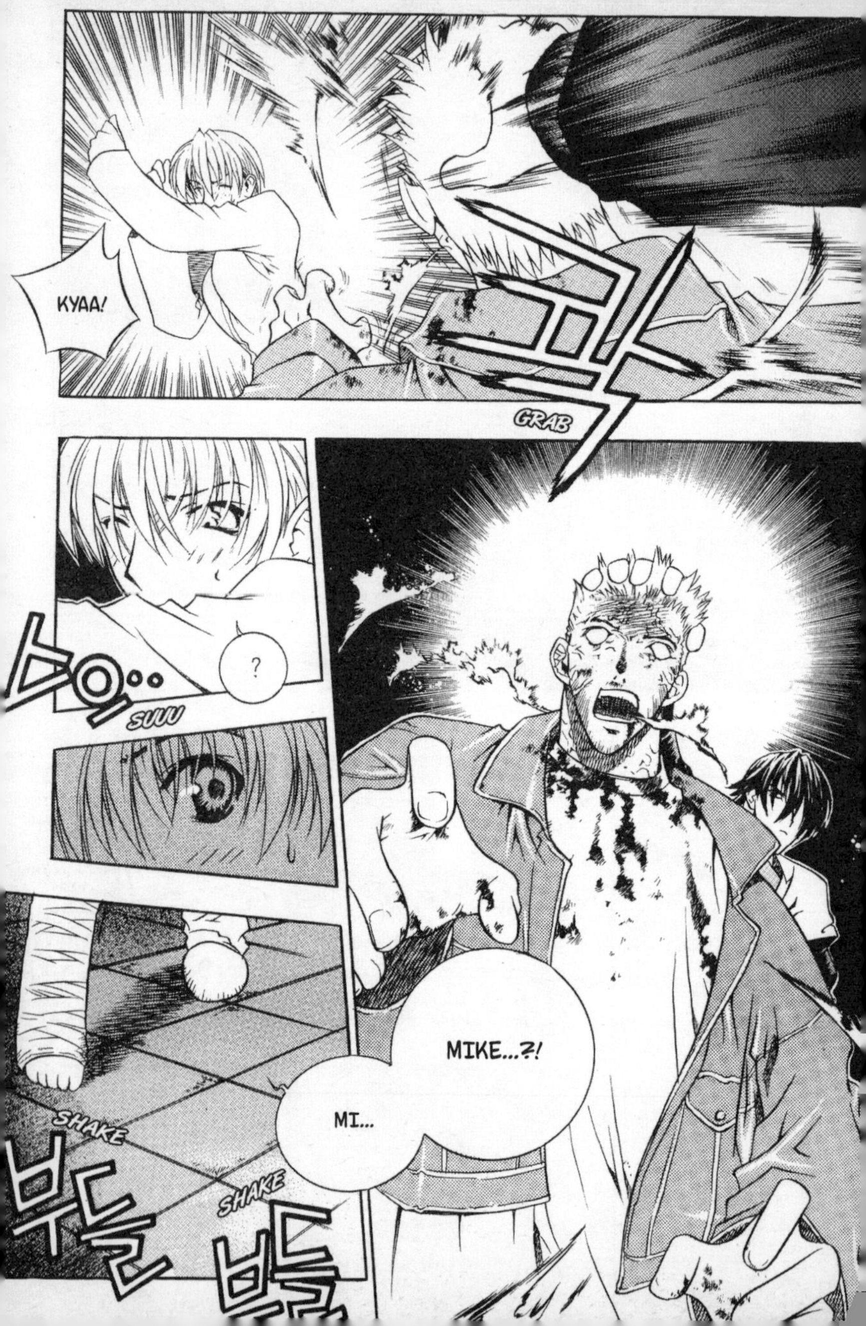
KYAA!
GRAB
?
SUUU
SHAKE
SHAKE
MI...
MIKE...?!

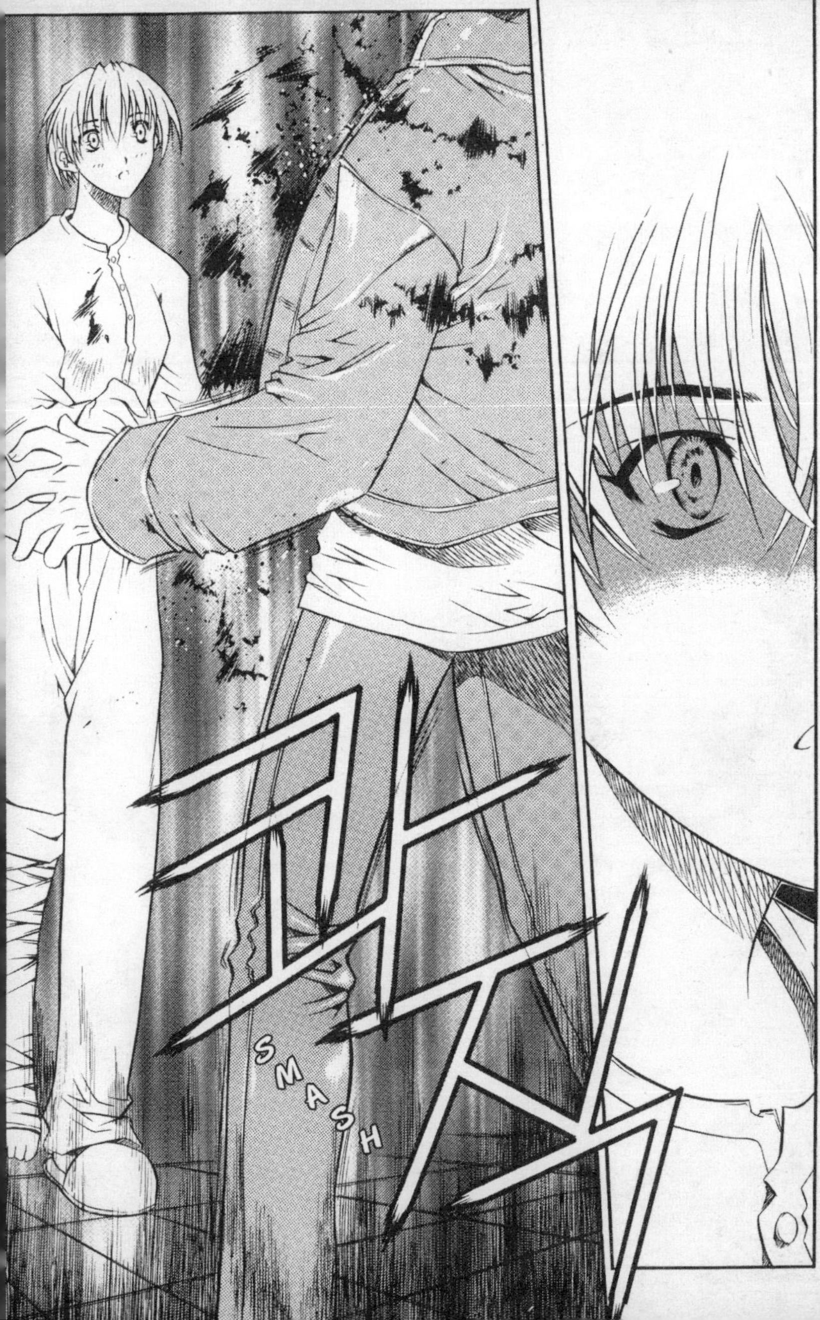
SMASH

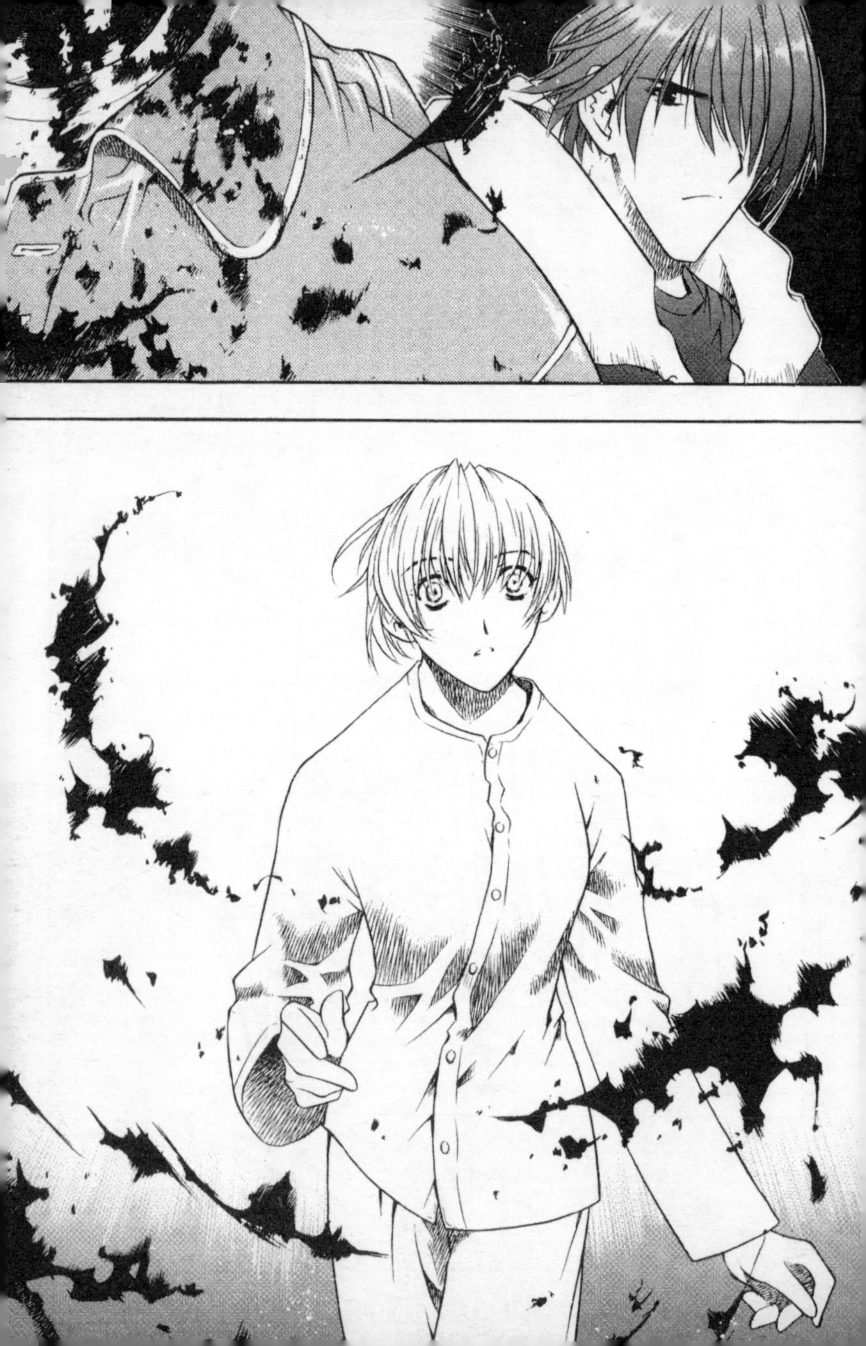

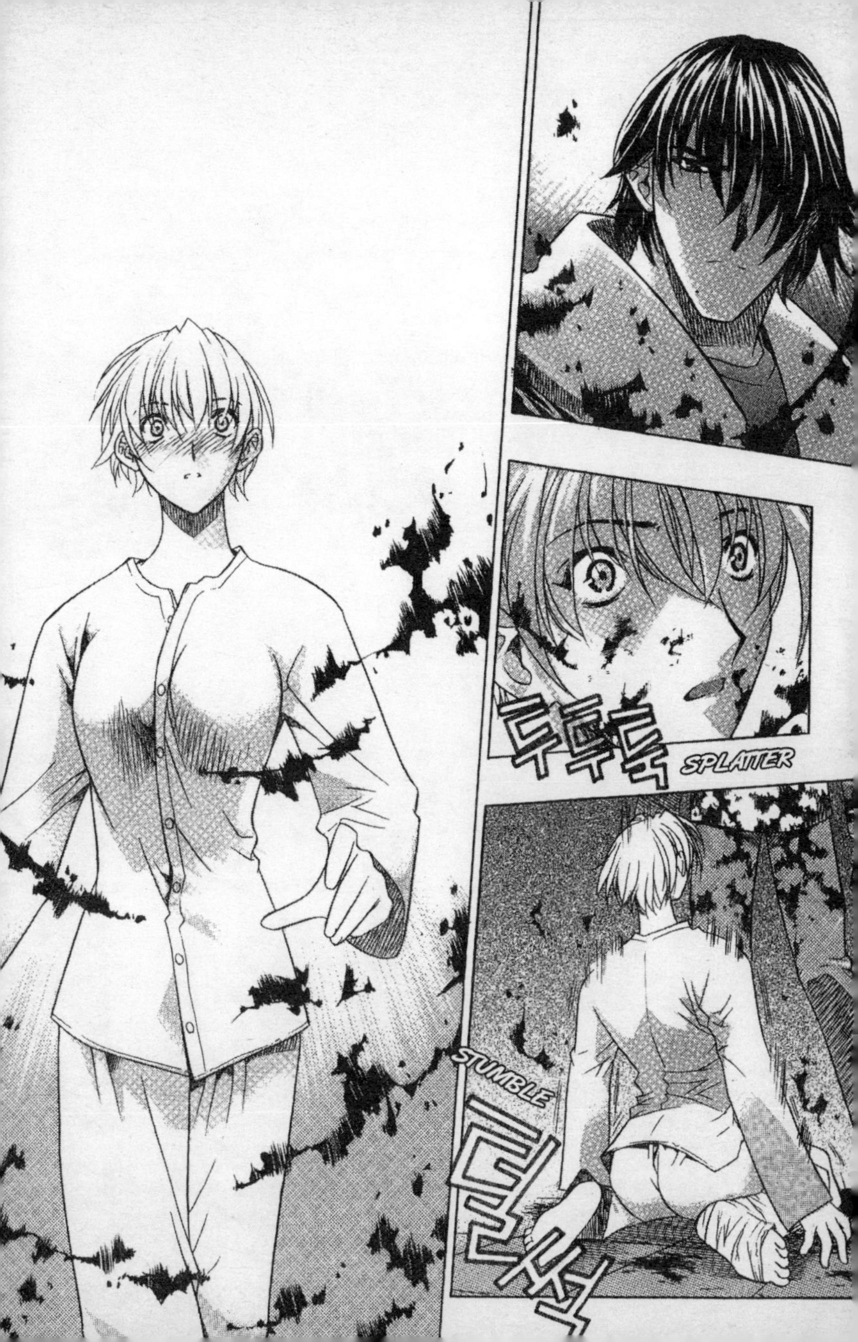
SPLATTER
STUMBLE

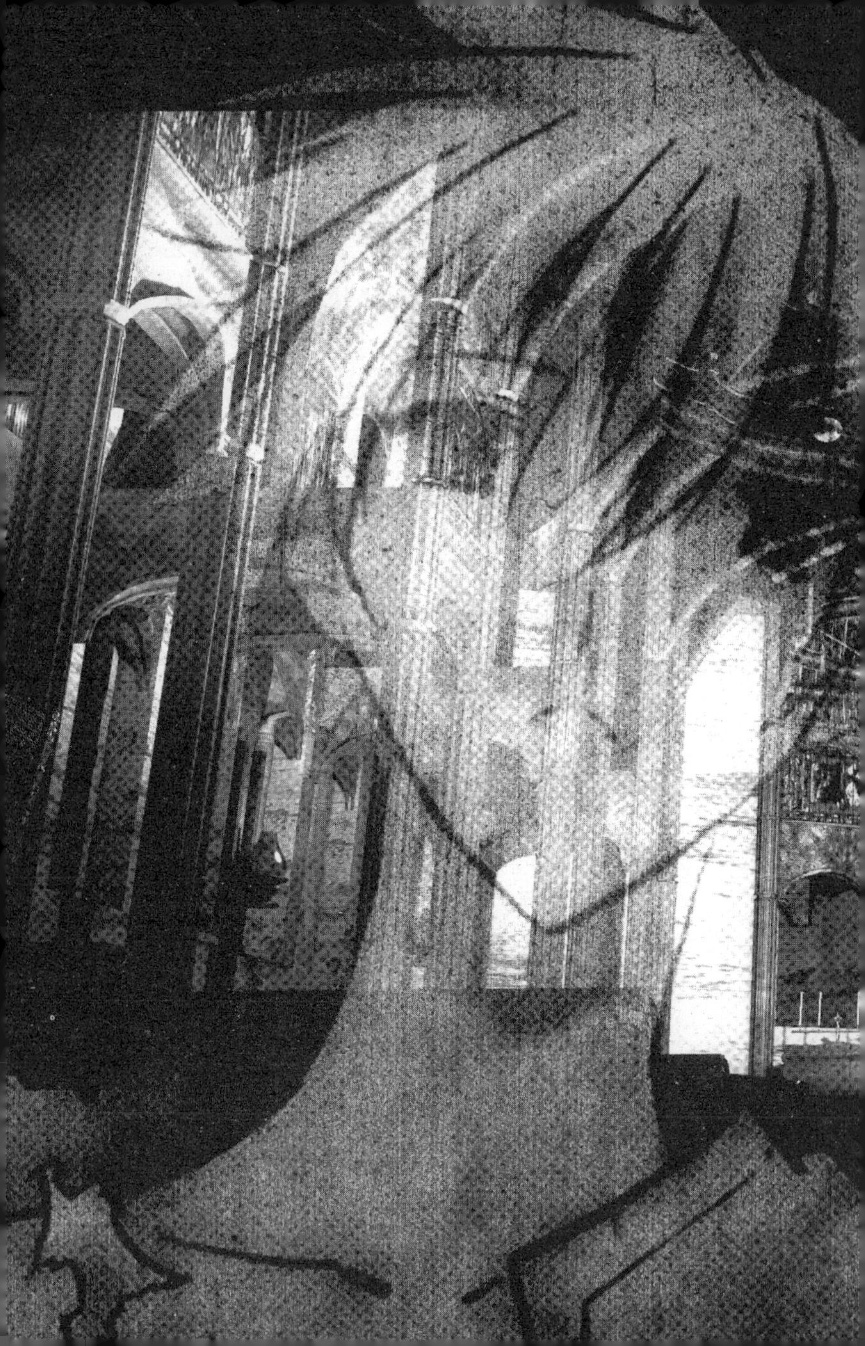

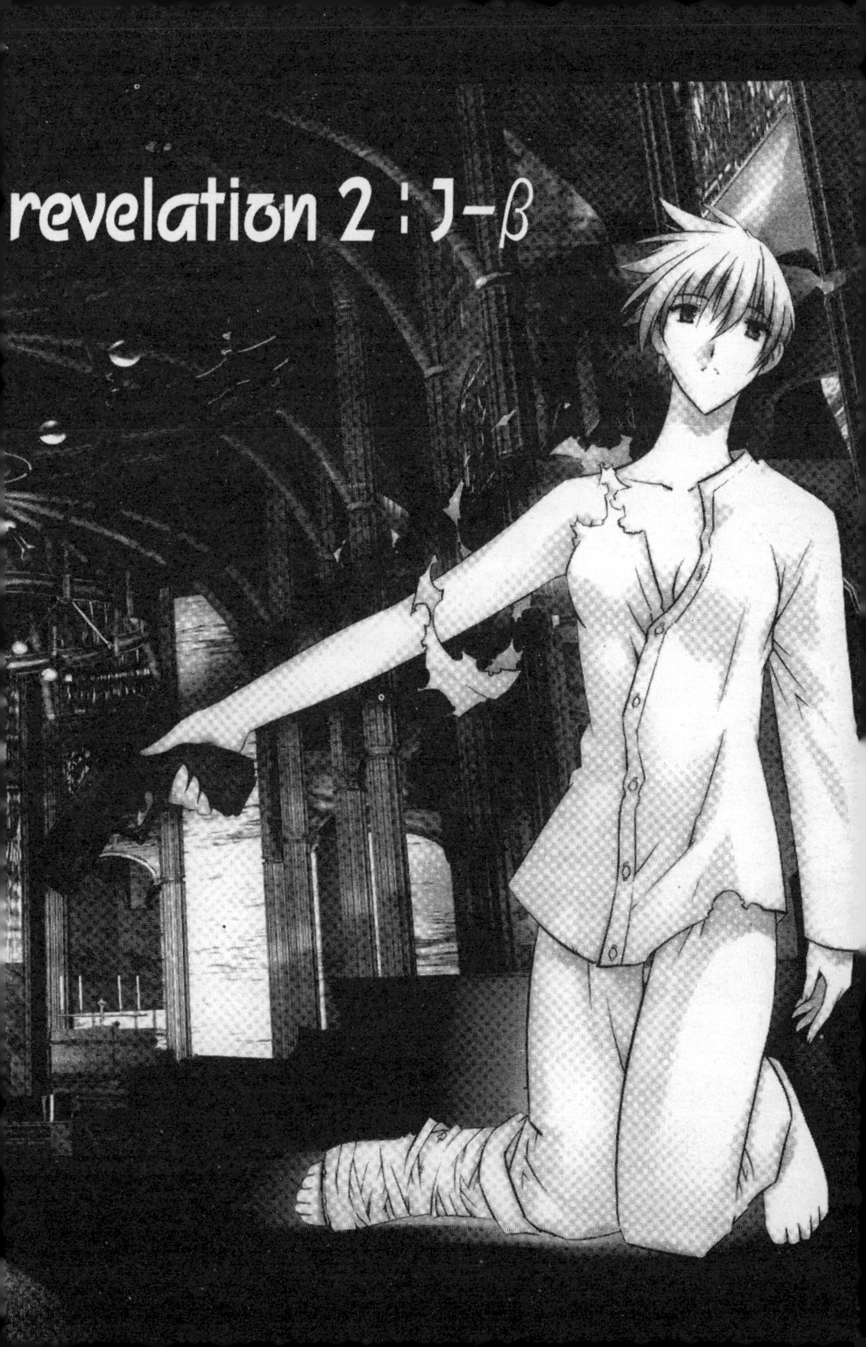
revelation 2 : J-β

NUDGE

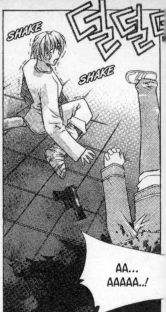

SHAKE

SHAKE

THUD

... ...

AA...
AAAAA..!

OOH, WHAT DO WE HAVE HERE? I DIDN'T THINK THERE'D BE PRETTY LADIES STILL LEFT IN THIS HOSPITAL!!

DASH

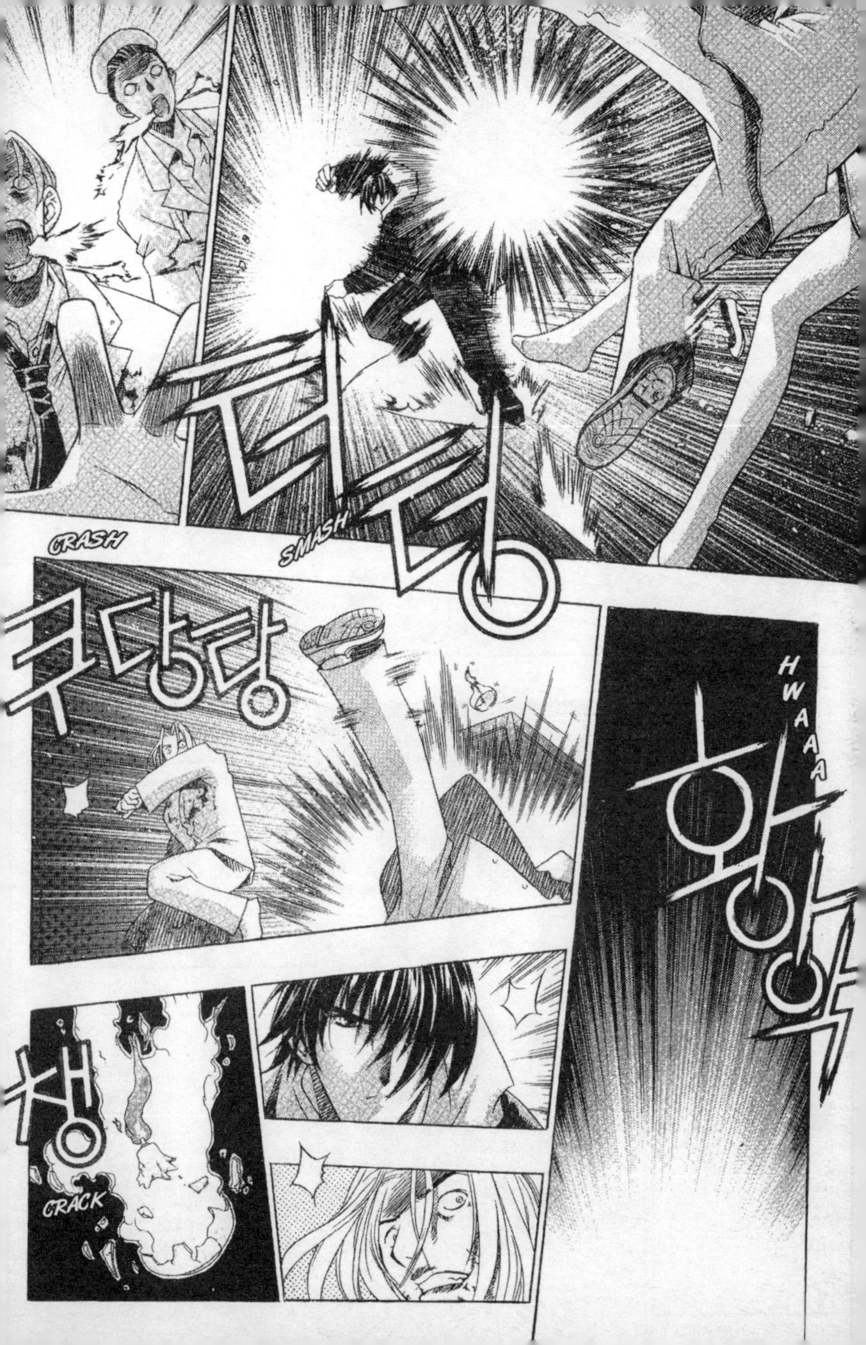
CRASH
SMASH
HWAAA
CRACK

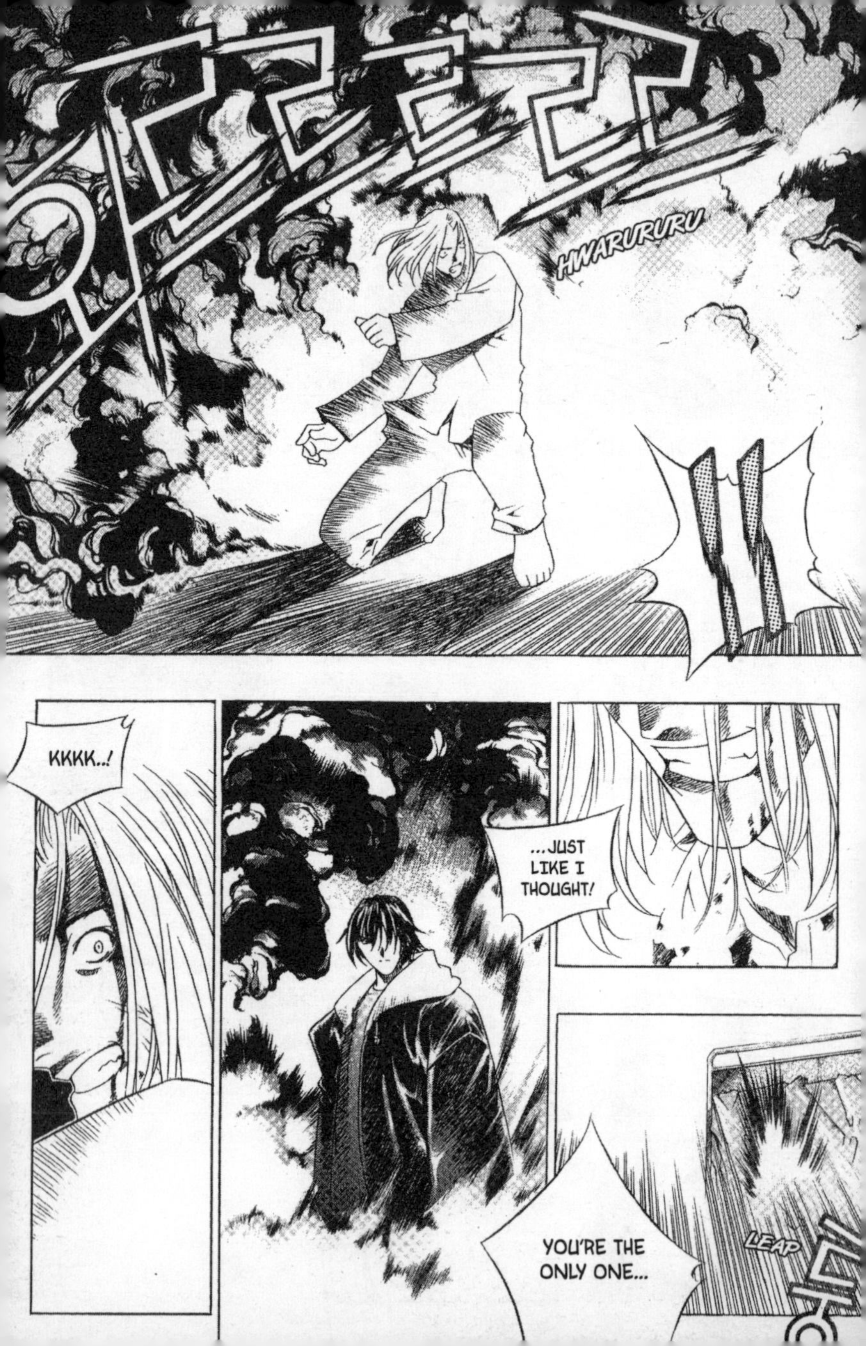
HWARURURU
KKKK..!
...JUST LIKE I THOUGHT!
YOU'RE THE ONLY ONE...
LEAP

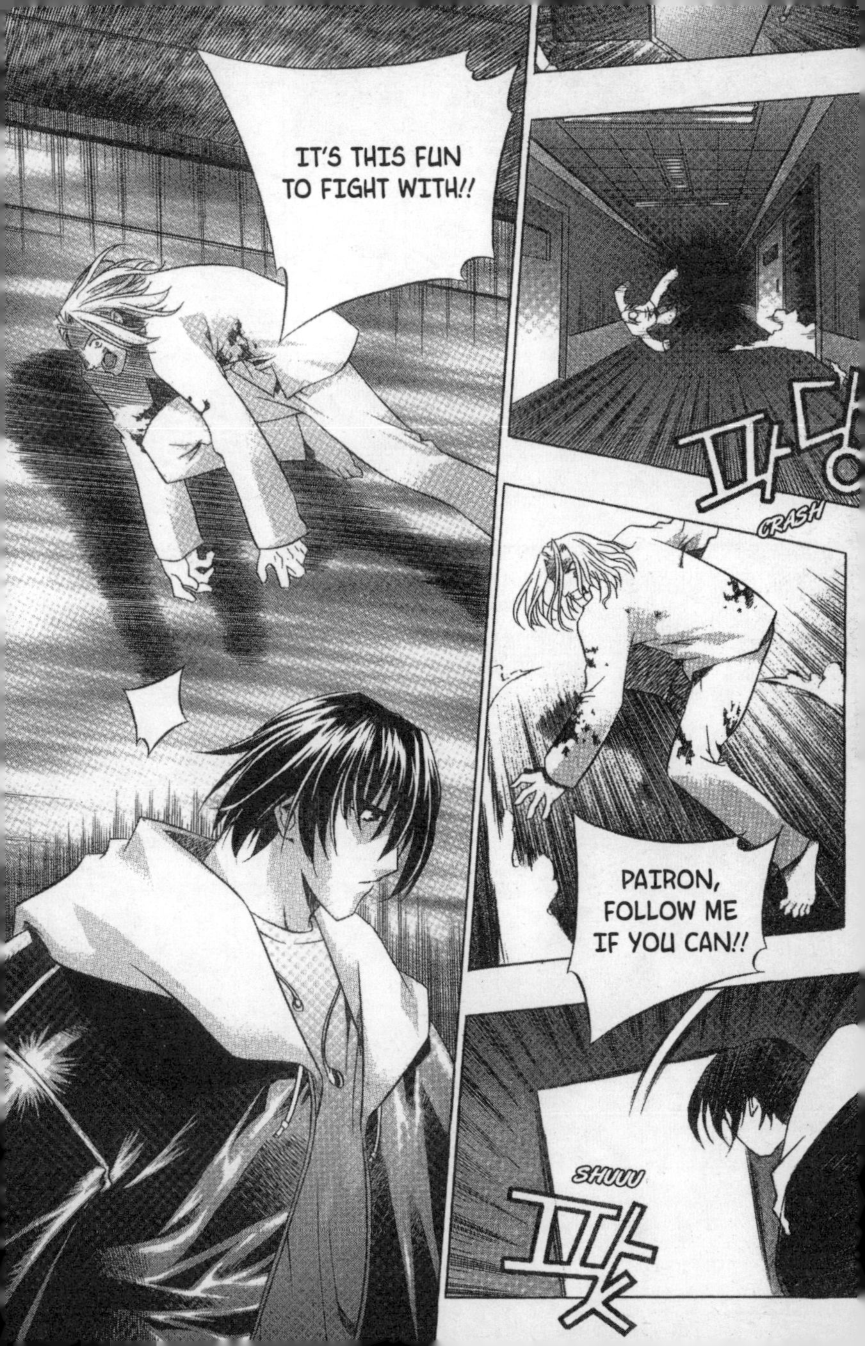
IT'S THIS FUN TO FIGHT WITH!!
파당
CRASH
PAIRON, FOLLOW ME IF YOU CAN!!
SHUUU

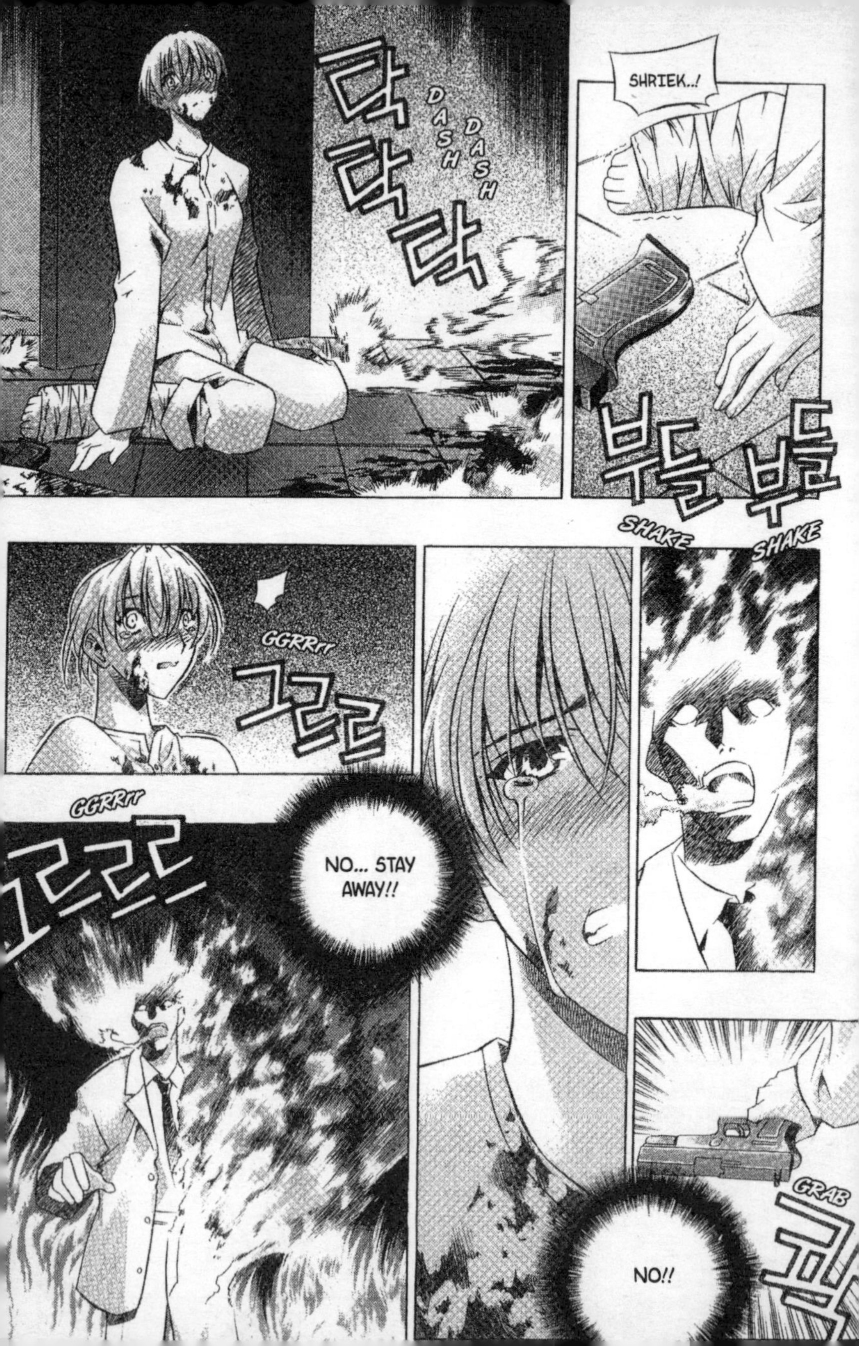
DASH DASH
SHRIEK..!
부들 부들
SHAKE SHAKE
GGRRrr
그르르
GGRRrr
그르르
NO... STAY AWAY!!
NO!!
GRAB
콱

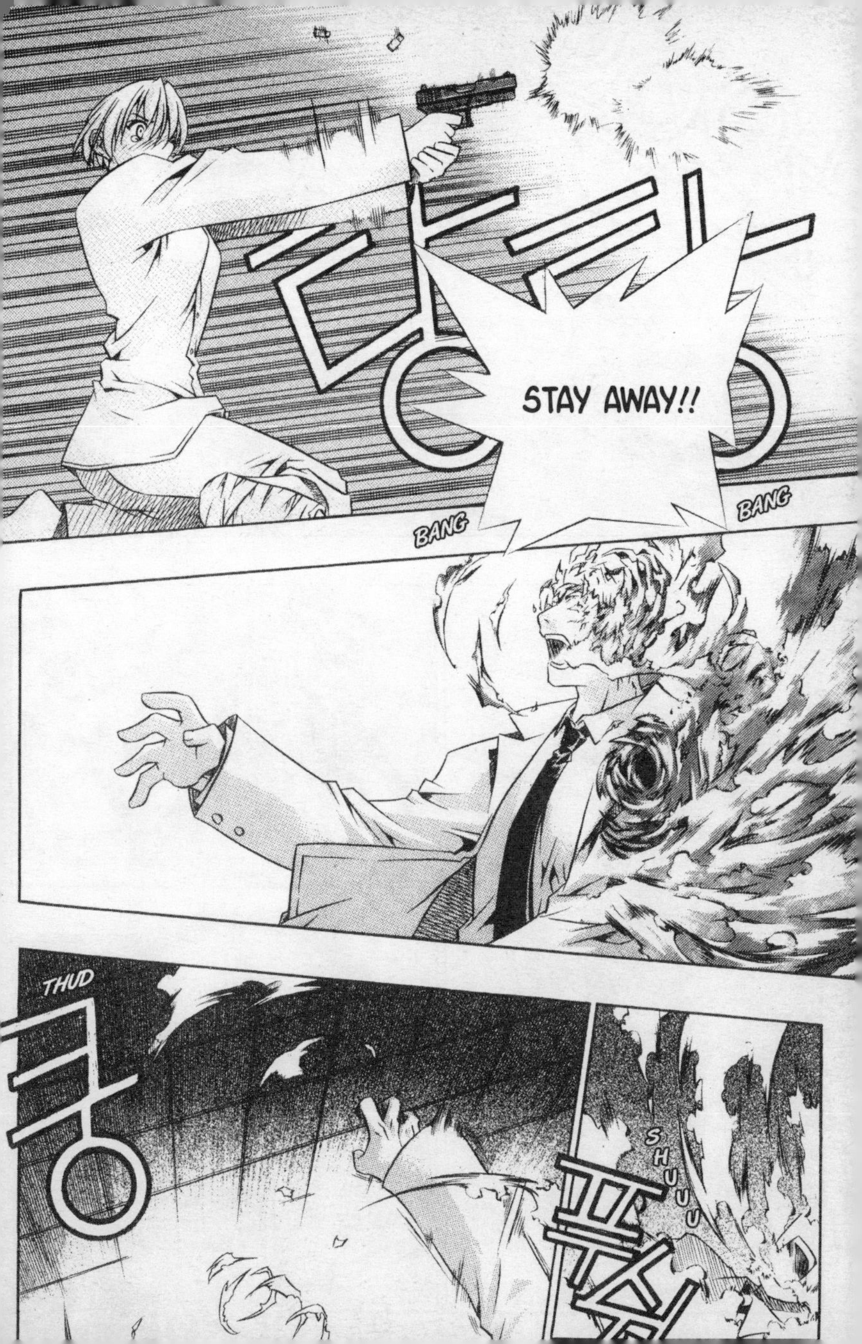
STAY AWAY!!
BANG
BANG
THUD
SHUUU

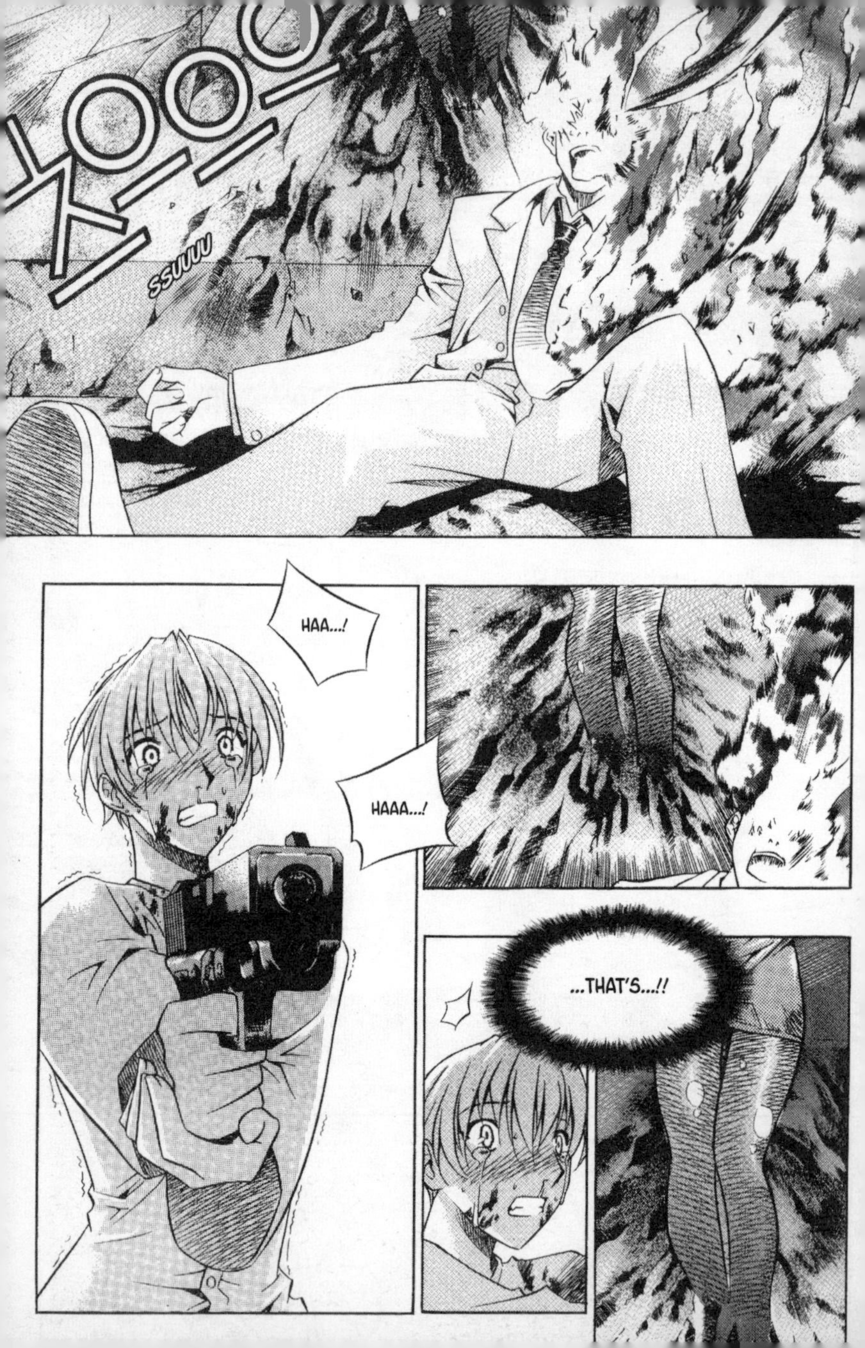
SSUUUU
HAA...!
HAAA...!
...THAT'S...!!

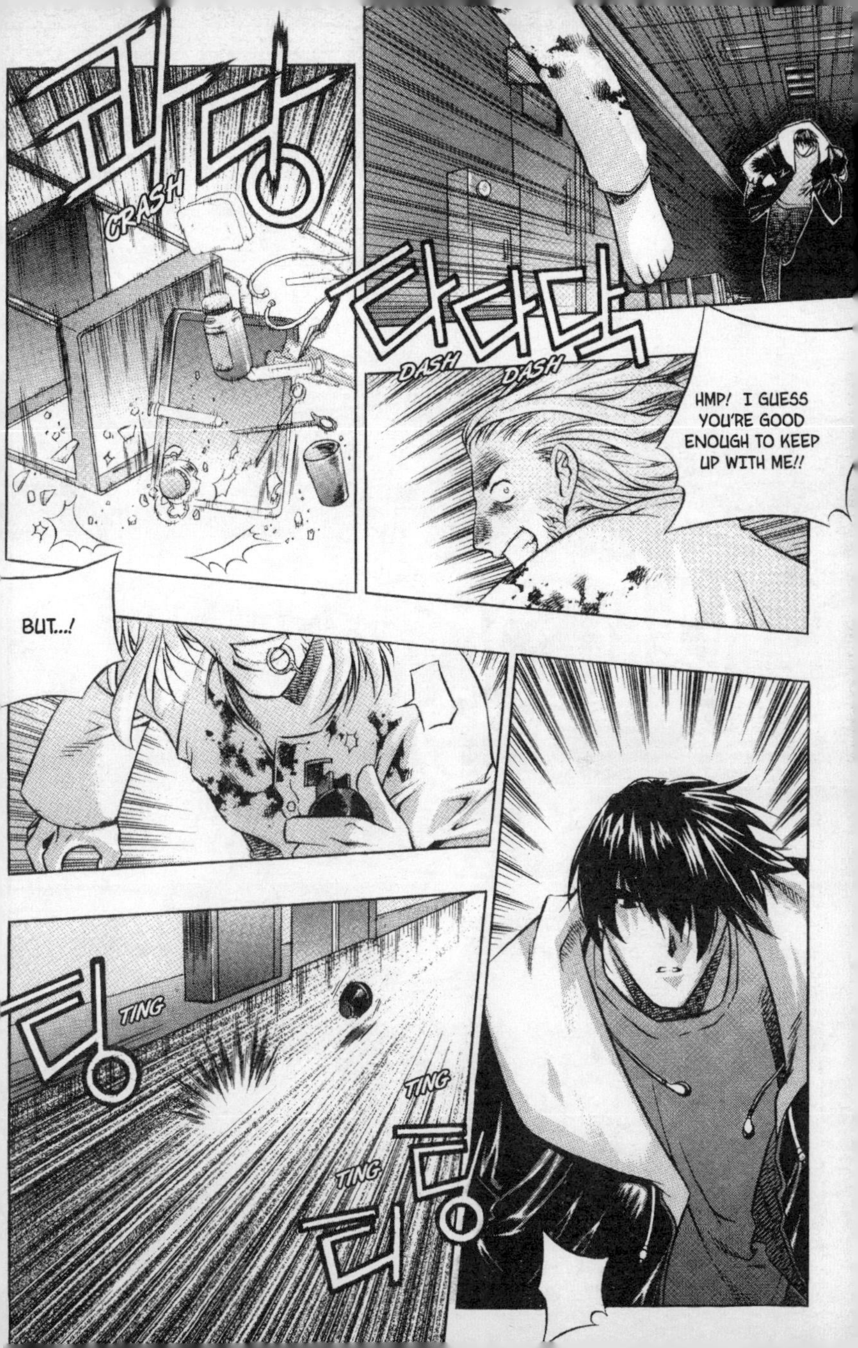
CRASH
DASH
DASH
HMP! I GUESS YOU'RE GOOD ENOUGH TO KEEP UP WITH ME!!
BUT...!
TING
TING
TING

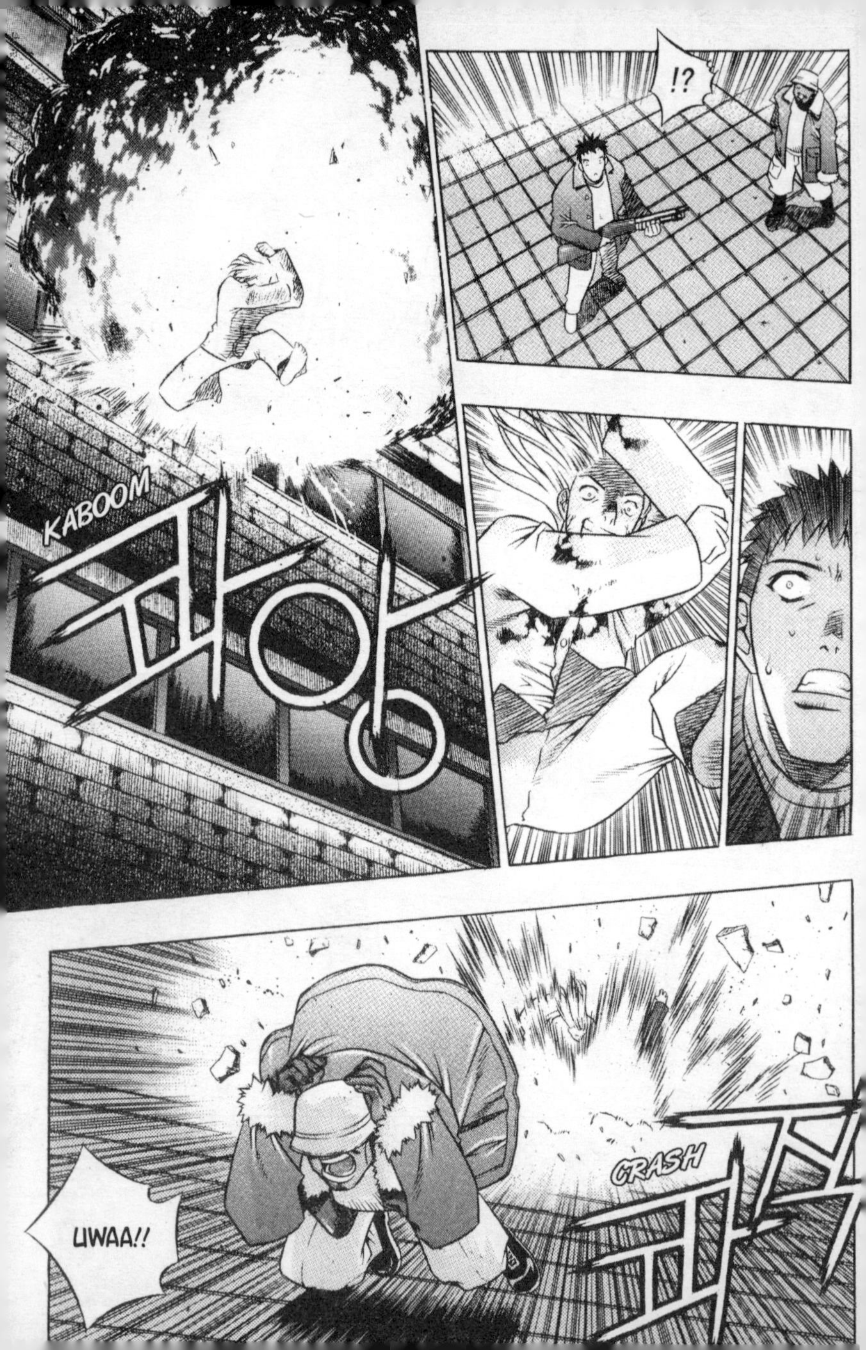
KABOOM
!?
UWAA!!
CRASH

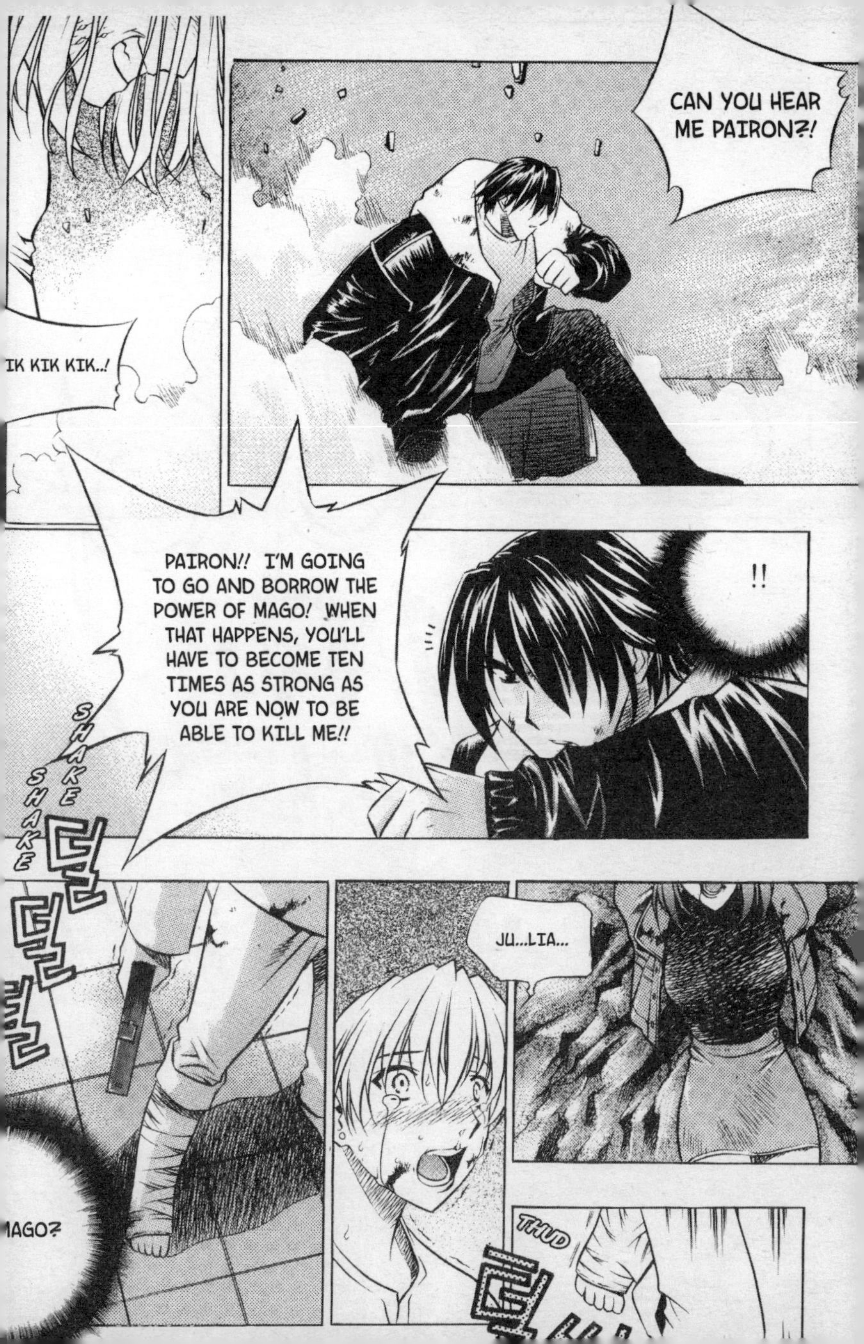
IK KIK KIK..!
CAN YOU HEAR ME PAIRON?!
PAIRON!! I'M GOING TO GO AND BORROW THE POWER OF MAGO! WHEN THAT HAPPENS, YOU'LL HAVE TO BECOME TEN TIMES AS STRONG AS YOU ARE NOW TO BE ABLE TO KILL ME!!
!!
SHAKE
SHAKE
SHAKE
MAGO?
JU...LIA...
THUD

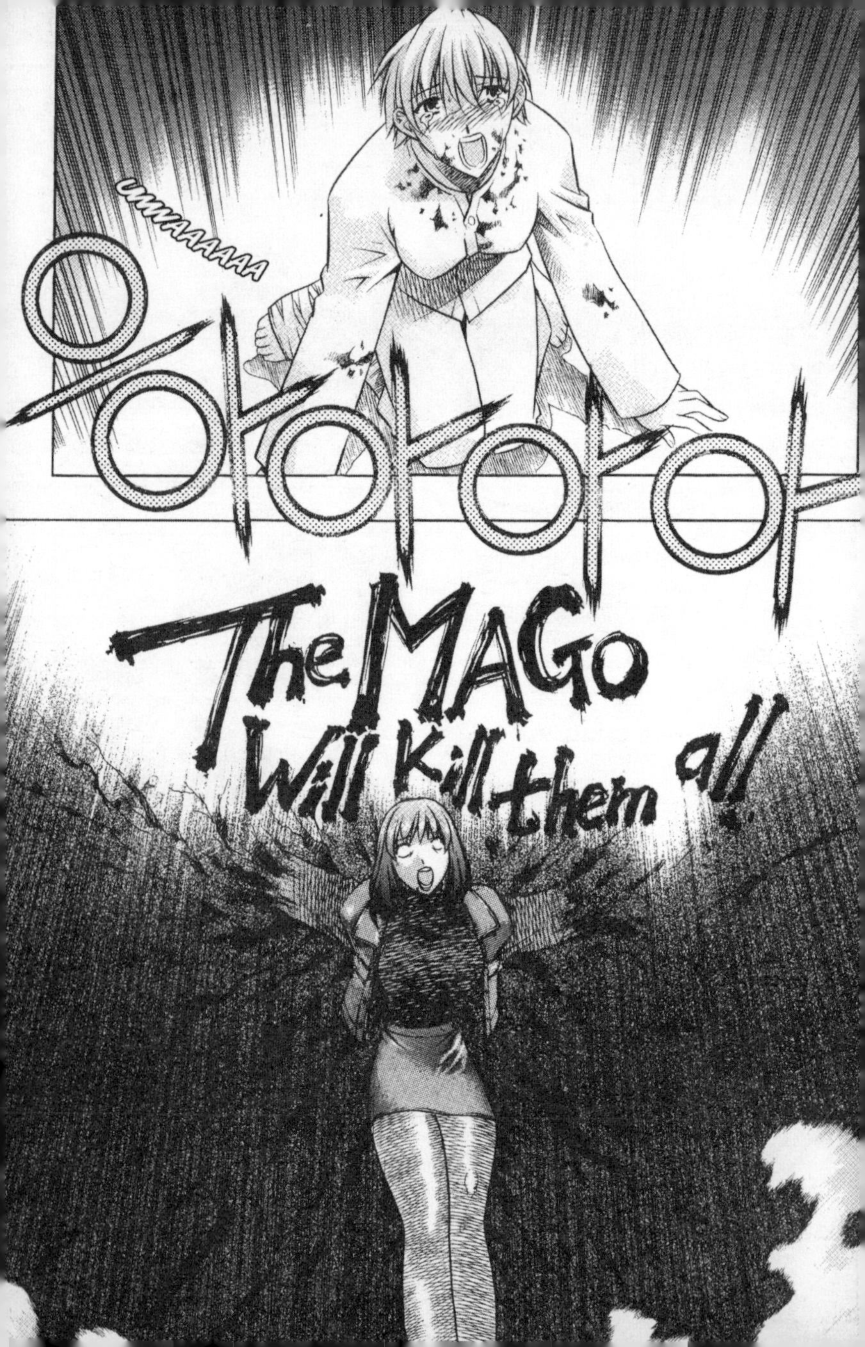
UWAAAAAAA
The MAGO Will Kill them all!

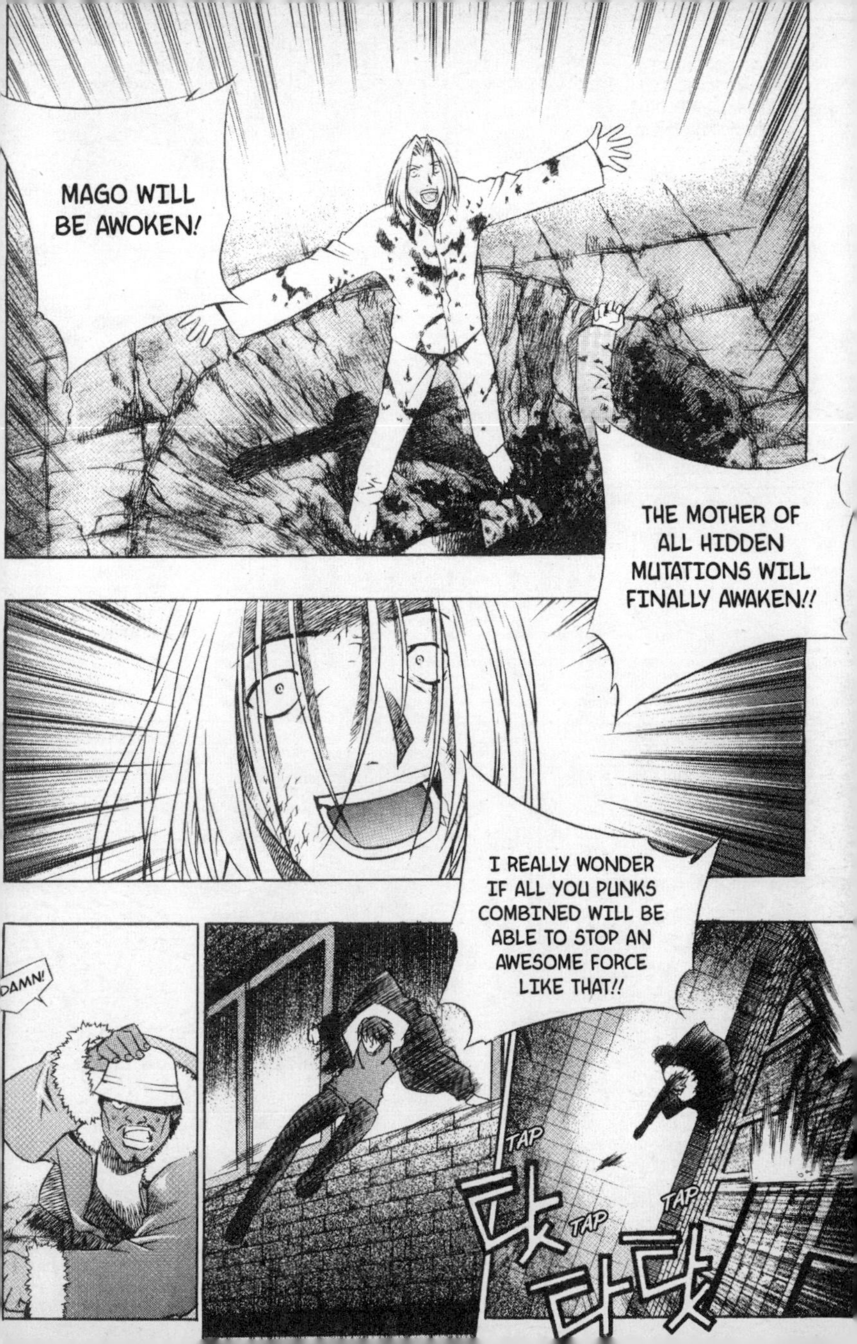
MAGO WILL BE AWOKEN!
THE MOTHER OF ALL HIDDEN MUTATIONS WILL FINALLY AWAKEN!!
I REALLY WONDER IF ALL YOU PUNKS COMBINED WILL BE ABLE TO STOP AN AWESOME FORCE LIKE THAT!!
DAMN!
TAP
TAP
TAP
닥
다닥

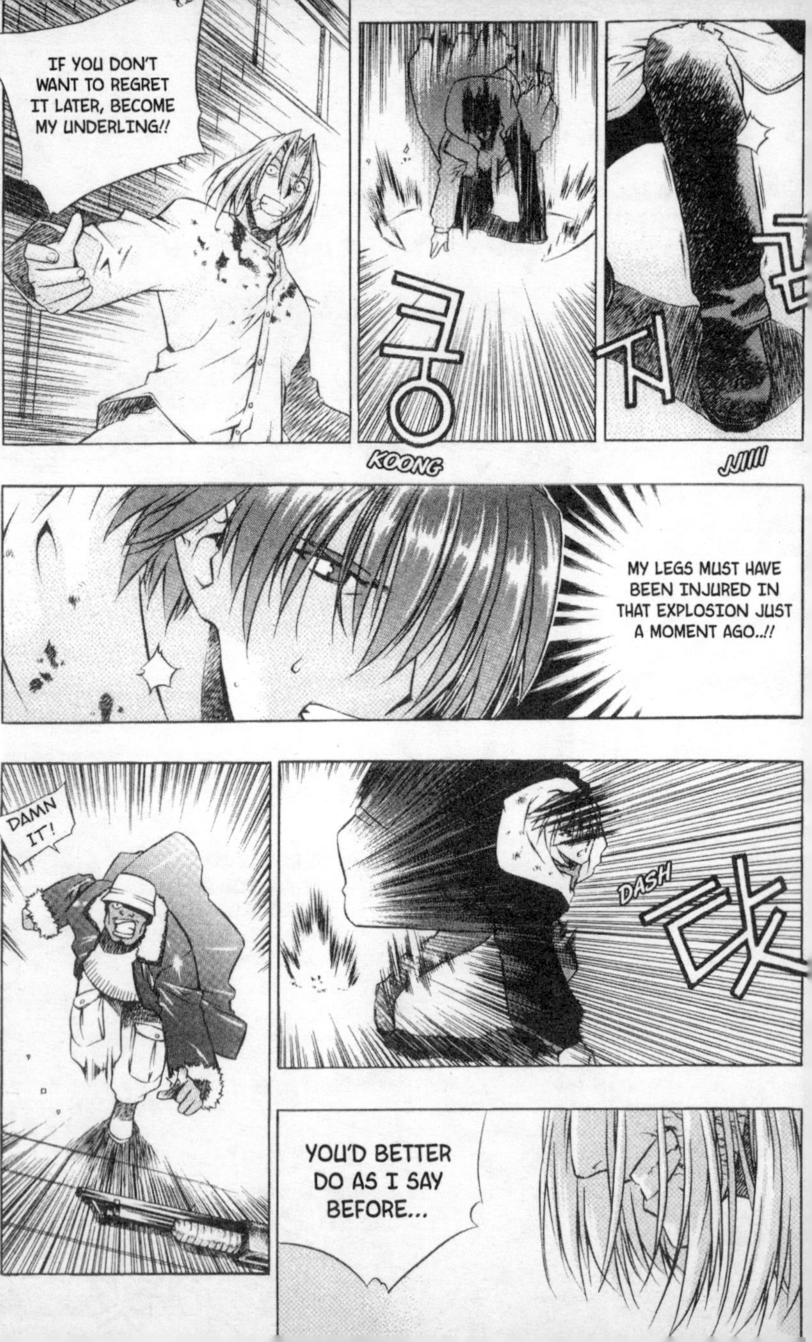
IF YOU DON'T WANT TO REGRET IT LATER, BECOME MY UNDERLING!!
KOONG
JJIIII
MY LEGS MUST HAVE BEEN INJURED IN THAT EXPLOSION JUST A MOMENT AGO..!!
DAMN IT!
DASH
YOU'D BETTER DO AS I SAY BEFORE...

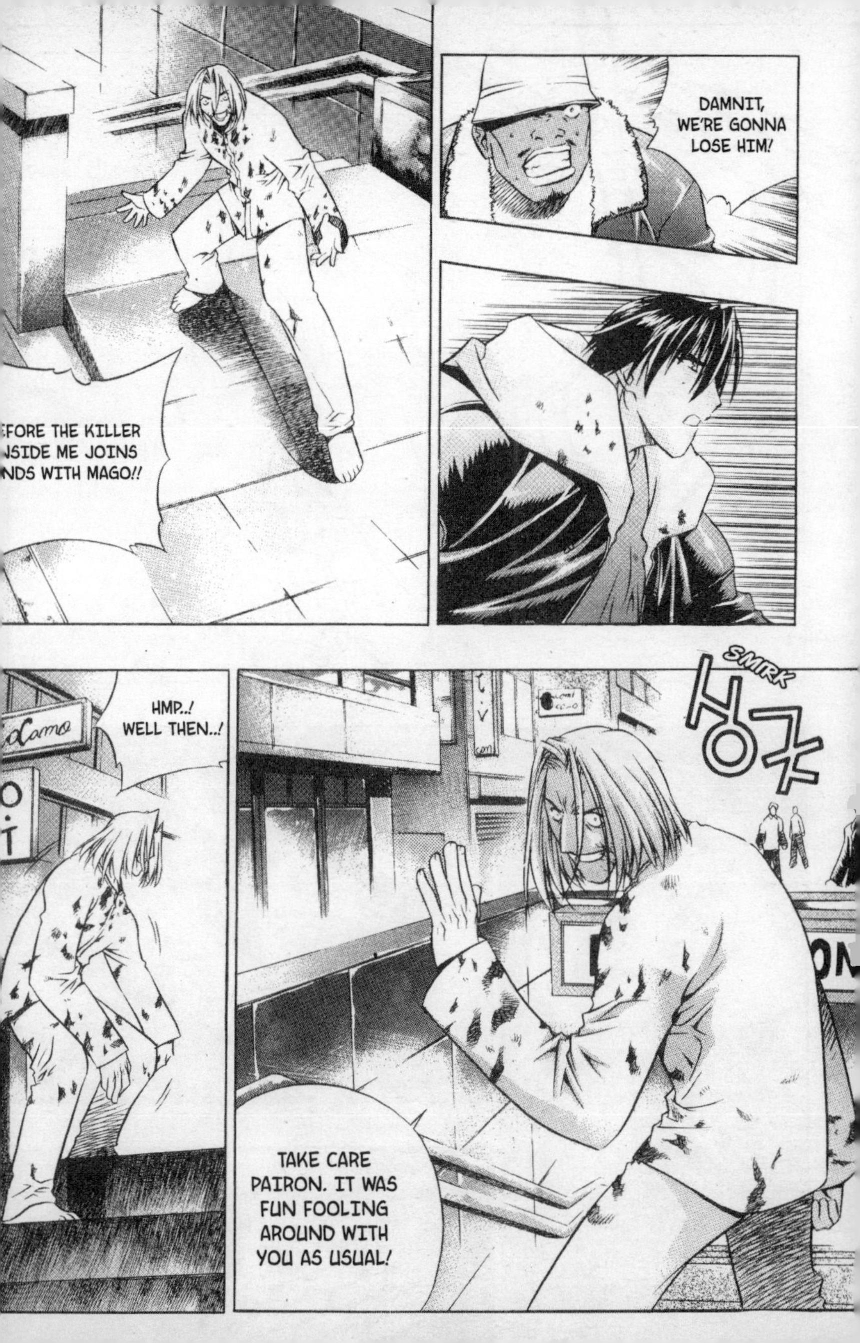
EFORE THE KILLER NSIDE ME JOINS NDS WITH MAGO!!
DAMNIT, WE'RE GONNA LOSE HIM!
HMP..! WELL THEN..!
SMRK
TAKE CARE PAIRON. IT WAS FUN FOOLING AROUND WITH YOU AS USUAL!

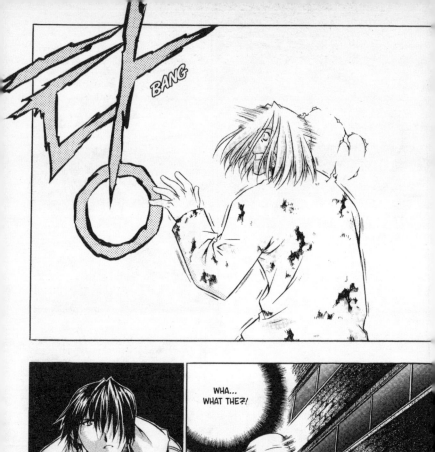

BANG

WHA...
WHAT THE?!

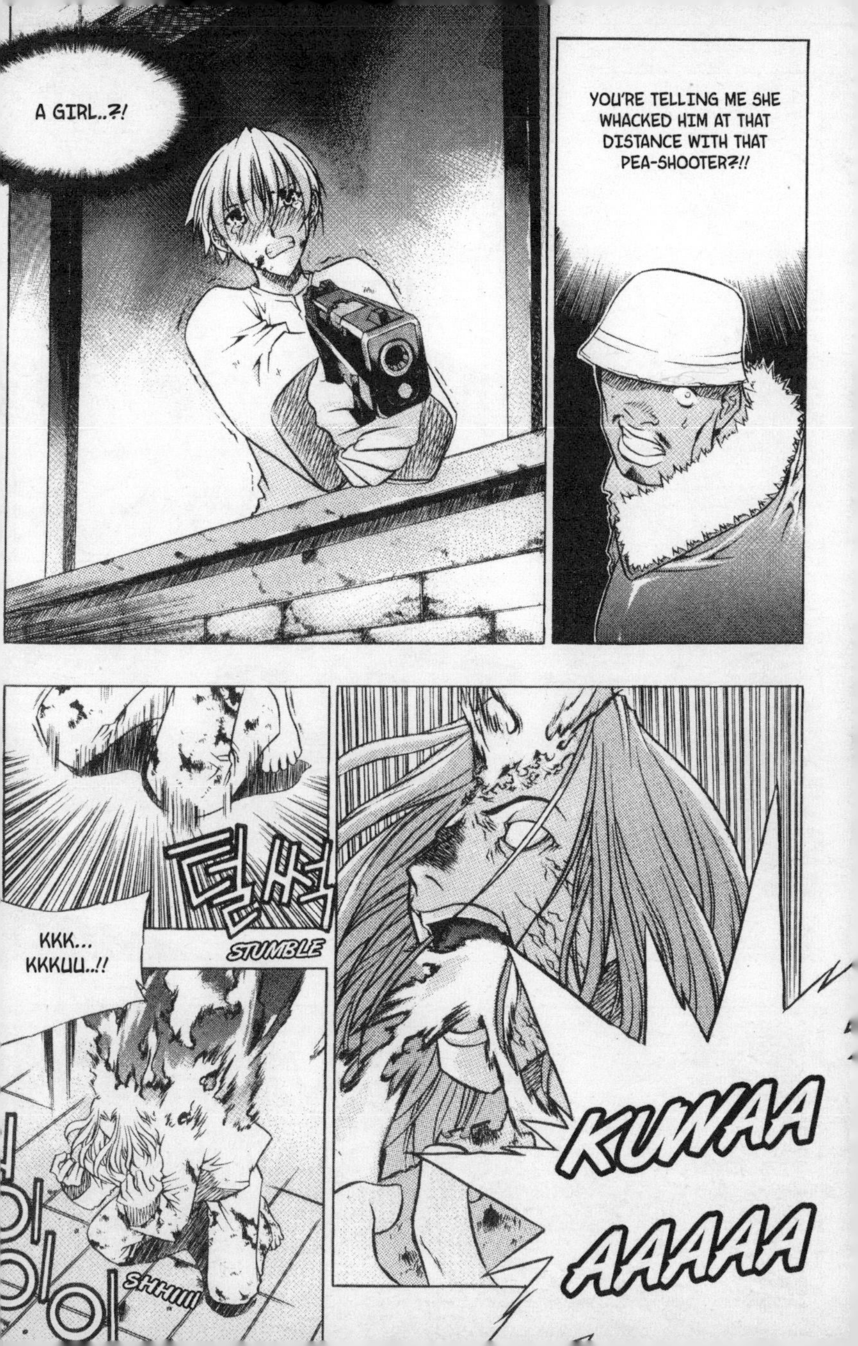
A GIRL..?!
YOU'RE TELLING ME SHE WHACKED HIM AT THAT DISTANCE WITH THAT PEA-SHOOTER?!!
STUMBLE
KKK... KKKUU..!!
SHHIIII
KUWAA AAAAA

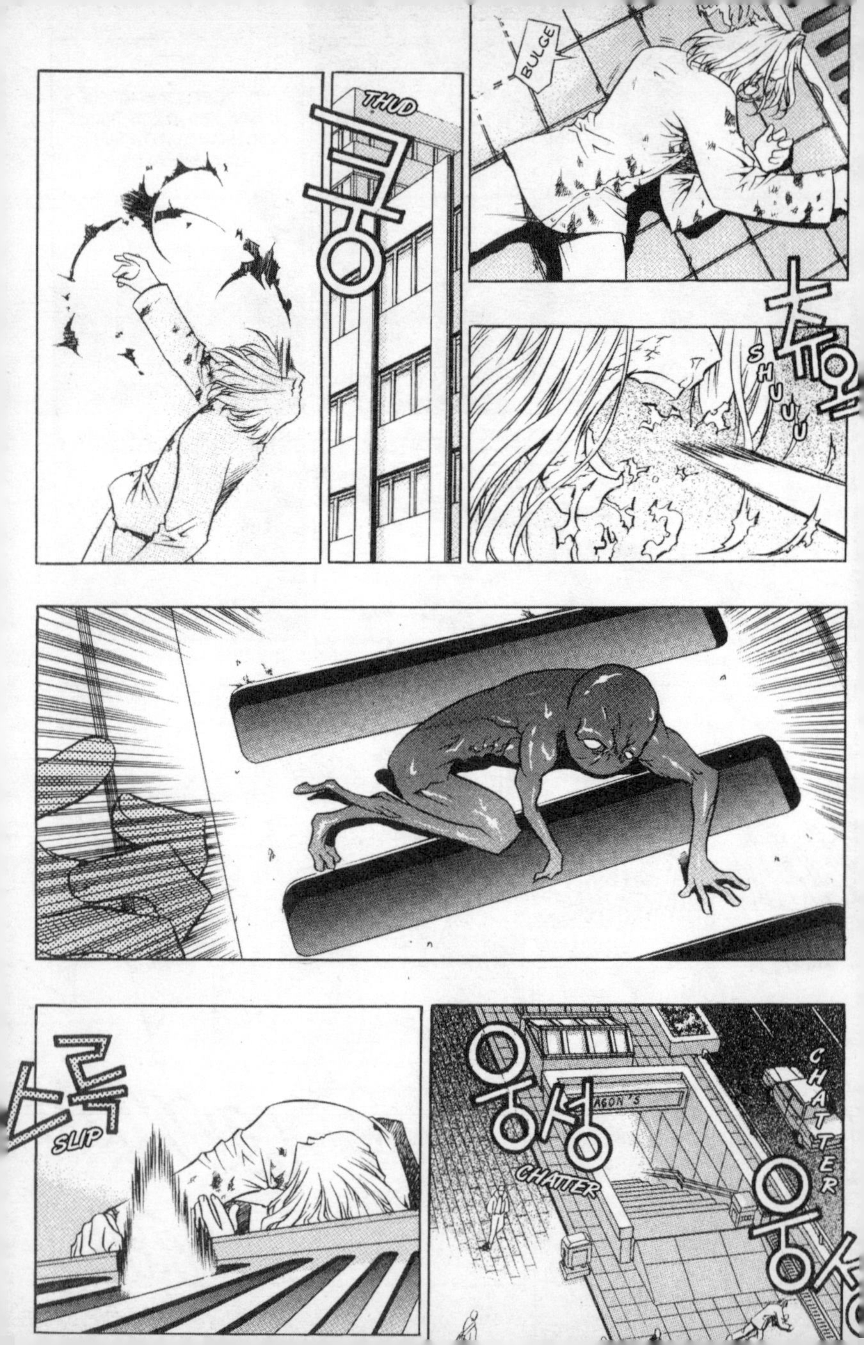
THUD
BULGE
SHUUU
SLIP
CHATTER
CHATTER

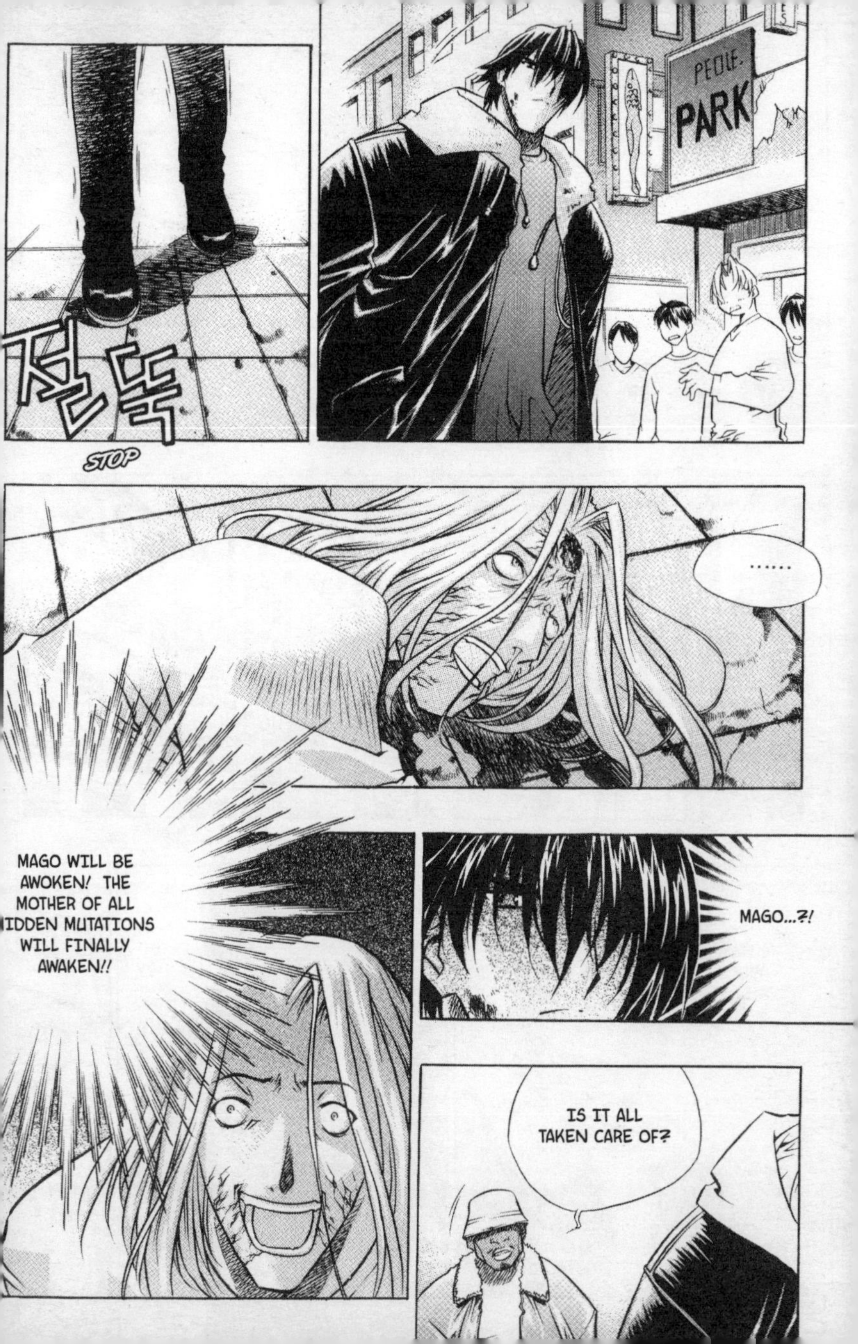
STOP
PEOLE.
PARK
......
MAGO WILL BE AWOKEN! THE MOTHER OF ALL IDDEN MUTATIONS WILL FINALLY AWAKEN!!
MAGO...?!
IS IT ALL TAKEN CARE OF?

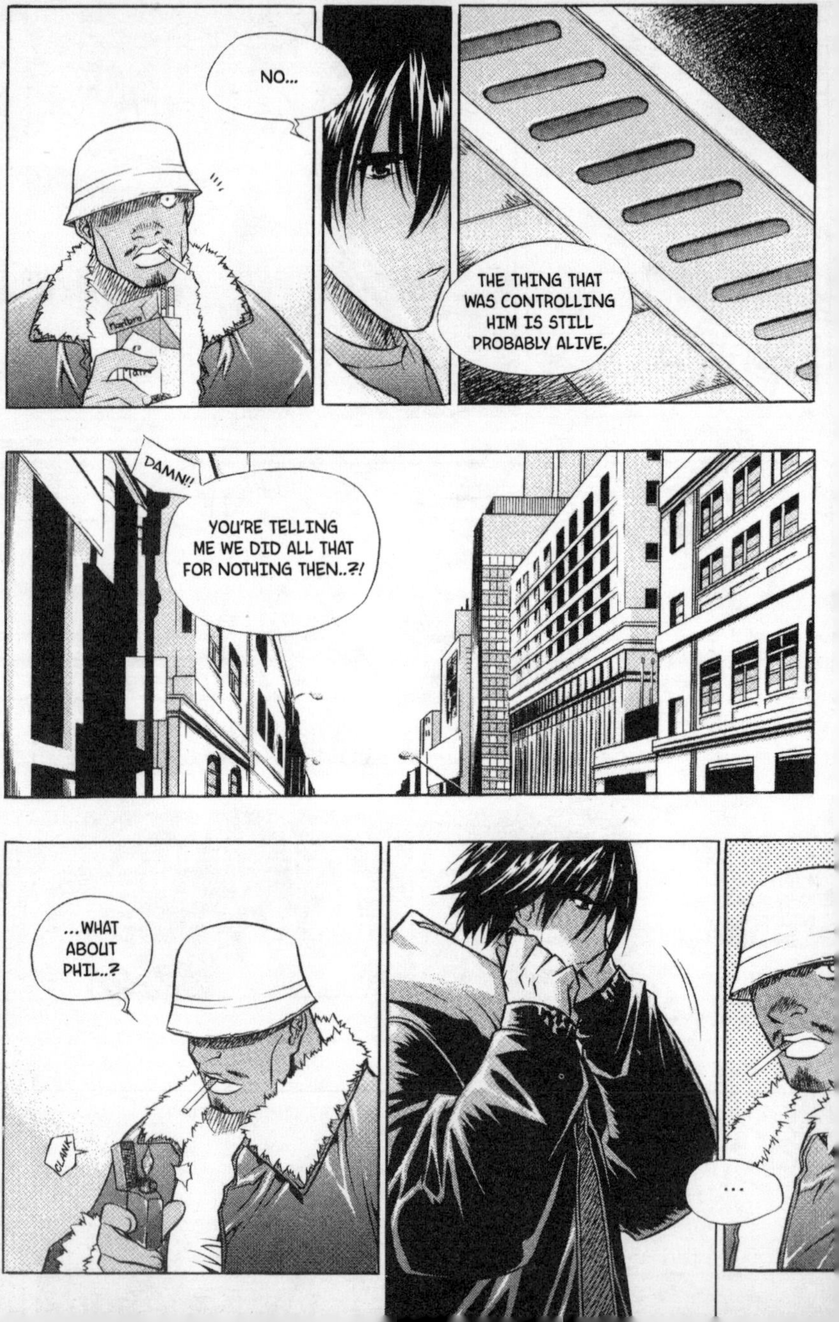
NO...
THE THING THAT WAS CONTROLLING HIM IS STILL PROBABLY ALIVE.
DAMN!!
YOU'RE TELLING ME WE DID ALL THAT FOR NOTHING THEN..?!
...WHAT ABOUT PHIL..?
CLANK
...

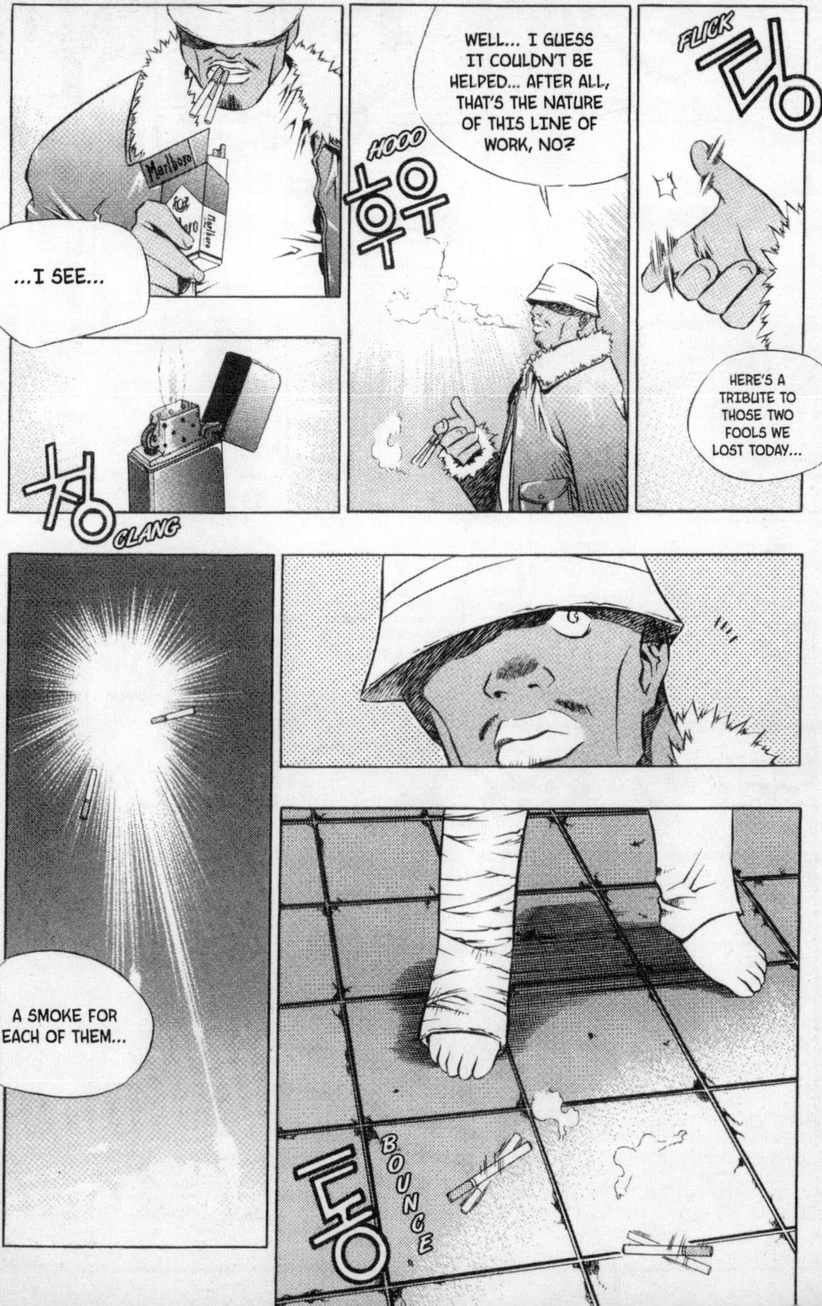
...I SEE...
CLANG
HOOO
WELL... I GUESS IT COULDN'T BE HELPED... AFTER ALL, THAT'S THE NATURE OF THIS LINE OF WORK, NO?
FLICK
HERE'S A TRIBUTE TO THOSE TWO FOOLS WE LOST TODAY...
A SMOKE FOR EACH OF THEM...
BOUNCE

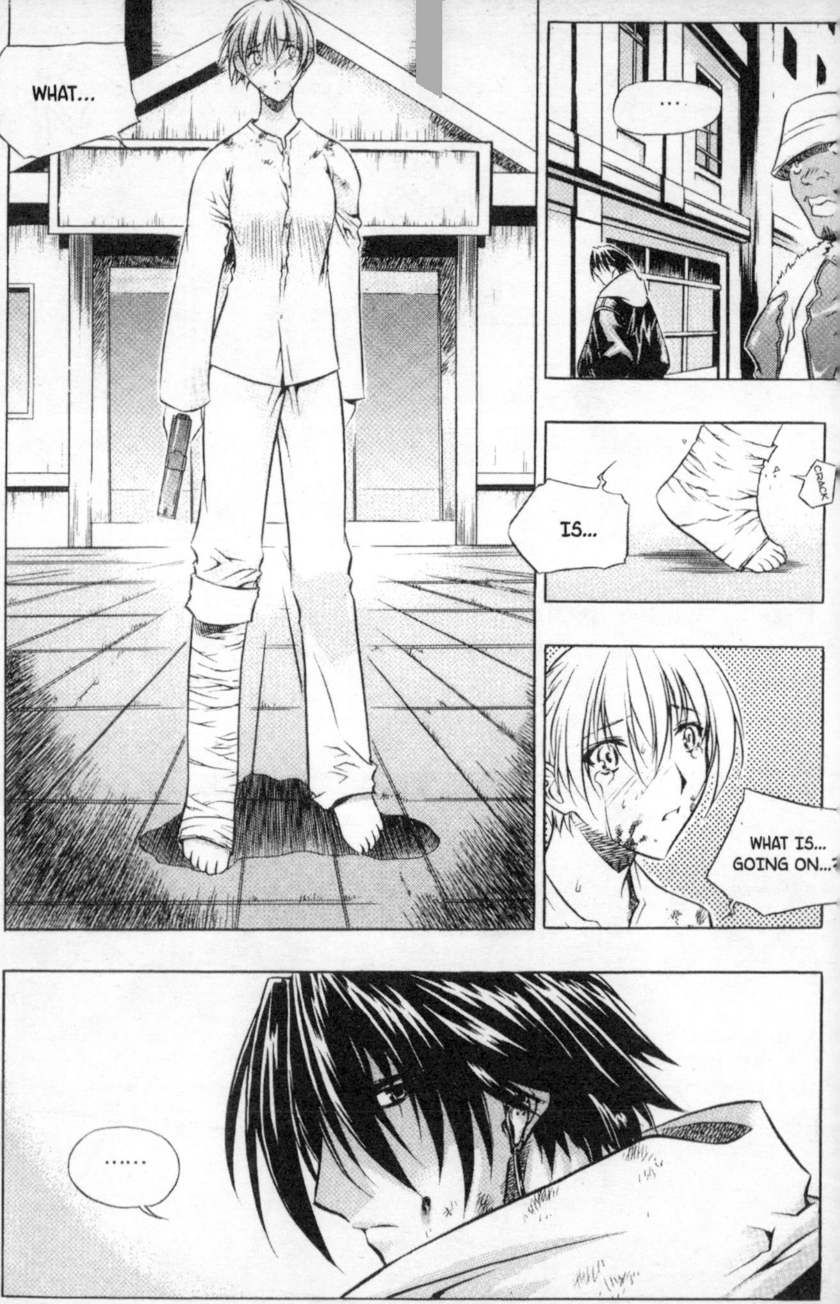
WHAT...
....
IS...
CRACK
WHAT IS... GOING ON...?
......

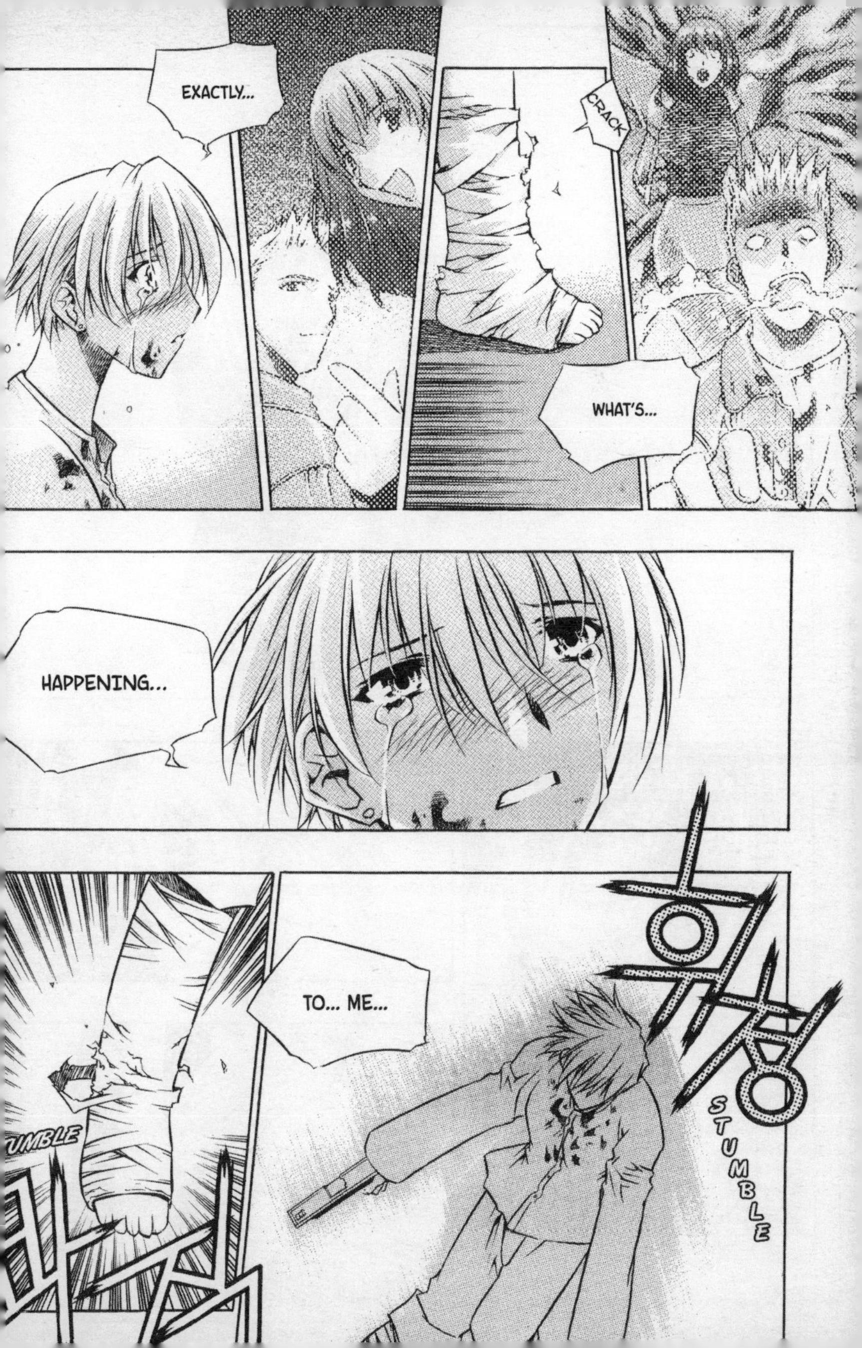
EXACTLY...
CRACK
WHAT'S...
HAPPENING...
UMBLE
TO... ME...
STUMBLE

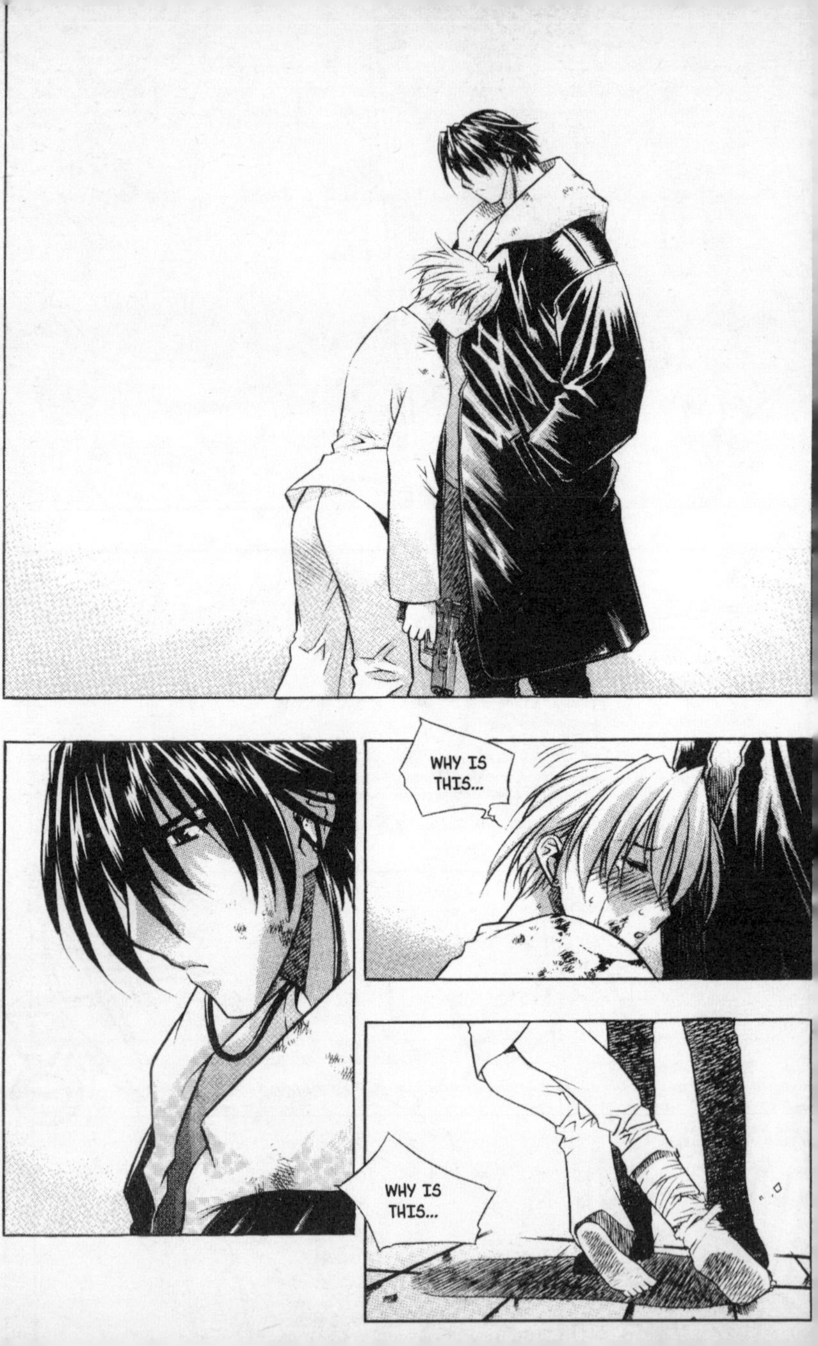
WHY IS THIS...
WHY IS THIS...

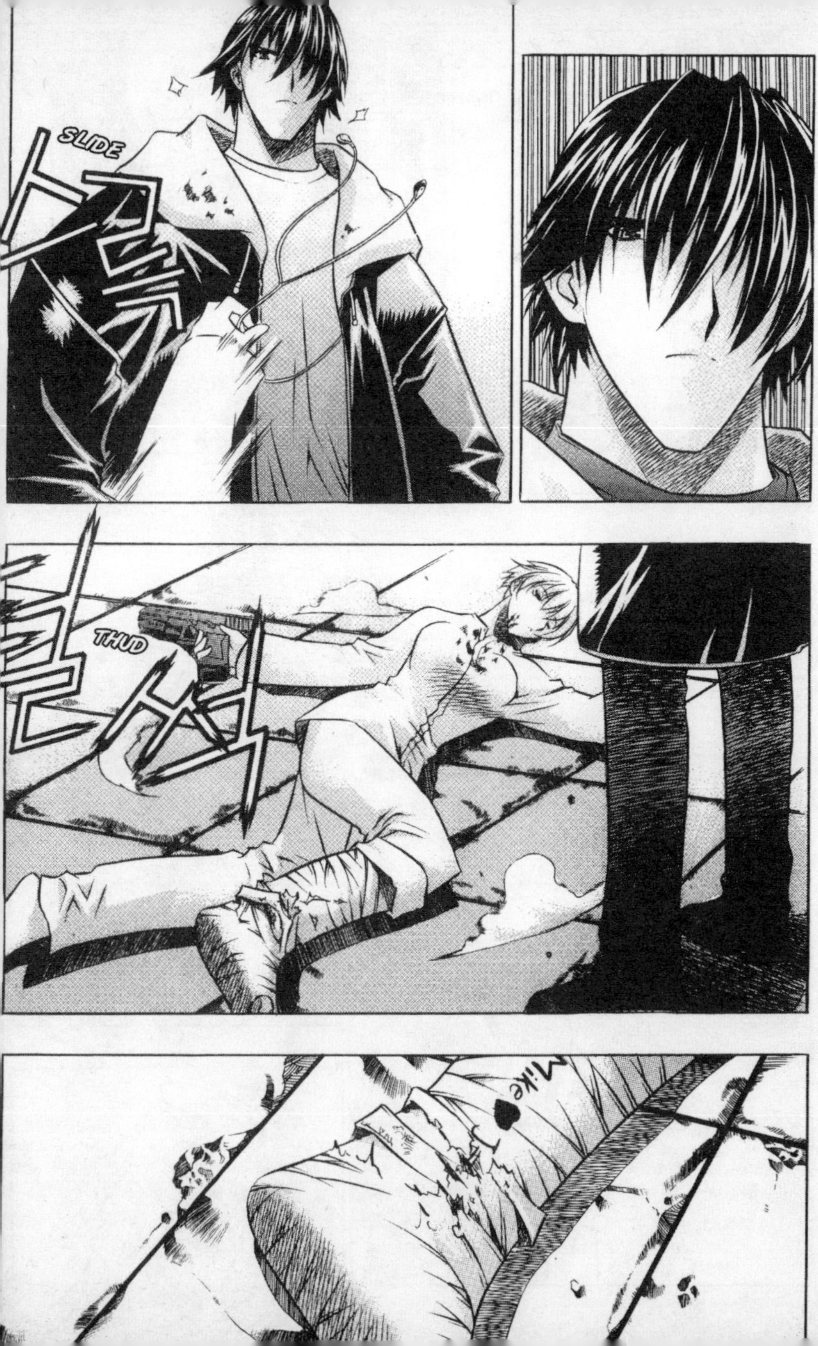
SLIDE
THUD
Mike

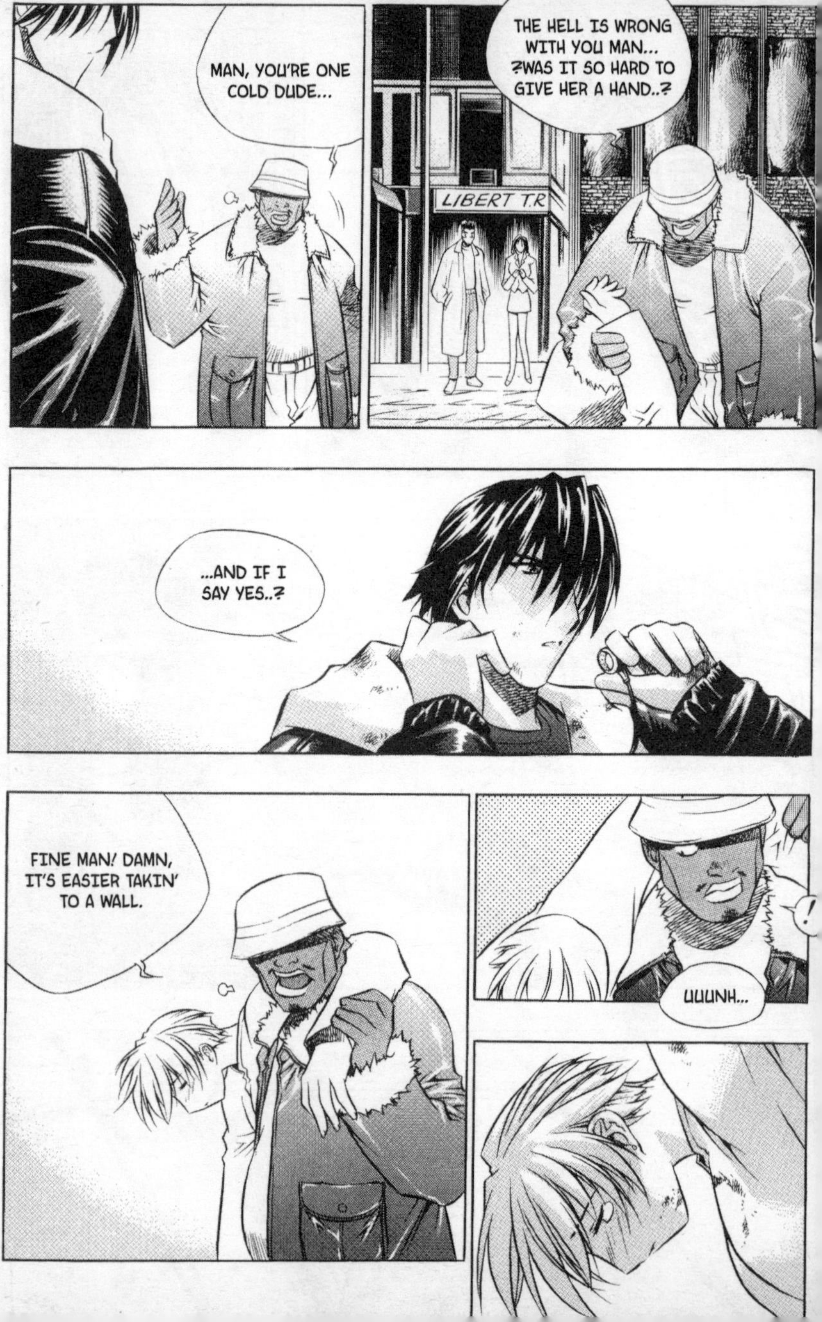

MAN, YOU'RE ONE COLD DUDE...
THE HELL IS WRONG WITH YOU MAN... ?WAS IT SO HARD TO GIVE HER A HAND..?
LIBERT T.R
...AND IF I SAY YES..?
FINE MAN! DAMN, IT'S EASIER TAKIN' TO A WALL.
!
UUUNH...

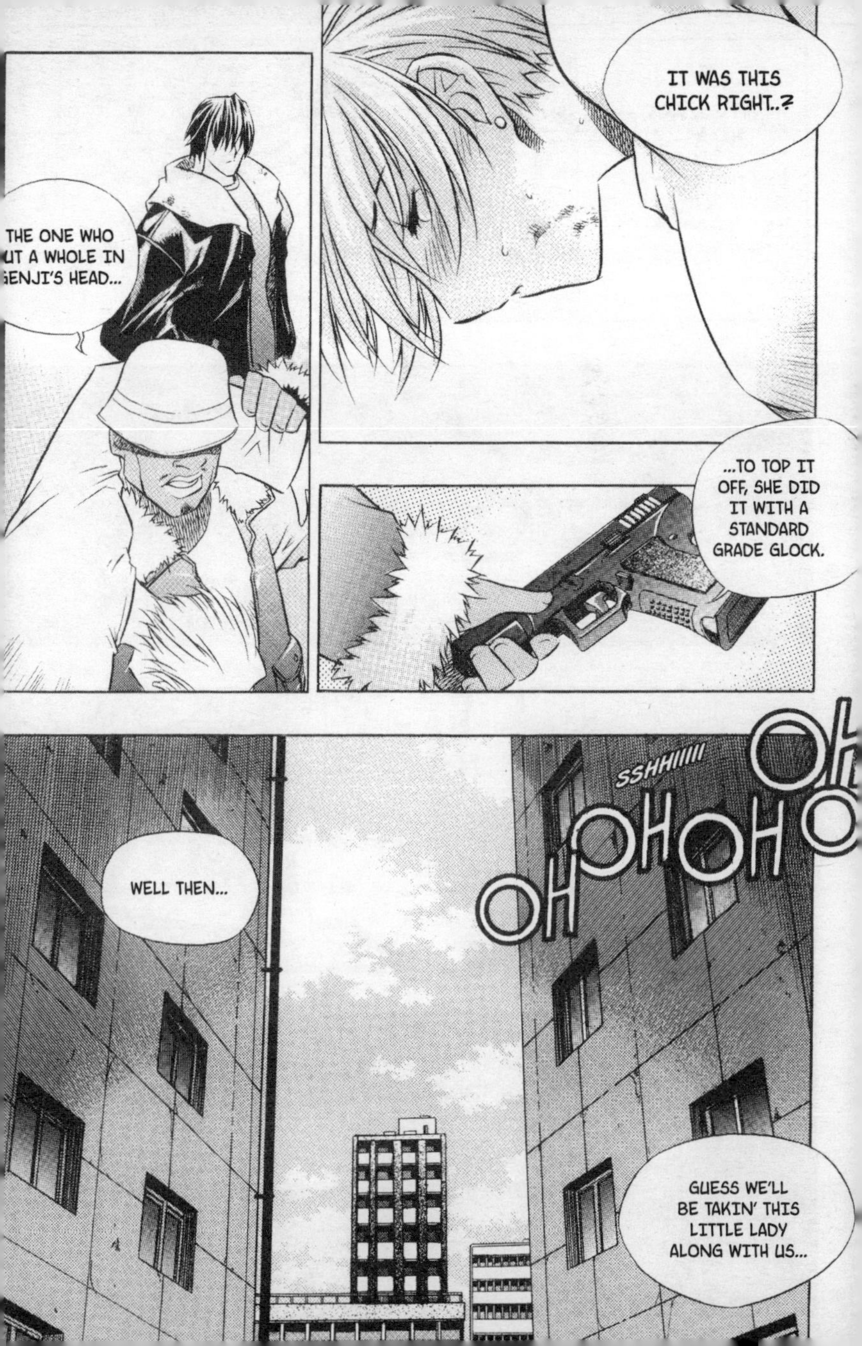
THE ONE WHO UT A WHOLE IN ENJI'S HEAD...
IT WAS THIS CHICK RIGHT..?
...TO TOP IT OFF, SHE DID IT WITH A STANDARD GRADE GLOCK.
WELL THEN...
SSHHIIIIII
OHOHOHOHOH
GUESS WE'LL BE TAKIN' THIS LITTLE LADY ALONG WITH US...

xmonth xday 2005
City : N.O.A.
Time : 3:30 pm
Case Number : xxx-xxxx
Incident Severity : b-
Infected Survivors : 4
Infected killed : 2

AT THE BEGINNING OF THE 21ST CENTURY, PEOPLE WITH ABILITIES
BEYOND THAT OF THE AVERAGE HUMAN STARTED APPEARING.

After cornering the
2nd generation mutation
within Genji Shizuma,
extermination attempt
failed. The parasite
successfully separated
from its host, while the
host was terminated.

THEY HAVE BECOME THE NEWLY EVOLVED HUMAN. HOWEVER, UNDER
THE EYES OF "NORMAL" HUMANS, THEY WERE LOOKED UPON AS
NOTHING MORE THAN FREAKISH MUTANTS.

Victims include among others, hospital workers and patients. The actual number of victims is undetermined but estimated to be extremely high. This concludes the report from the incident. Debriefing to take place later.

NOT BEING ACCEPTED ANYWHERE, THESE EVOLVED PEOPLE BECAME EXILES, WANDERING AIMLESSLY. WHEREVER THEY WENT THEY BECAME FOREIGNERS.

After clean up of the victims, it is requested that the issue of responsibility and that of the survivor be addressed as soon as possible. That is all.

THESE PEOPLE WITH SPECIAL ABILITIES WERE MORE COMMONLY REFERRED TO AS HAVING "MUTATIONS."

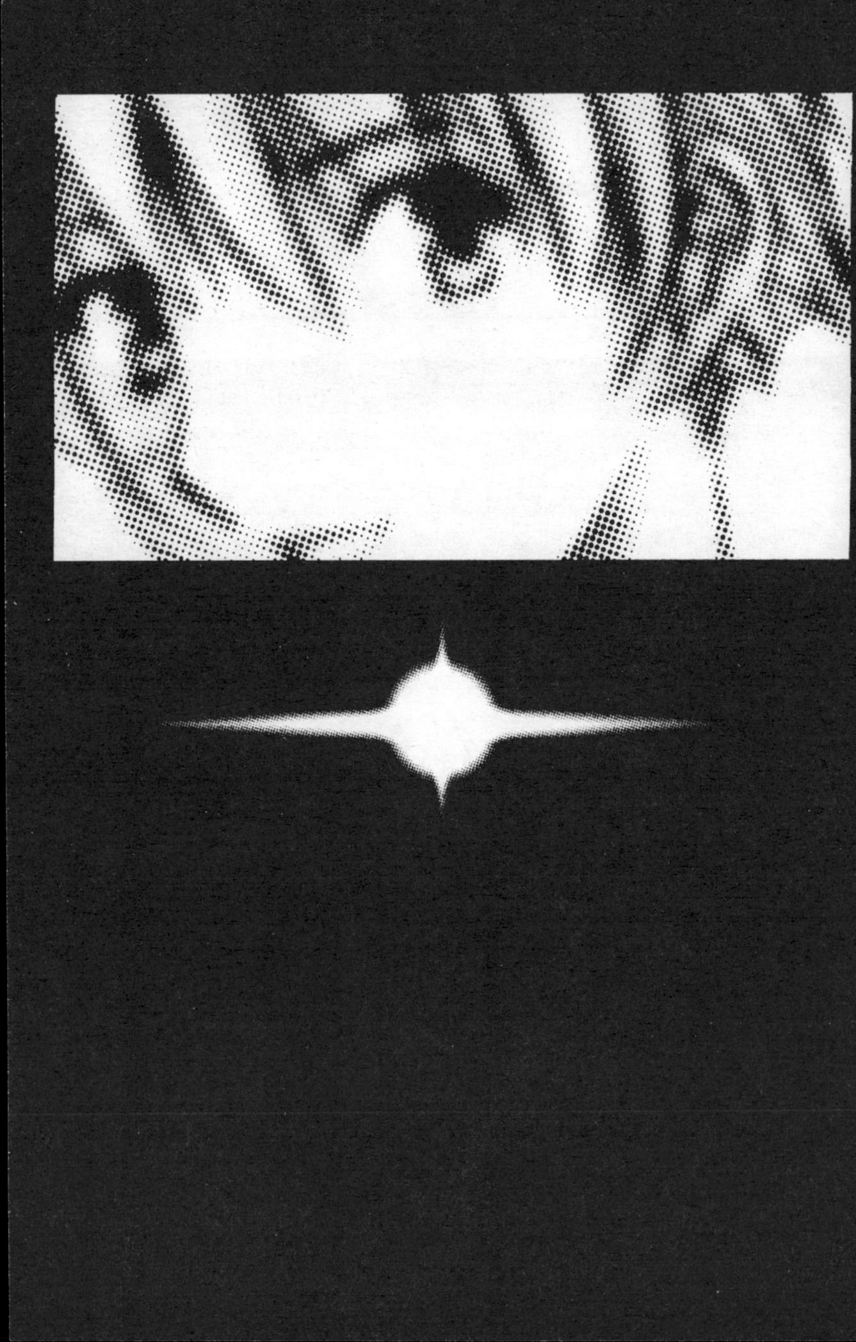

Jay Berell, age : 20
Date : xmonth xday 2005
An incident which occurred at a hospital in the suburban outskirts of N.O.A. City was caused by a 2nd generation mutation, code named "Shizuma Genji." As a result, a woman with powers deriving from a mutation was discovered. After analysis of the report, Jay Berell is to be inducted into the Peigenz Organization.

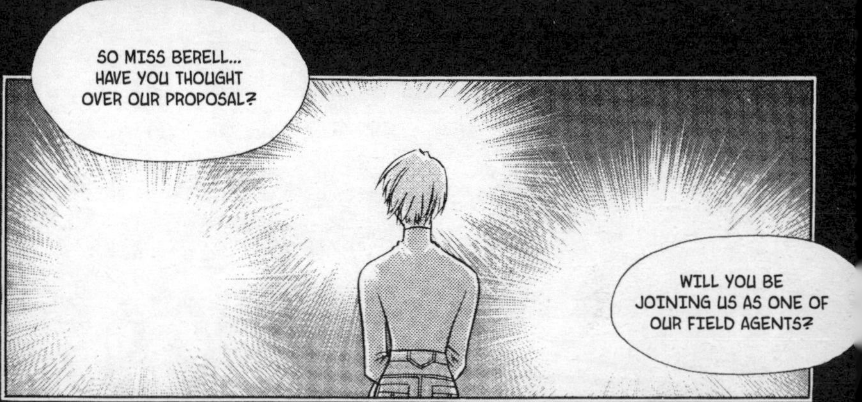
SO MISS BERELL... HAVE YOU THOUGHT OVER OUR PROPOSAL?
WILL YOU BE JOINING US AS ONE OF OUR FIELD AGENTS?

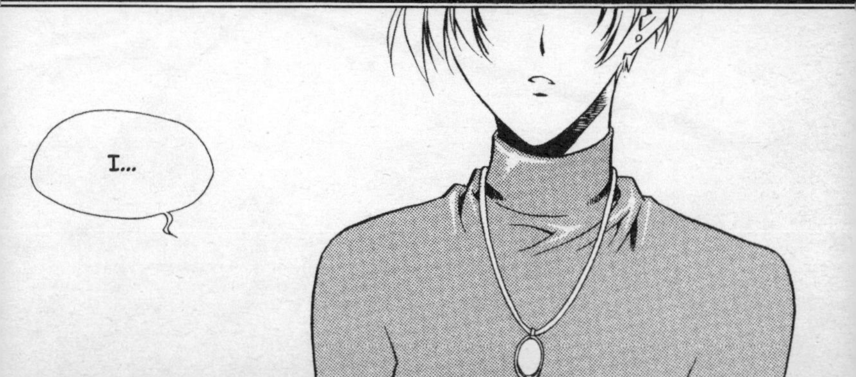
I...

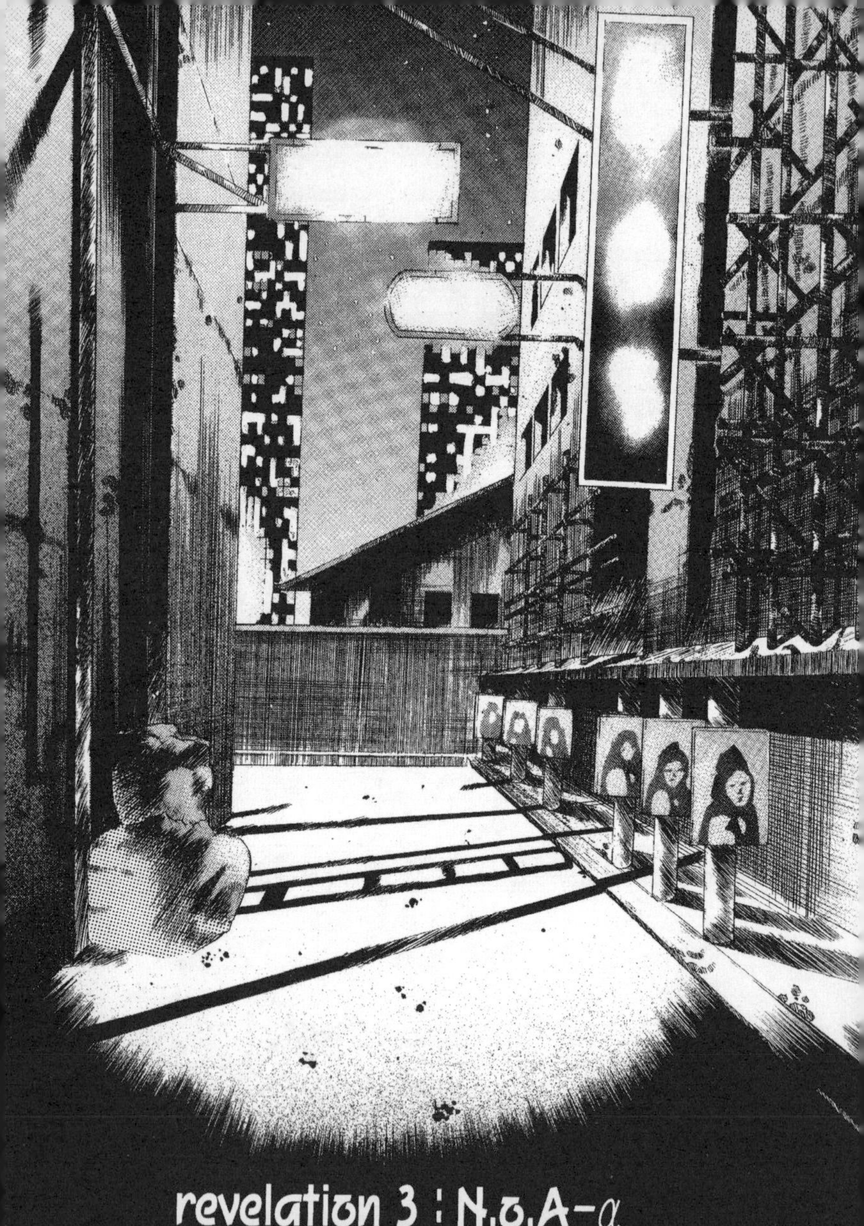

revelation 3 : N.o.A-α

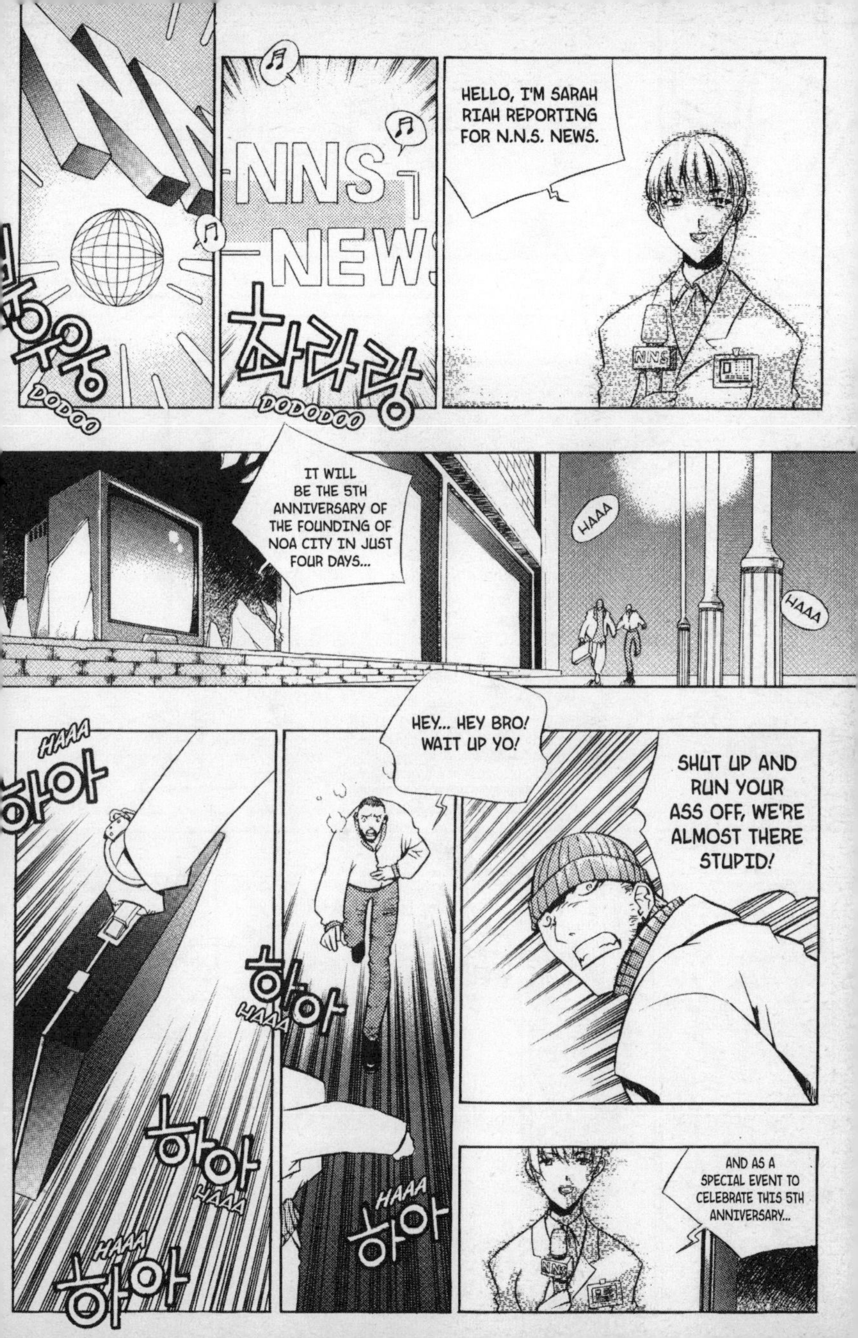
DODOO
NNS NEWS
차라랑
DODODOO
HELLO, I'M SARAH RIAH REPORTING FOR N.N.S. NEWS.
NNS
IT WILL BE THE 5TH ANNIVERSARY OF THE FOUNDING OF NOA CITY IN JUST FOUR DAYS...
HAAA
HAAA
HAAA
하아
하아
HAAA
하아
HAAA
HAAA
하아
HEY... HEY BRO! WAIT UP YO!
하아
HAAA
HAAA
하아
SHUT UP AND RUN YOUR ASS OFF, WE'RE ALMOST THERE STUPID!
AND AS A SPECIAL EVENT TO CELEBRATE THIS 5TH ANNIVERSARY...
NNS

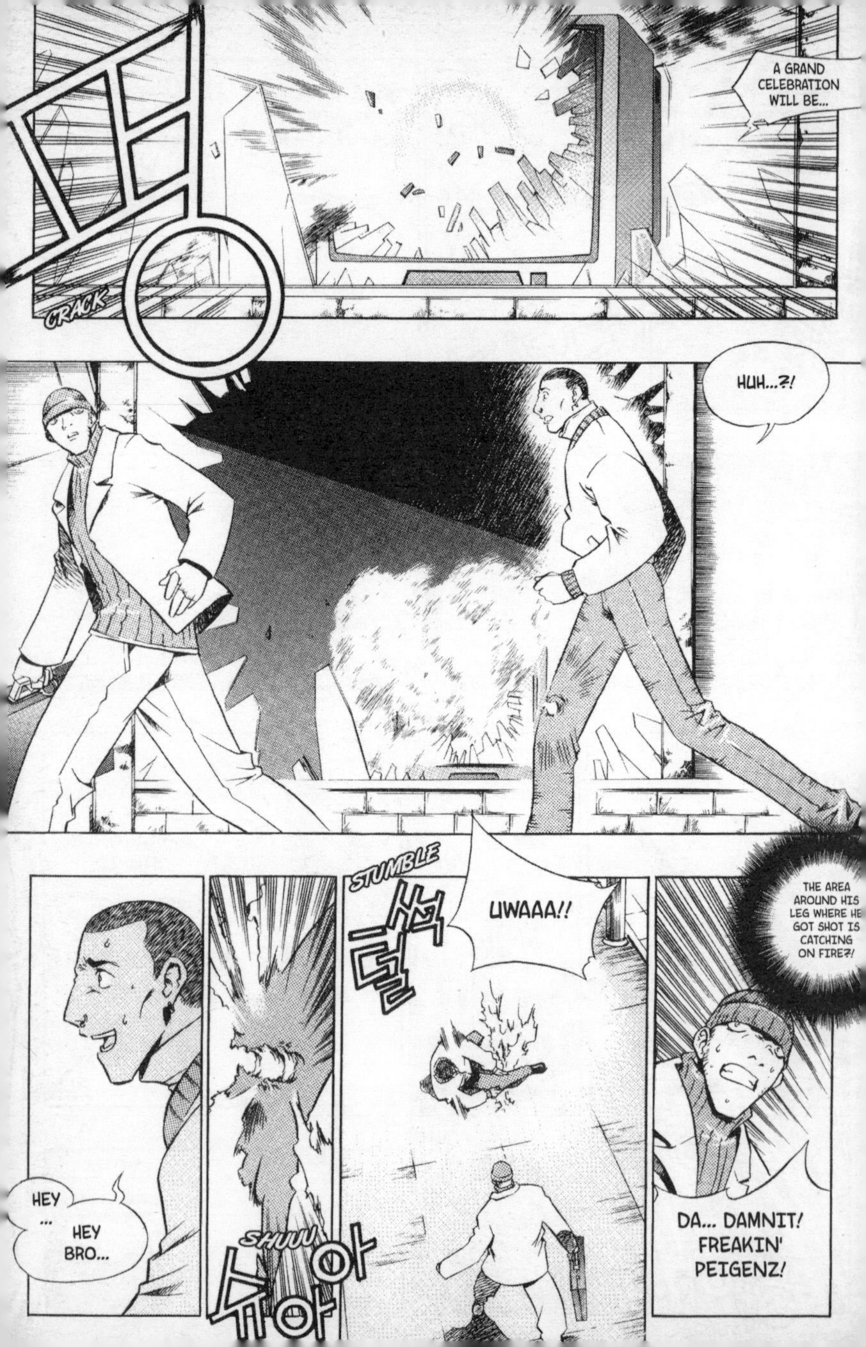
CRACK
A GRAND CELEBRATION WILL BE...
HUH...?!
HEY ... HEY BRO...
SHUUU
STUMBLE
UWAAA!!
THE AREA AROUND HIS LEG WHERE HE GOT SHOT IS CATCHING ON FIRE?!
DA... DAMNIT! FREAKIN' PEIGENZ!

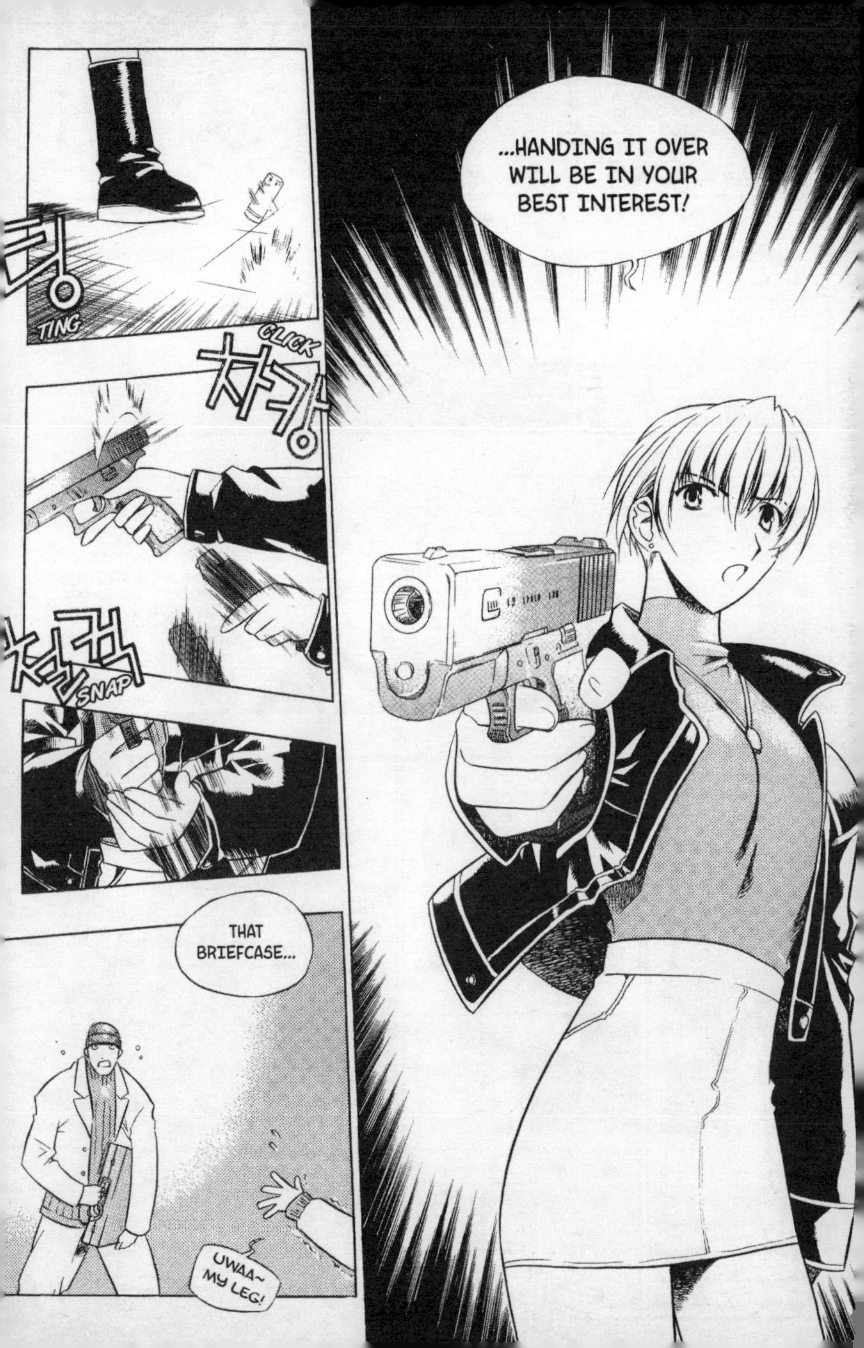
TING
CLICK
SNAP
THAT BRIEFCASE...
UWAA~ MY LEG!
...HANDING IT OVER WILL BE IN YOUR BEST INTEREST!

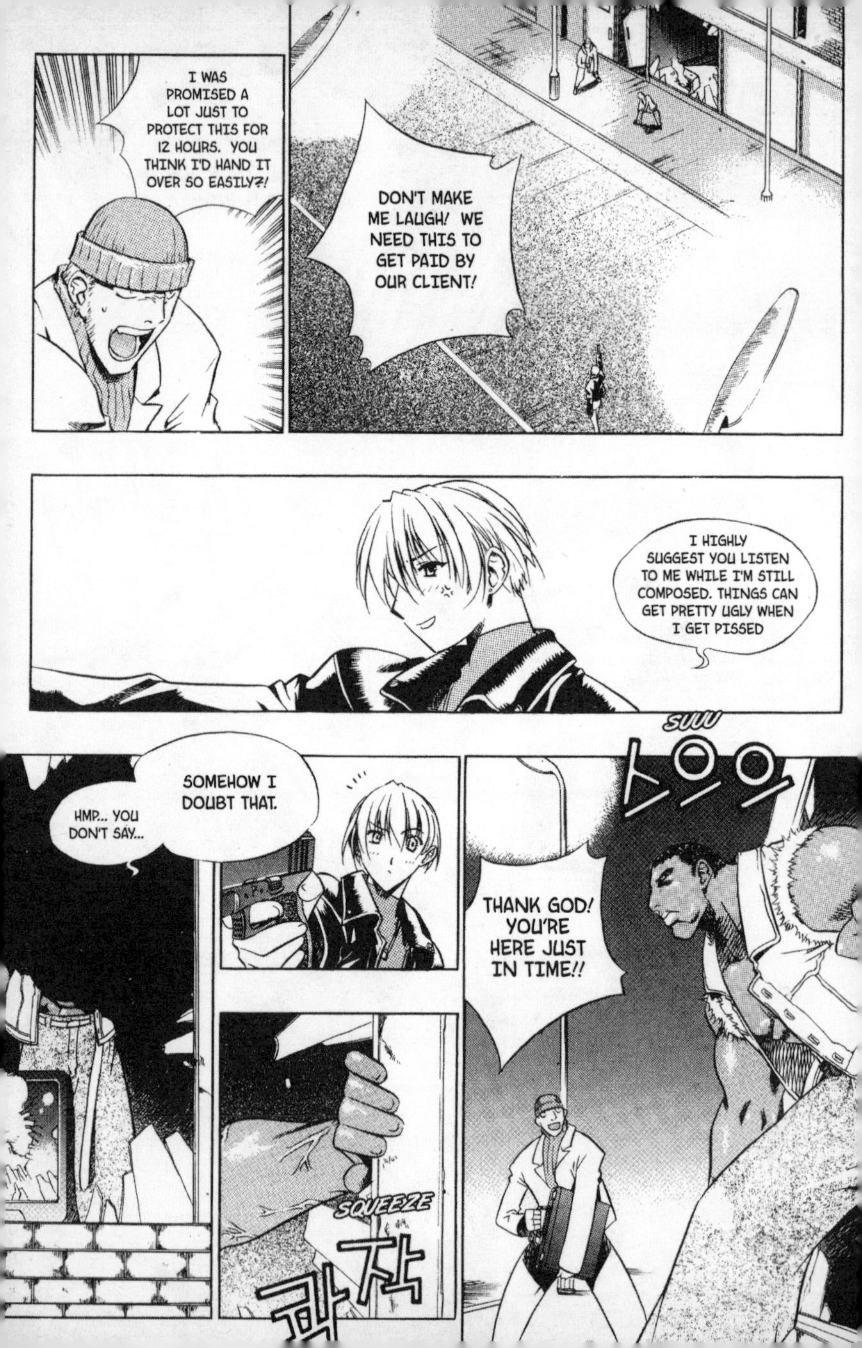
I WAS PROMISED A LOT JUST TO PROTECT THIS FOR 12 HOURS. YOU THINK I'D HAND IT OVER SO EASILY?!
DON'T MAKE ME LAUGH! WE NEED THIS TO GET PAID BY OUR CLIENT!
I HIGHLY SUGGEST YOU LISTEN TO ME WHILE I'M STILL COMPOSED. THINGS CAN GET PRETTY UGLY WHEN I GET PISSED
HMP... YOU DON'T SAY...
SOMEHOW I DOUBT THAT.
SQUEEZE
SUUU
THANK GOD! YOU'RE HERE JUST IN TIME!!

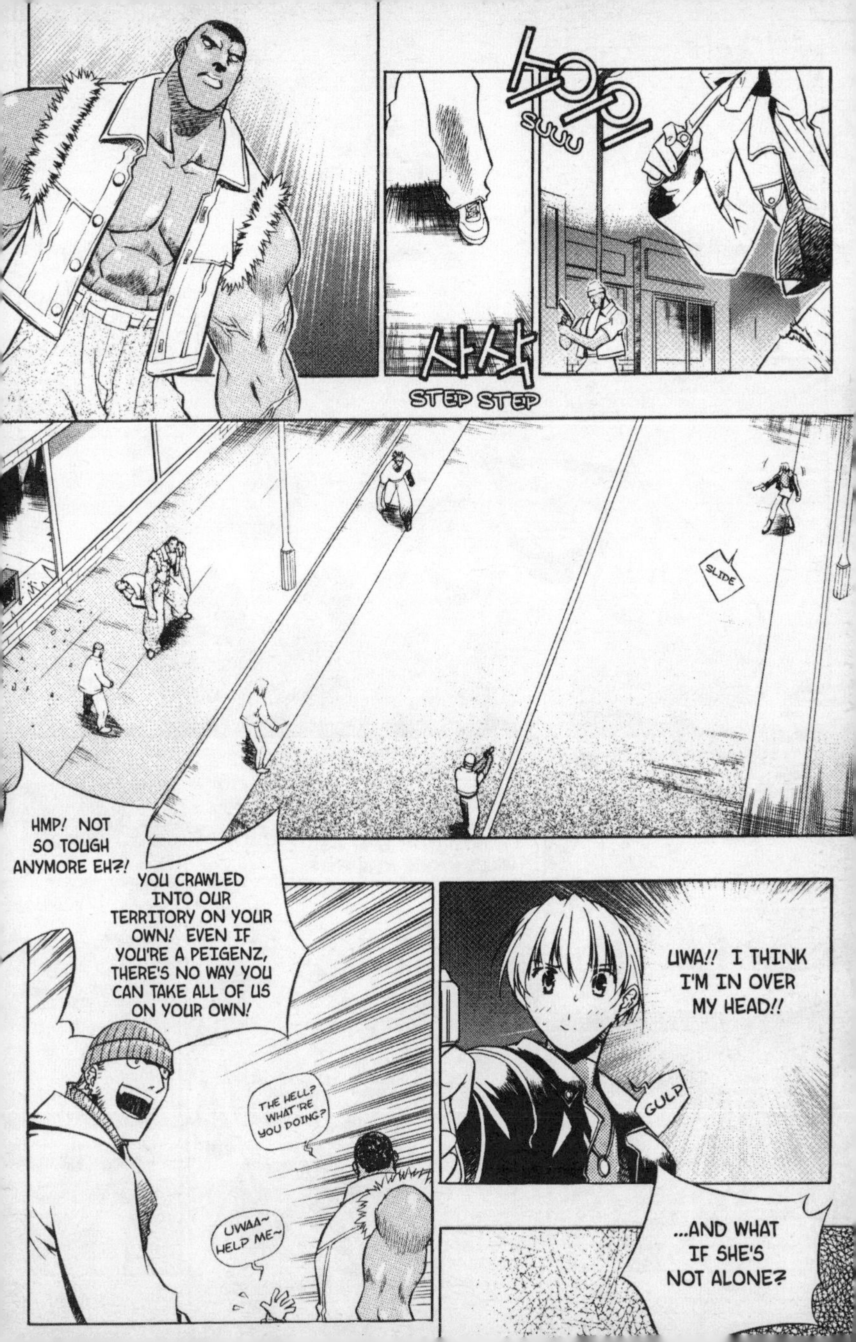

스으윽
SUUU
사사삭
STEP STEP
SLIDE
HMP! NOT SO TOUGH ANYMORE EH?!
YOU CRAWLED INTO OUR TERRITORY ON YOUR OWN! EVEN IF YOU'RE A PEIGENZ, THERE'S NO WAY YOU CAN TAKE ALL OF US ON YOUR OWN!
THE HELL? WHAT'RE YOU DOING?
UWAA~ HELP ME~
UWA!! I THINK I'M IN OVER MY HEAD!!
GULP
...AND WHAT IF SHE'S NOT ALONE?

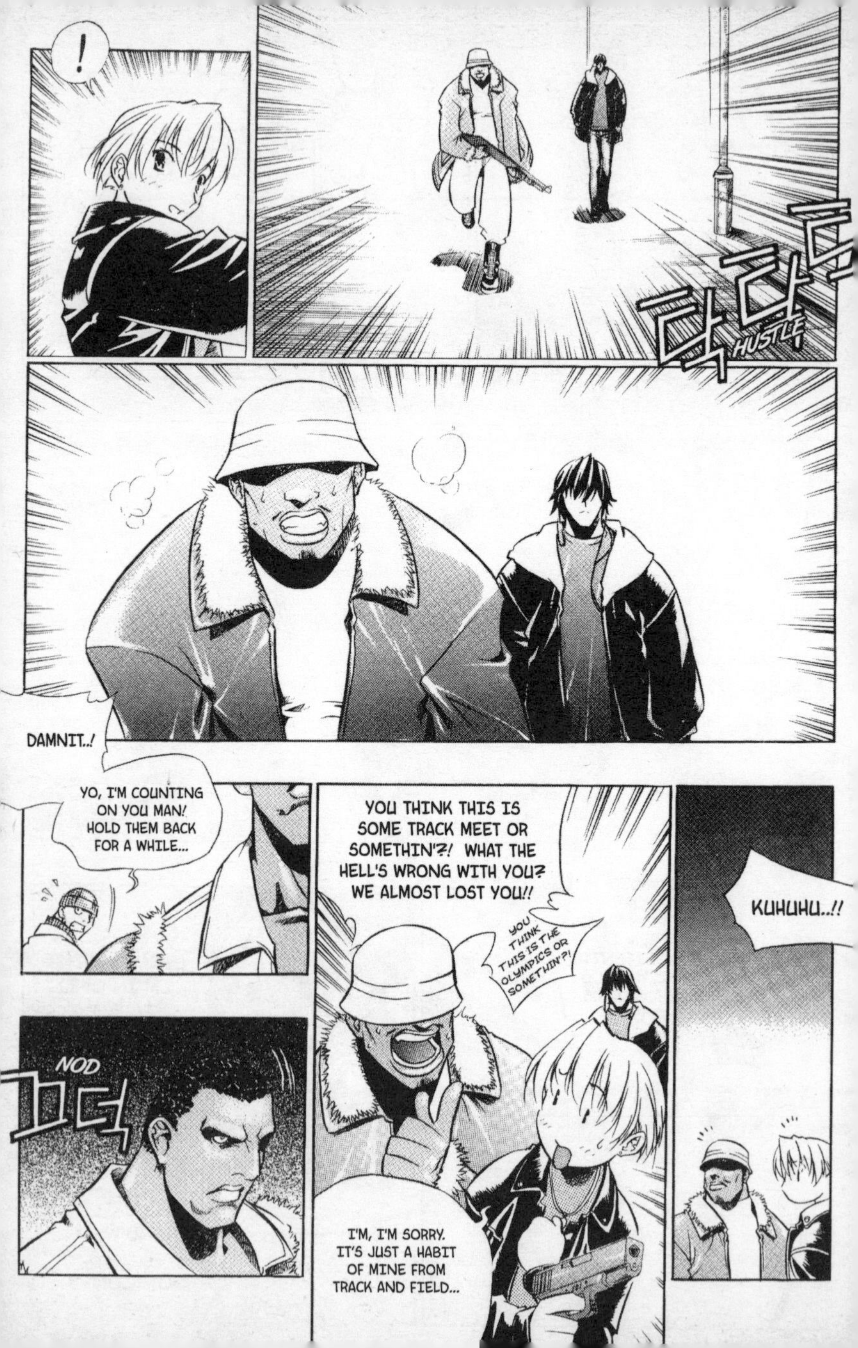
!
HUSTLE
DAMNIT..!
YO, I'M COUNTING ON YOU MAN! HOLD THEM BACK FOR A WHILE...
NOD
YOU THINK THIS IS SOME TRACK MEET OR SOMETHIN'?! WHAT THE HELL'S WRONG WITH YOU? WE ALMOST LOST YOU!!
YOU THINK THIS IS THE OLYMPICS OR SOMETHIN'?!
I'M, I'M SORRY. IT'S JUST A HABIT OF MINE FROM TRACK AND FIELD...
KUHUHU..!!

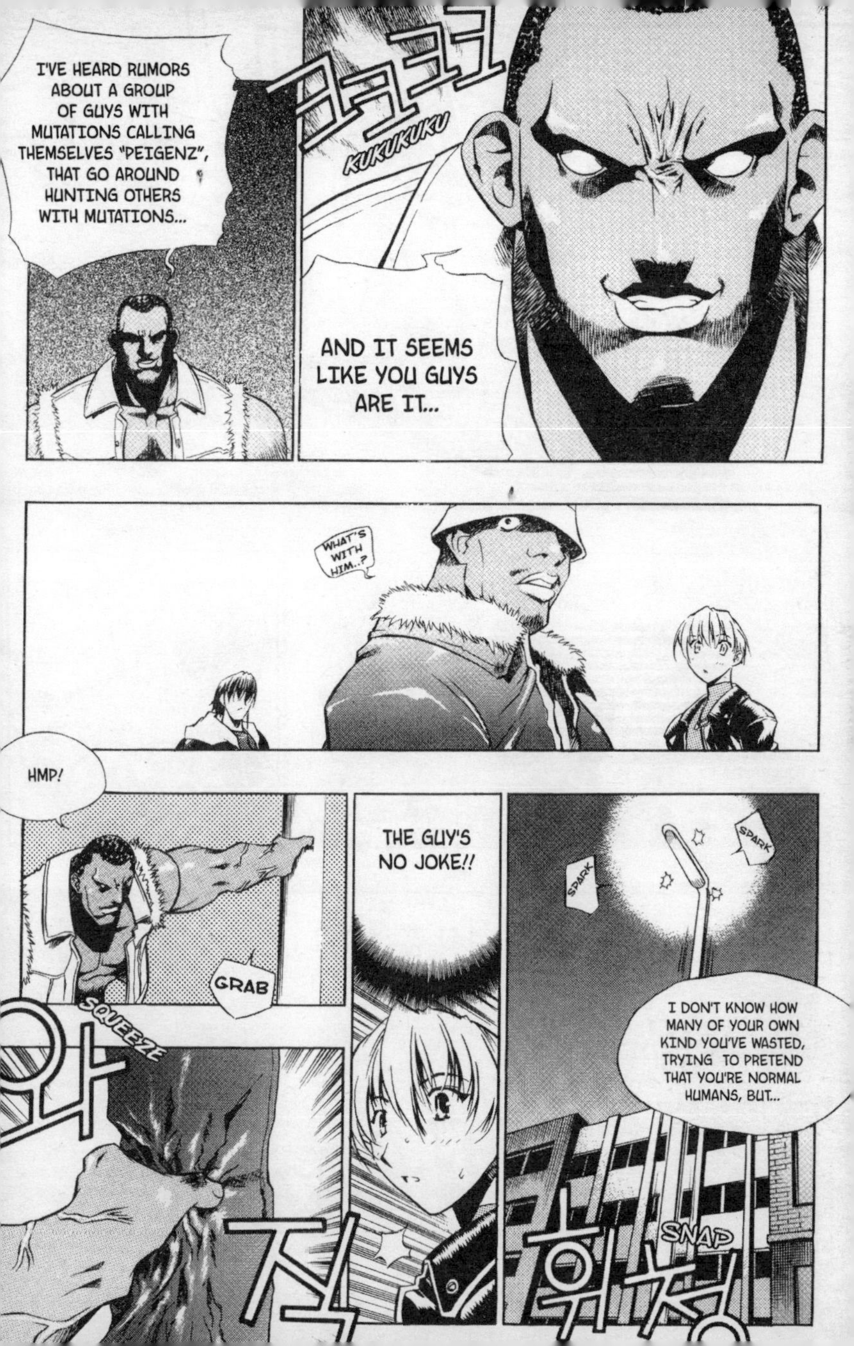
I'VE HEARD RUMORS ABOUT A GROUP OF GUYS WITH MUTATIONS CALLING THEMSELVES "PEIGENZ", THAT GO AROUND HUNTING OTHERS WITH MUTATIONS...
KUKUKUKU
AND IT SEEMS LIKE YOU GUYS ARE IT...
WHAT'S WITH HIM..?
HMP!
GRAB
SQUEEZE
THE GUY'S NO JOKE!!
SPARK
SPARK
I DON'T KNOW HOW MANY OF YOUR OWN KIND YOU'VE WASTED, TRYING TO PRETEND THAT YOU'RE NORMAL HUMANS, BUT...
SNAP

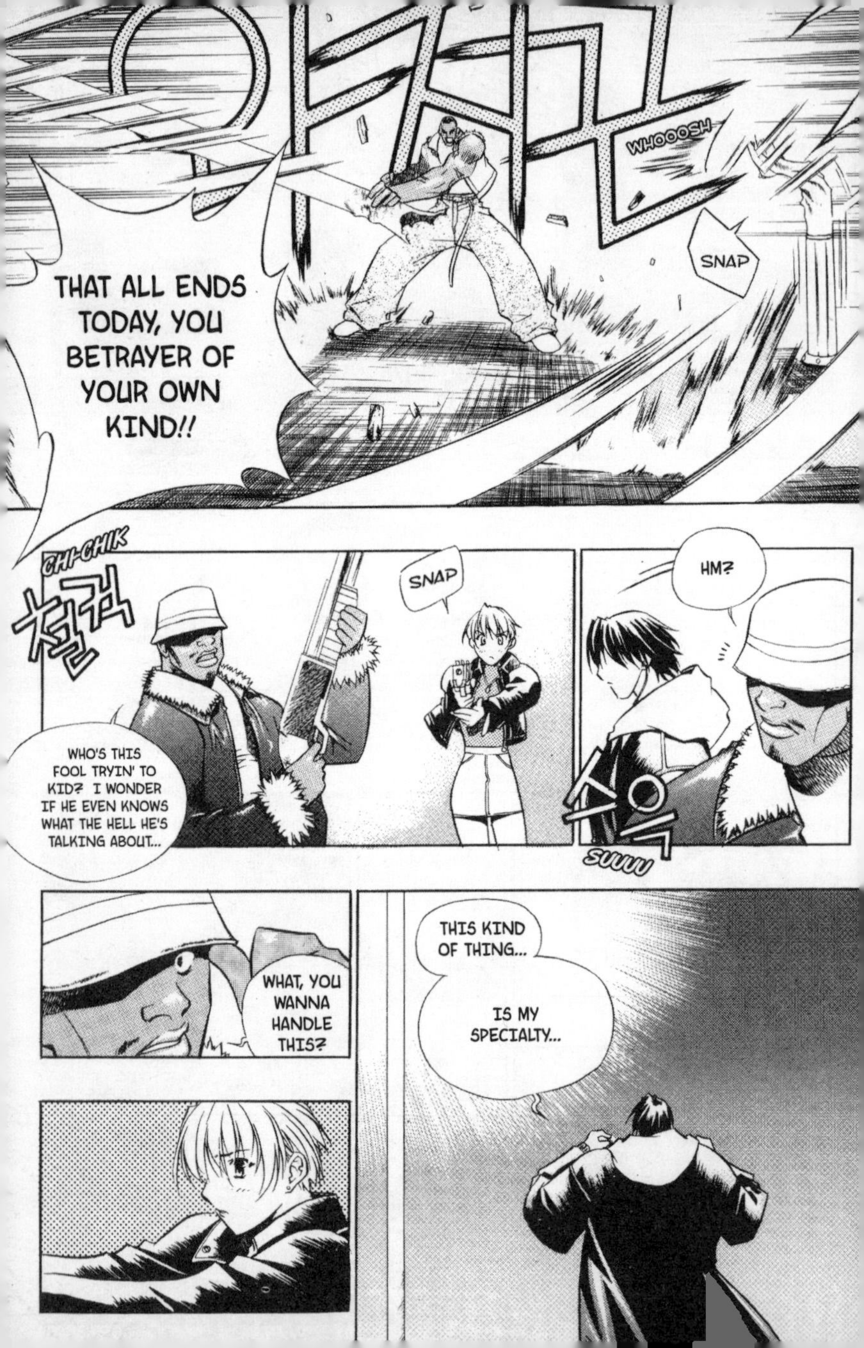
WHOOOSH
SNAP
THAT ALL ENDS TODAY, YOU BETRAYER OF YOUR OWN KIND!!
CHI-CHIK
철컥
WHO'S THIS FOOL TRYIN' TO KID? I WONDER IF HE EVEN KNOWS WHAT THE HELL HE'S TALKING ABOUT...
SNAP
HM?
SUUU
WHAT, YOU WANNA HANDLE THIS?
THIS KIND OF THING...
IS MY SPECIALTY...

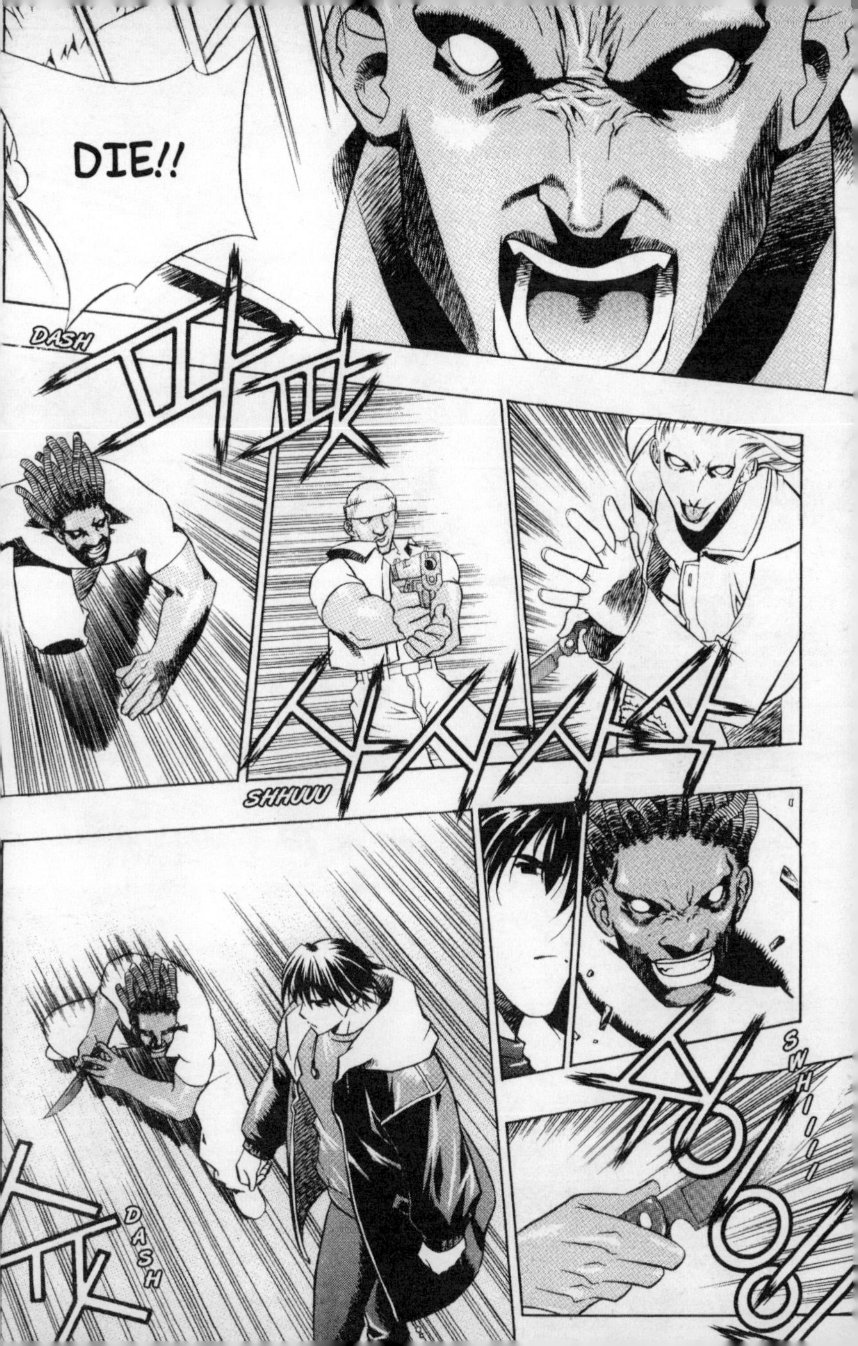
DIE!!
DASH
SHHUUU
DASH
SWHIIII

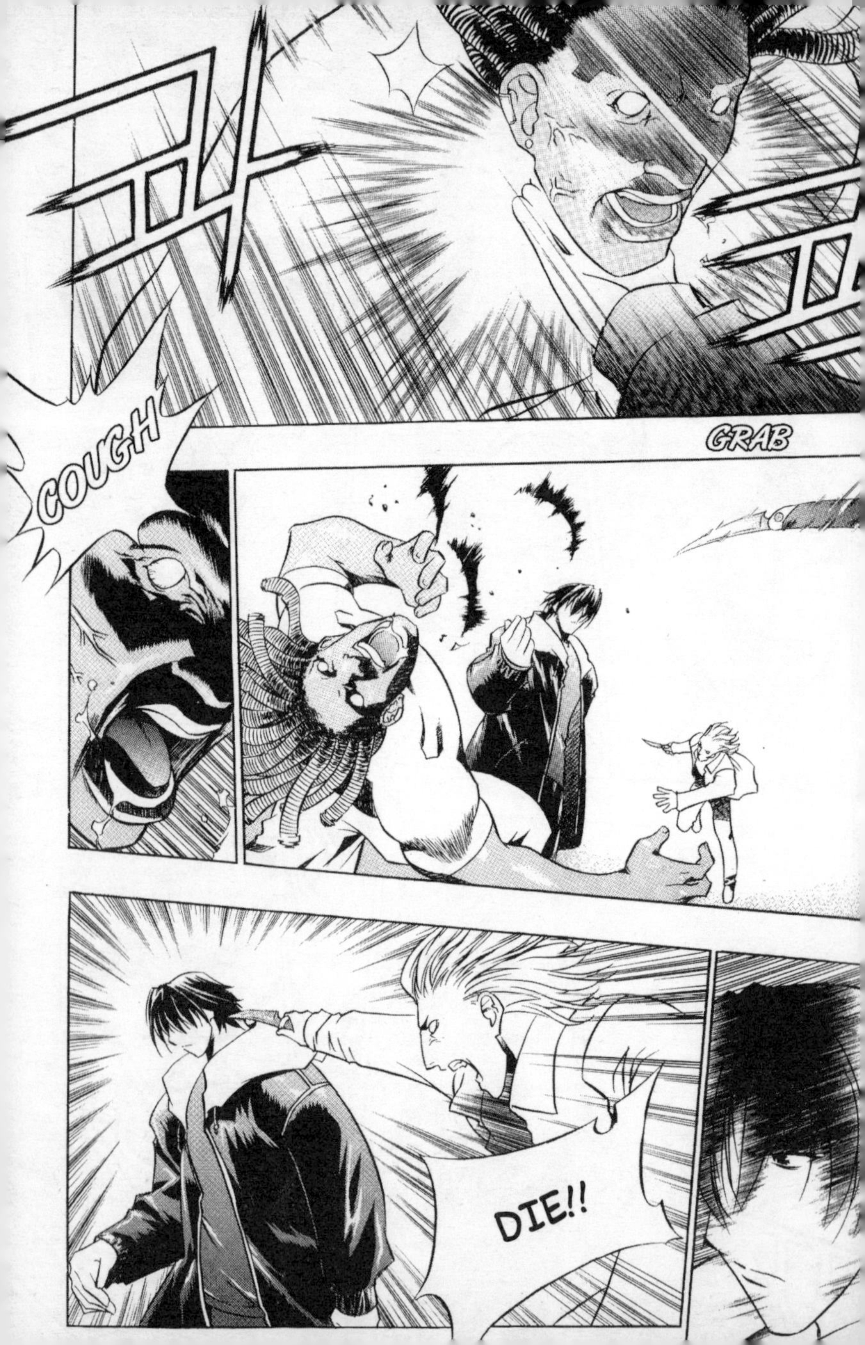
COUGH
GRAB
DIE!!

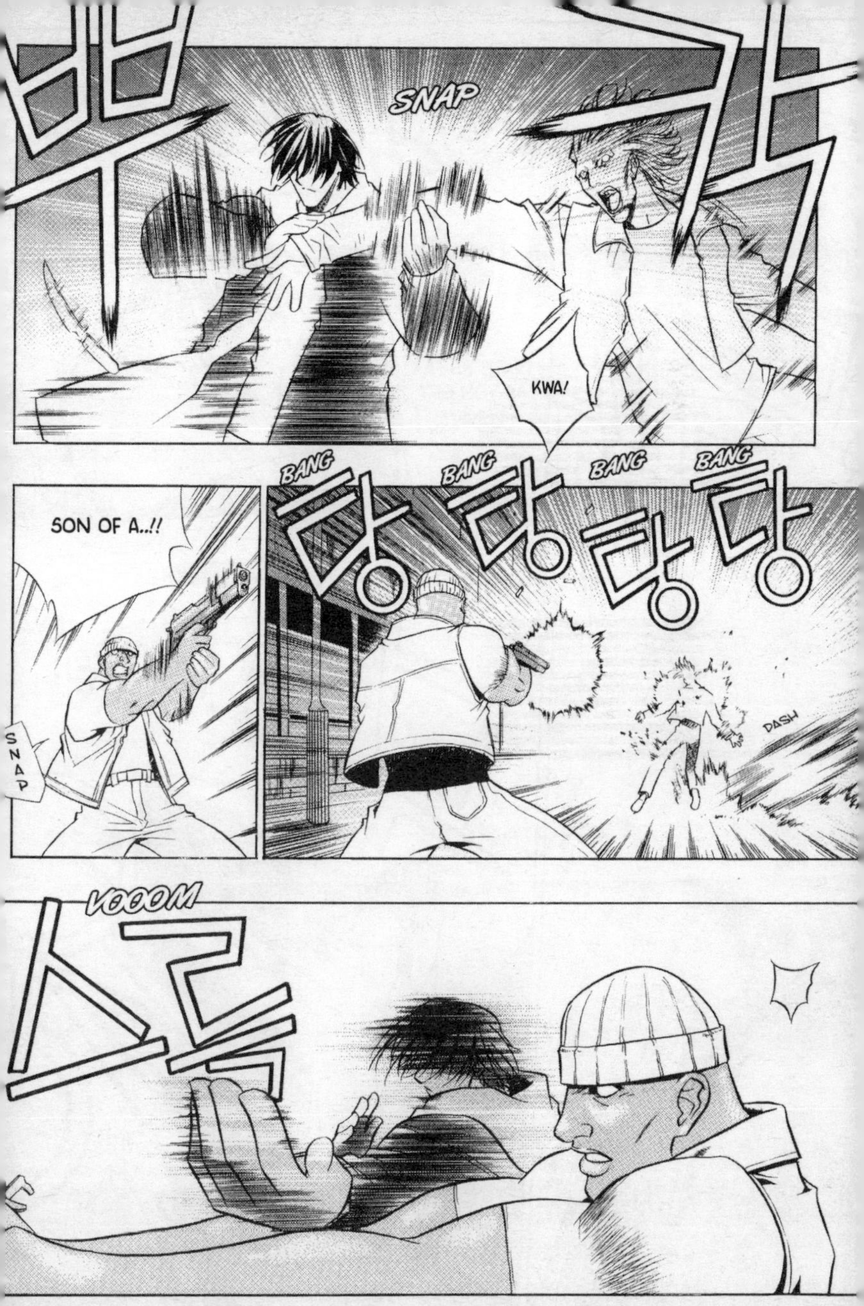
SNAP
KWA!
SON OF A..!!
SNAP
BANG 당
BANG 당
BANG 당
BANG 당
DASH
VOOOM

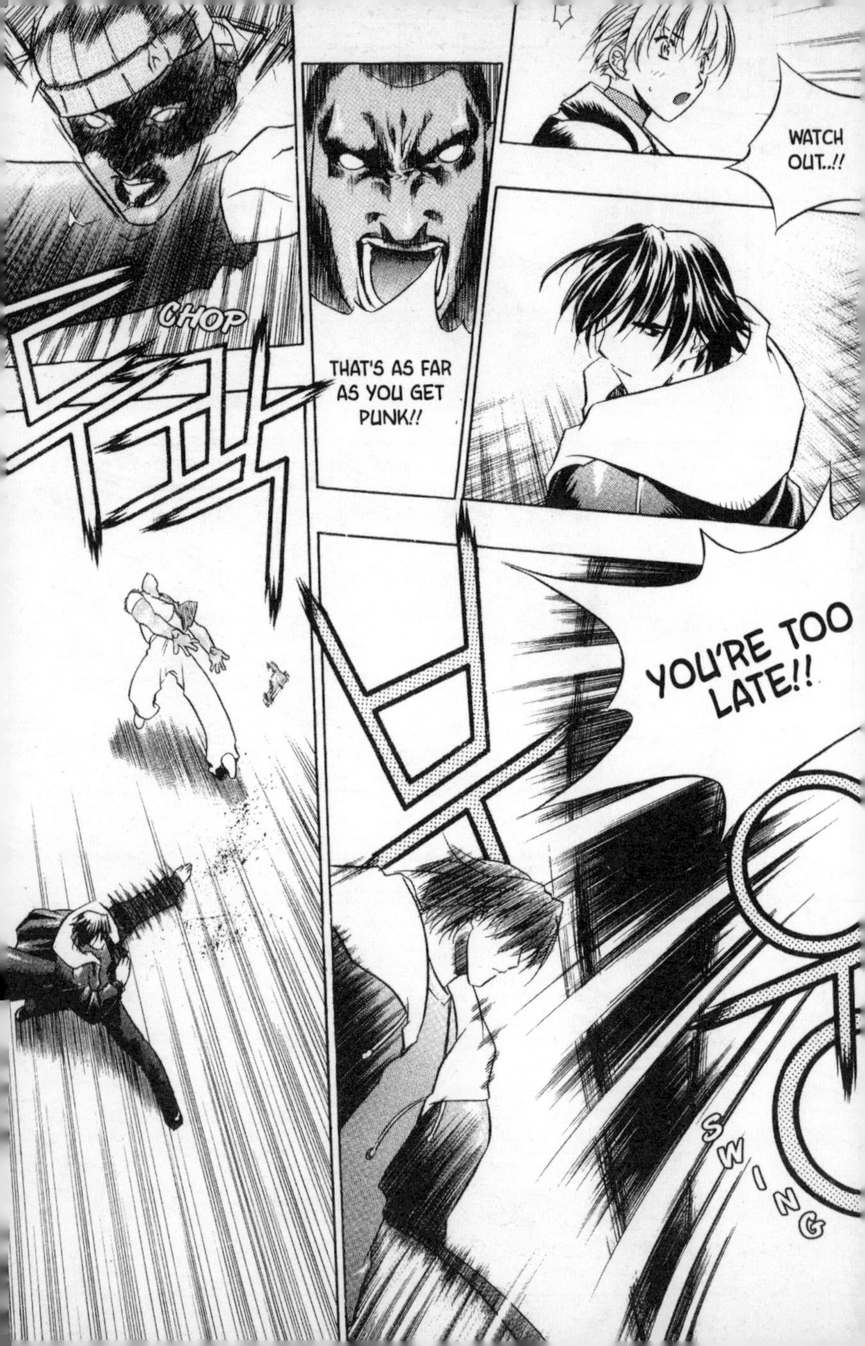
CHOP
THAT'S AS FAR AS YOU GET PUNK!!
WATCH OUT..!!
YOU'RE TOO LATE!!
SWING

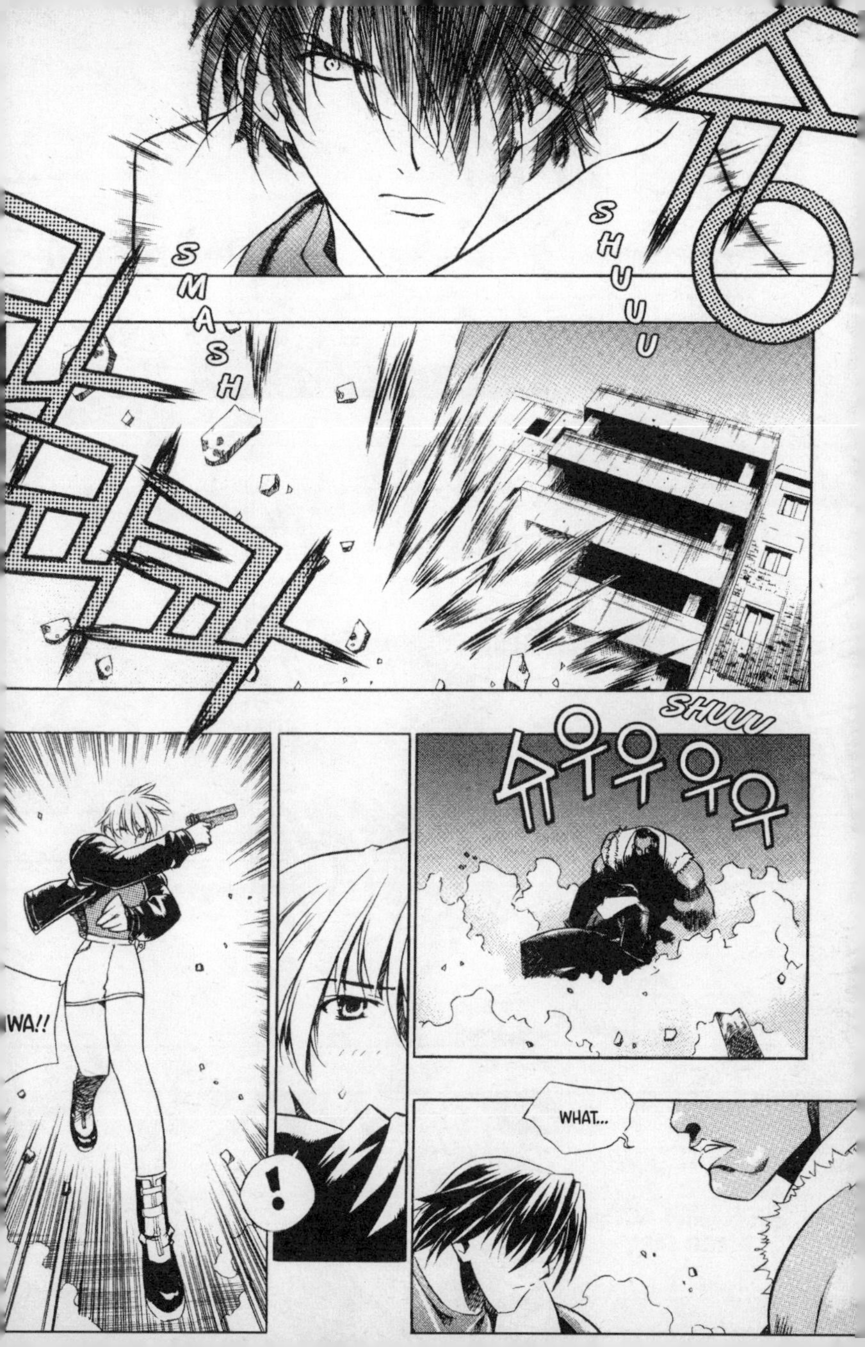
SMASH
SHUUU
WA!!
!
SHUUU
WHAT...

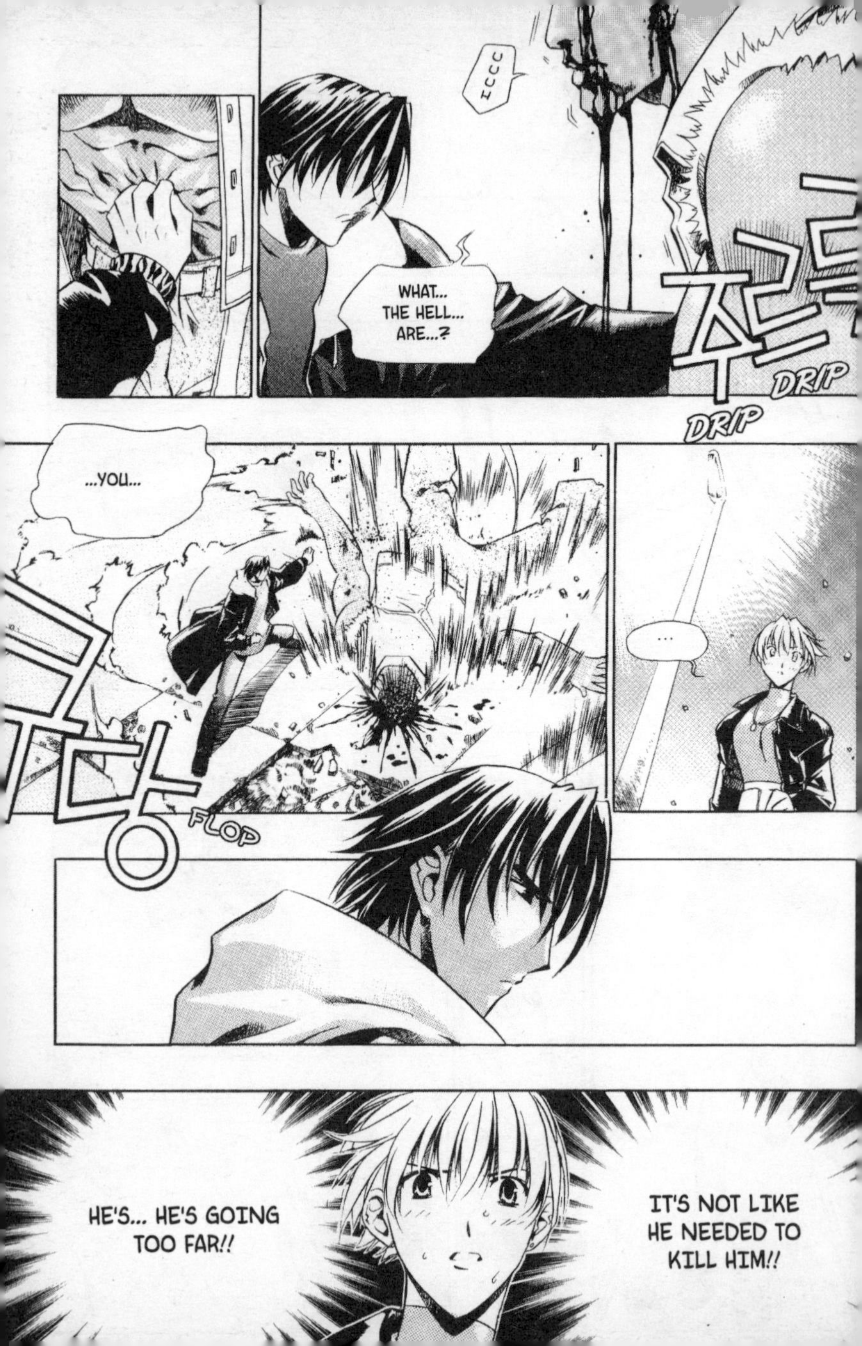
ICCC
WHAT... THE HELL... ARE...?
DRIP
DRIP
...YOU...
FLOP
...
HE'S... HE'S GOING TOO FAR!!
IT'S NOT LIKE HE NEEDED TO KILL HIM!!

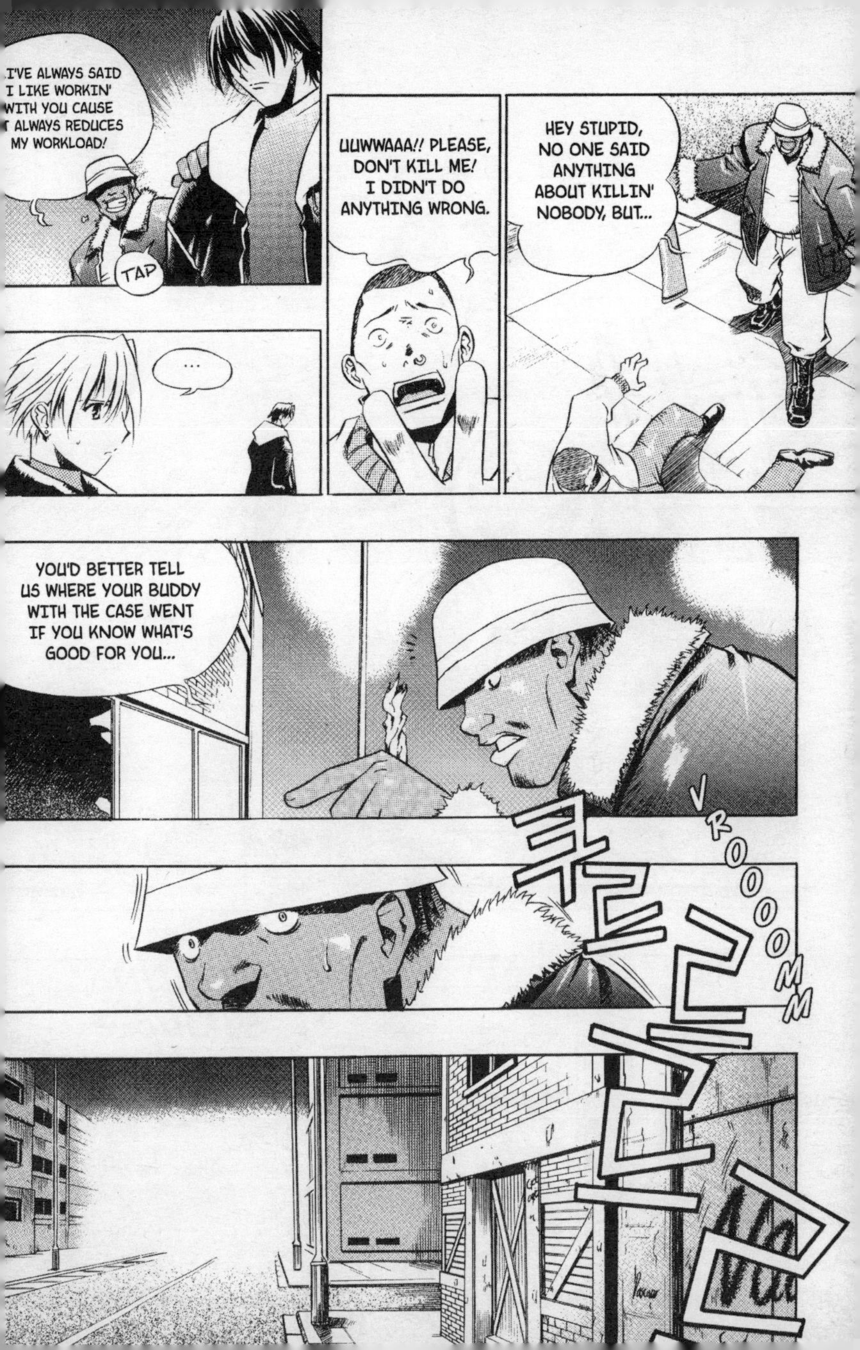
I'VE ALWAYS SAID I LIKE WORKIN' WITH YOU CAUSE T ALWAYS REDUCES MY WORKLOAD!
TAP
...
UUWWAAA!! PLEASE, DON'T KILL ME! I DIDN'T DO ANYTHING WRONG.
HEY STUPID, NO ONE SAID ANYTHING ABOUT KILLIN' NOBODY, BUT...
YOU'D BETTER TELL US WHERE YOUR BUDDY WITH THE CASE WENT IF YOU KNOW WHAT'S GOOD FOR YOU...
VROOOOMM

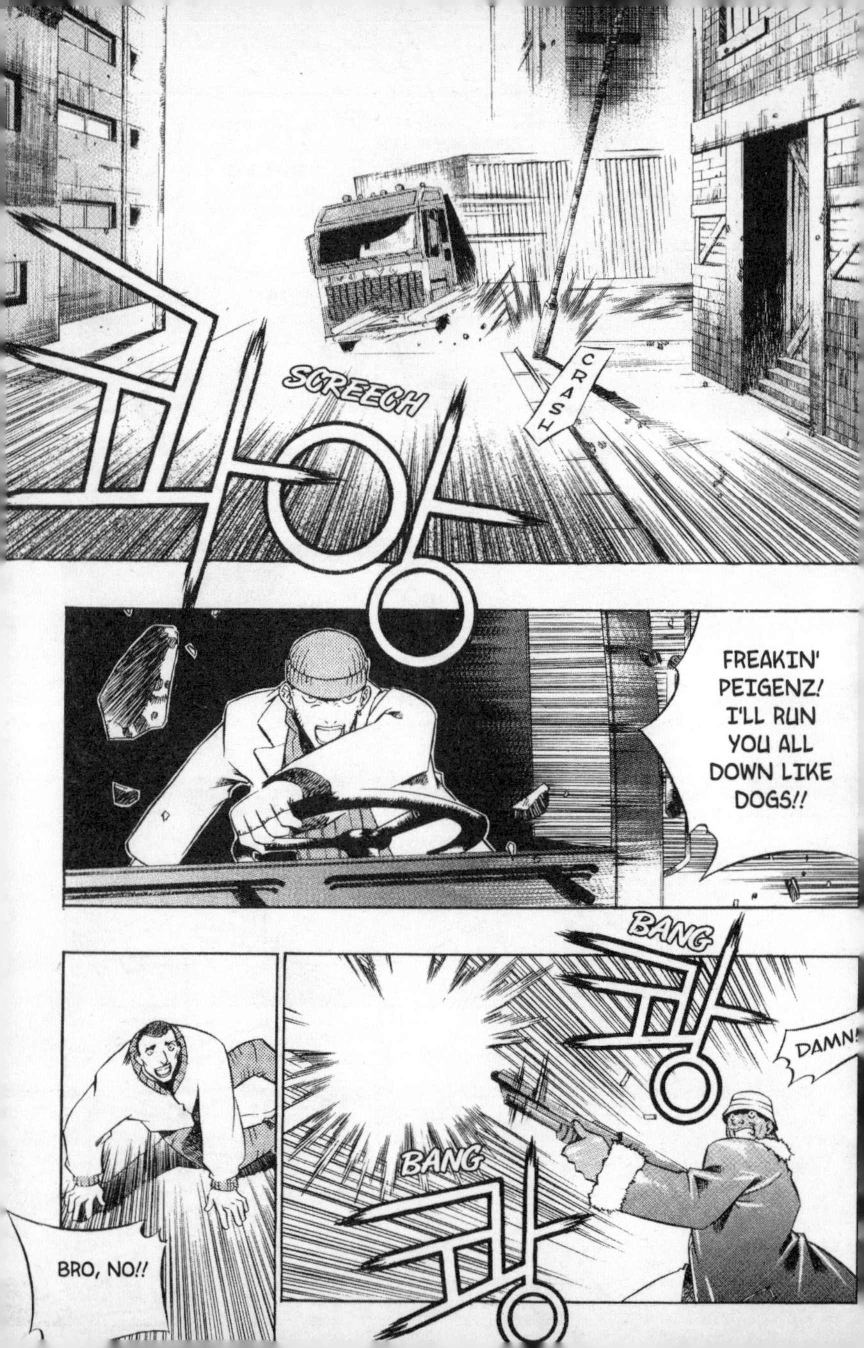
SCREECH
CRASH
FREAKIN' PEIGENZ! I'LL RUN YOU ALL DOWN LIKE DOGS!!
BANG
DAMN!
BANG
BRO, NO!!

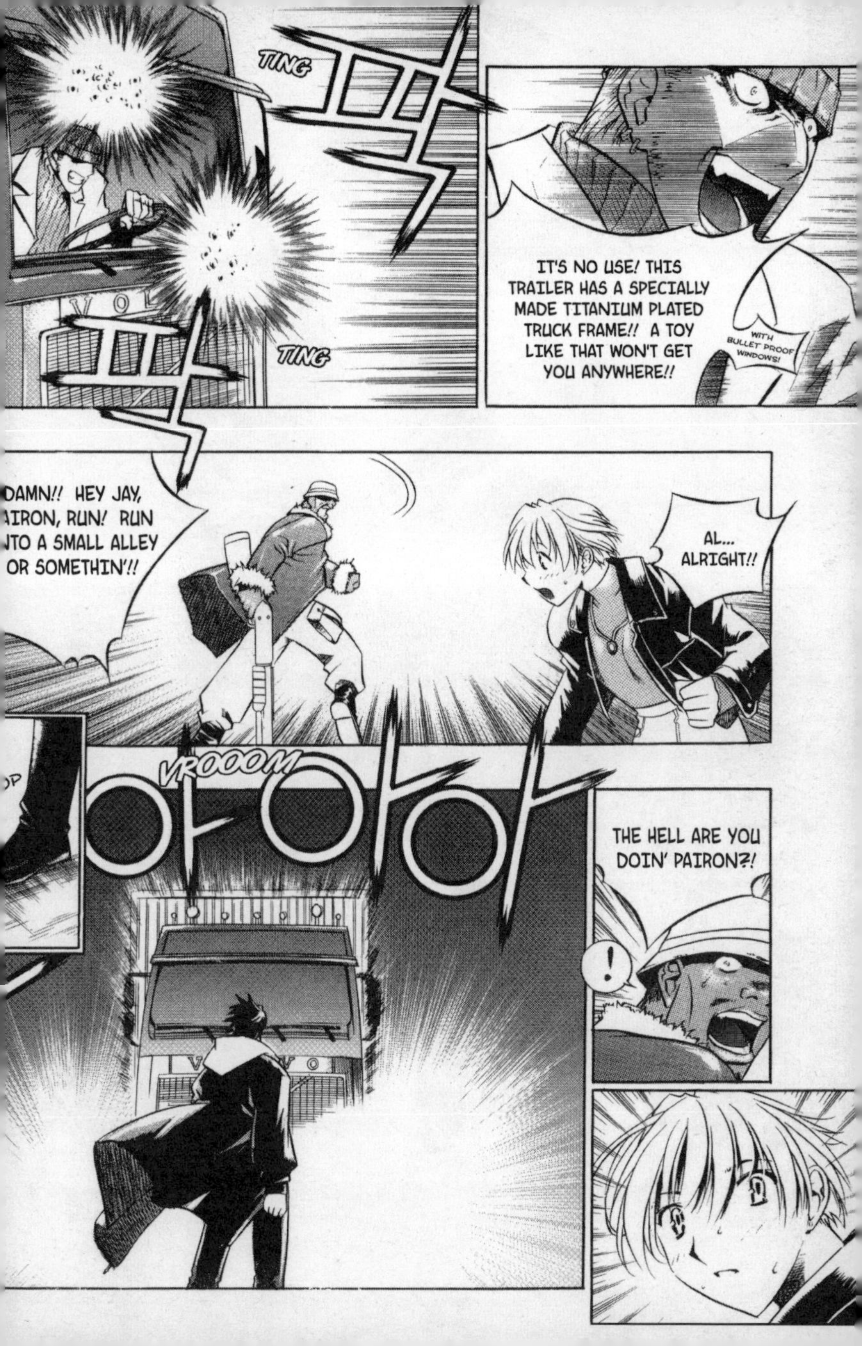
TING
TING
IT'S NO USE! THIS TRAILER HAS A SPECIALLY MADE TITANIUM PLATED TRUCK FRAME!! A TOY LIKE THAT WON'T GET YOU ANYWHERE!!
WITH BULLET PROOF WINDOWS!
DAMN!! HEY JAY, AIRON, RUN! RUN NTO A SMALL ALLEY OR SOMETHIN'!!
AL... ALRIGHT!!
VROOOM
THE HELL ARE YOU DOIN' PAIRON?!
!

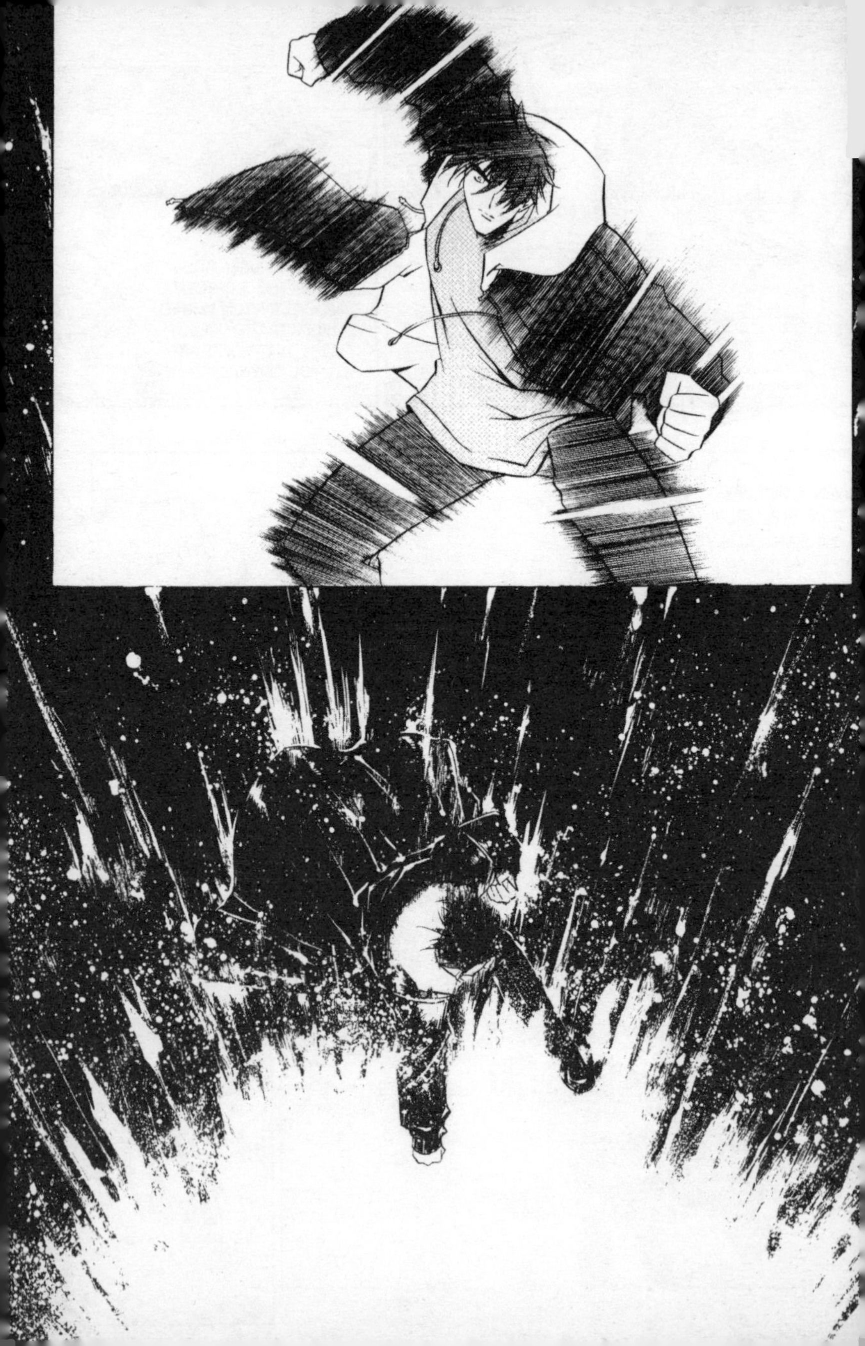

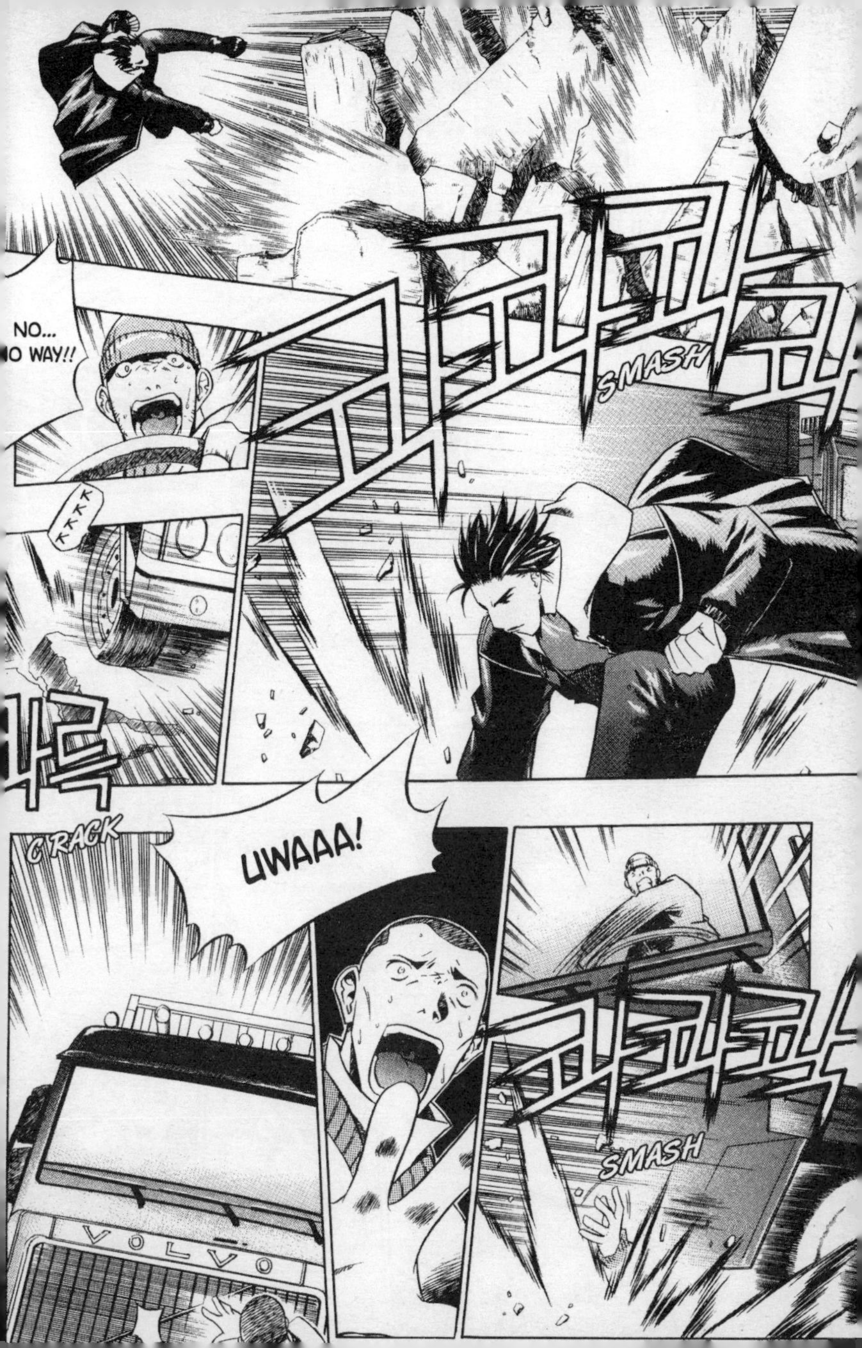
SMASH
NO...
O WAY!!
CRACK
UWAAA!
VOLVO
SMASH

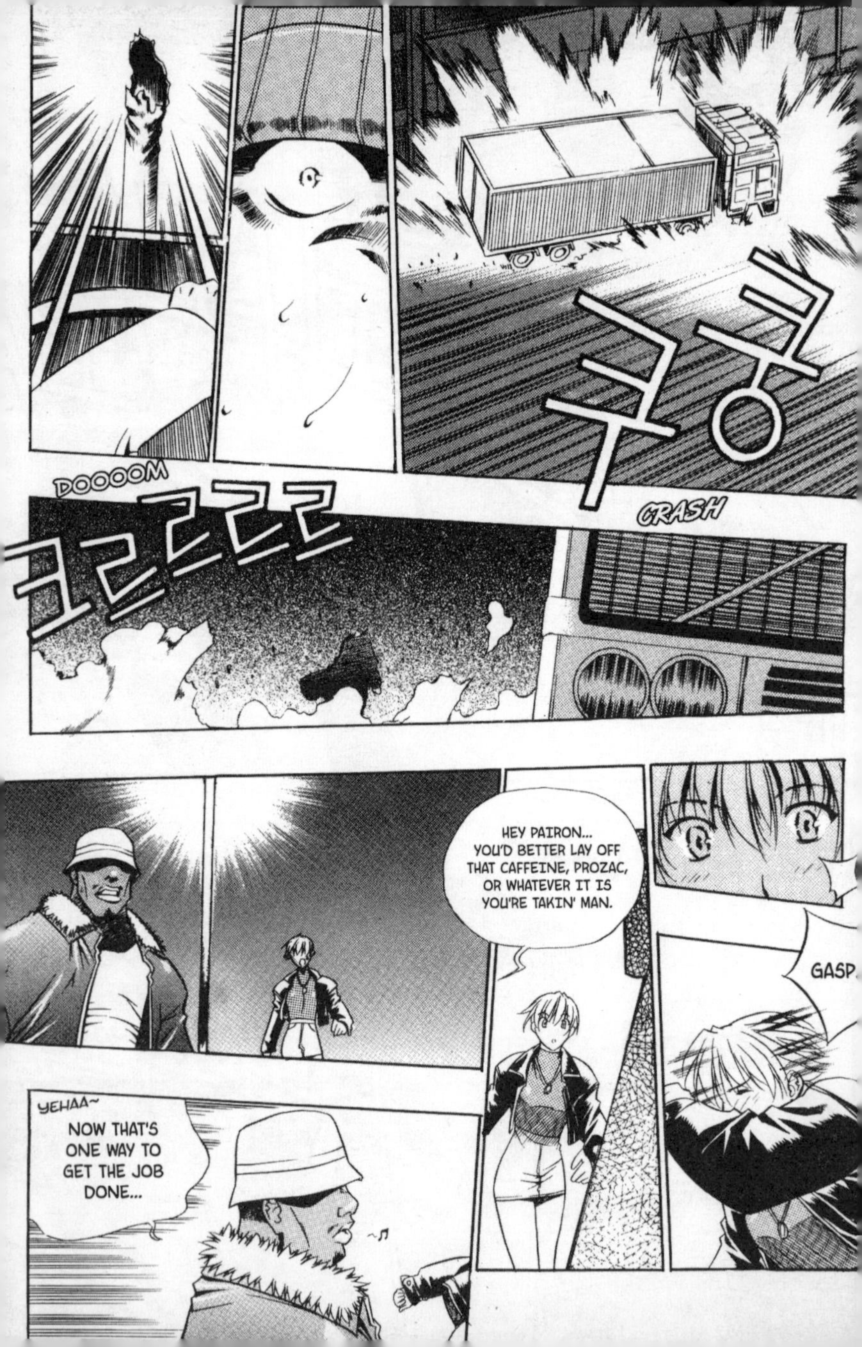
DOOOOM
CRASH
HEY PAIRON... YOU'D BETTER LAY OFF THAT CAFFEINE, PROZAC, OR WHATEVER IT IS YOU'RE TAKIN' MAN.
GASP.
YEHAA~
NOW THAT'S ONE WAY TO GET THE JOB DONE...

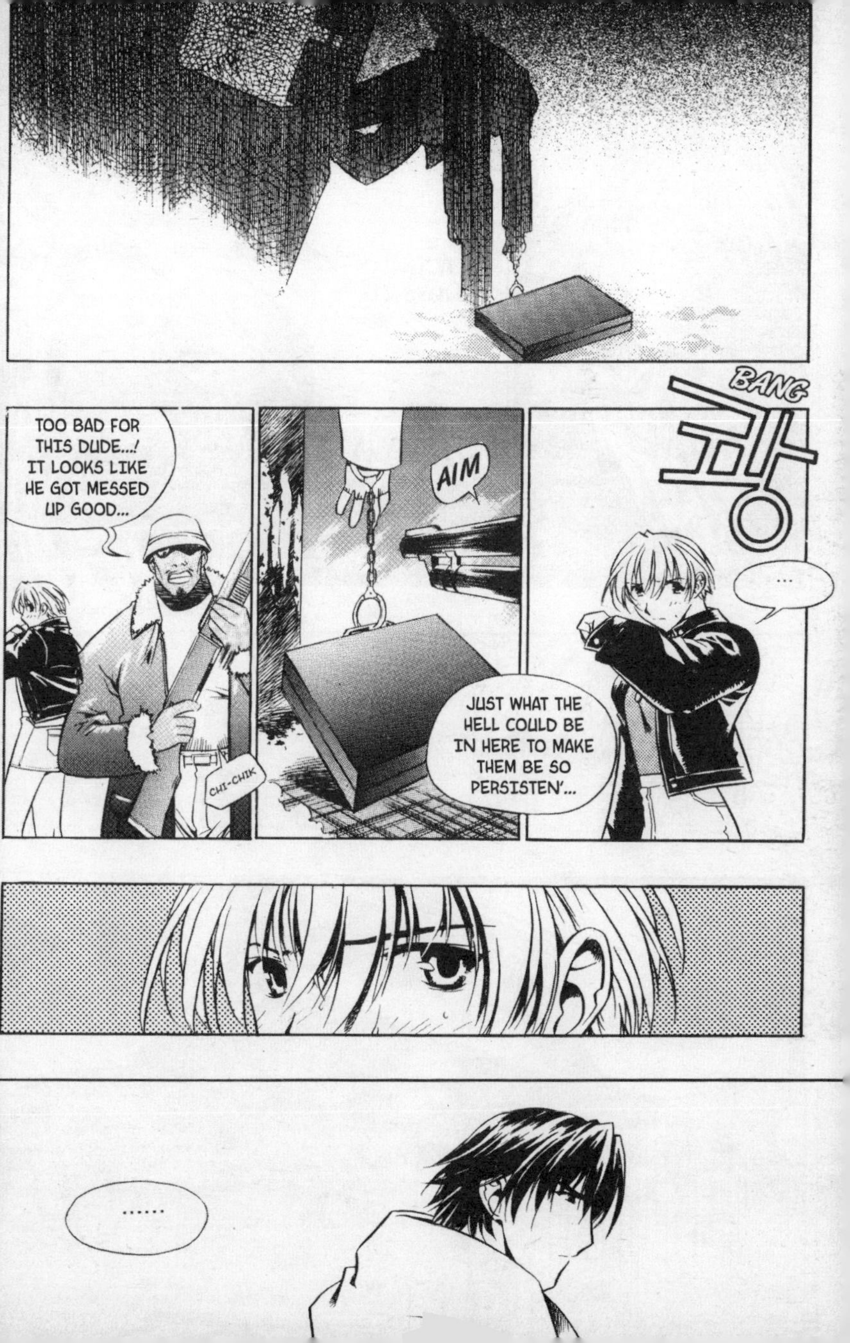
TOO BAD FOR THIS DUDE...! IT LOOKS LIKE HE GOT MESSED UP GOOD...
CHI-CHIK
AIM
JUST WHAT THE HELL COULD BE IN HERE TO MAKE THEM BE SO PERSISTEN'...
BANG
쾅
...
......

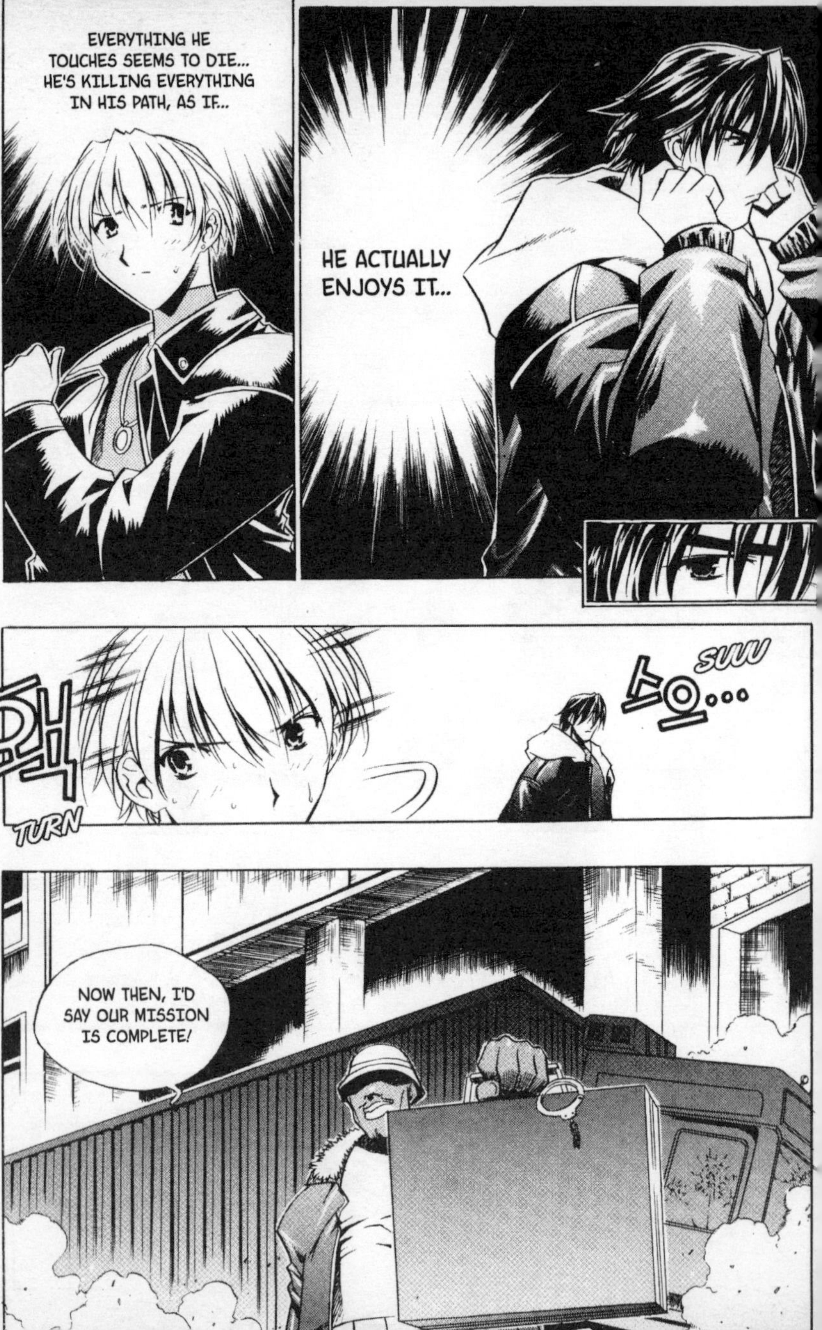
EVERYTHING HE TOUCHES SEEMS TO DIE... HE'S KILLING EVERYTHING IN HIS PATH, AS IF...
HE ACTUALLY ENJOYS IT...
홱
TURN
스으...
SUUU
NOW THEN, I'D SAY OUR MISSION IS COMPLETE!

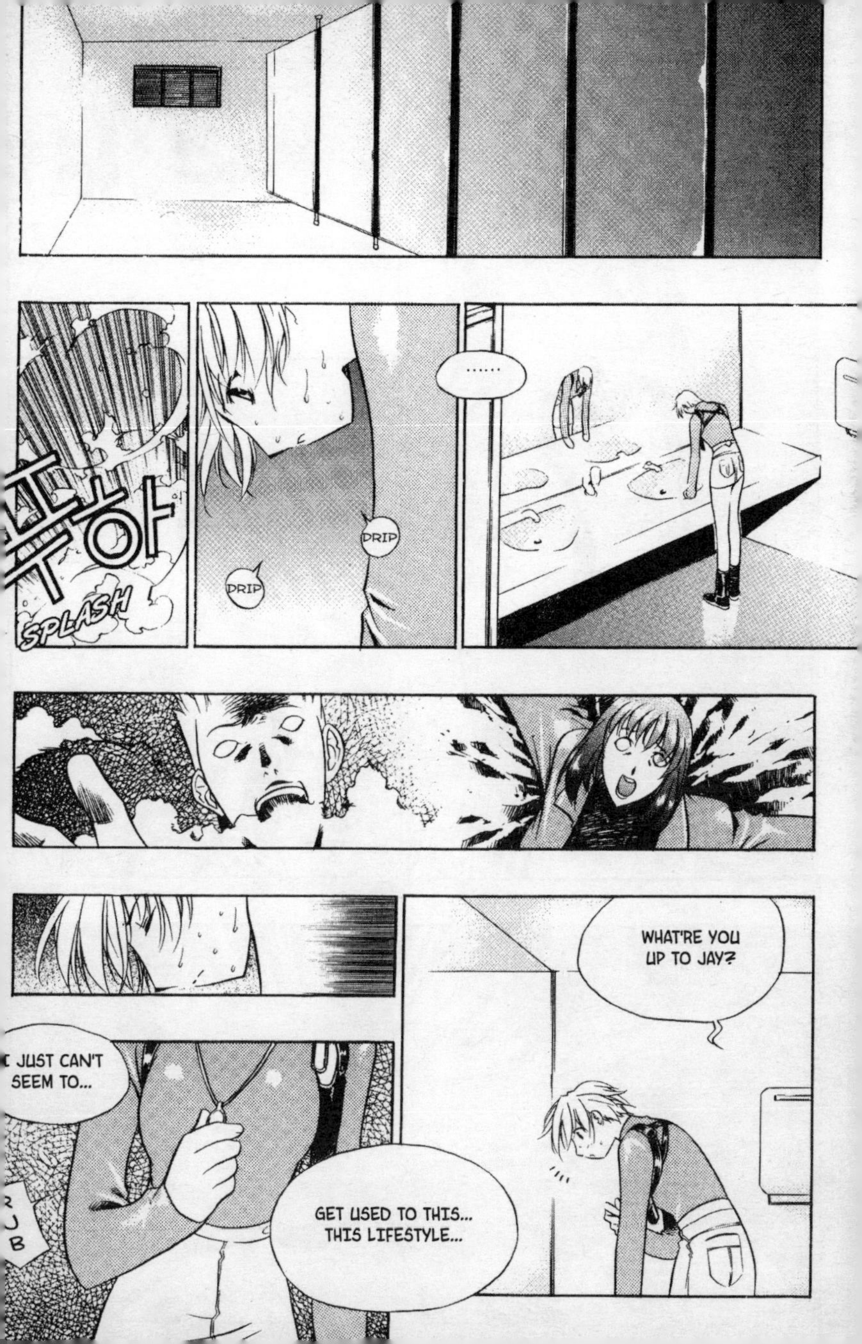

쏴아
SPLASH
DRIP
DRIP
....
WHAT'RE YOU UP TO JAY?
I JUST CAN'T SEEM TO...
RUB
GET USED TO THIS... THIS LIFESTYLE...

I'M... I'M SORRY.

WHAT'S SHE DOING?

ENTHIA IS CALLING. SHE'S ORDERING AN EMERGENCY MEETING.

RE... REALLY?

ALRIGHT, I'LL BE JUST BEHIND YOU, MAYO.

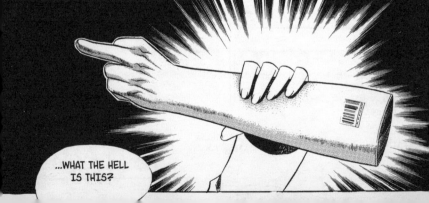

...WHAT THE HELL IS THIS?

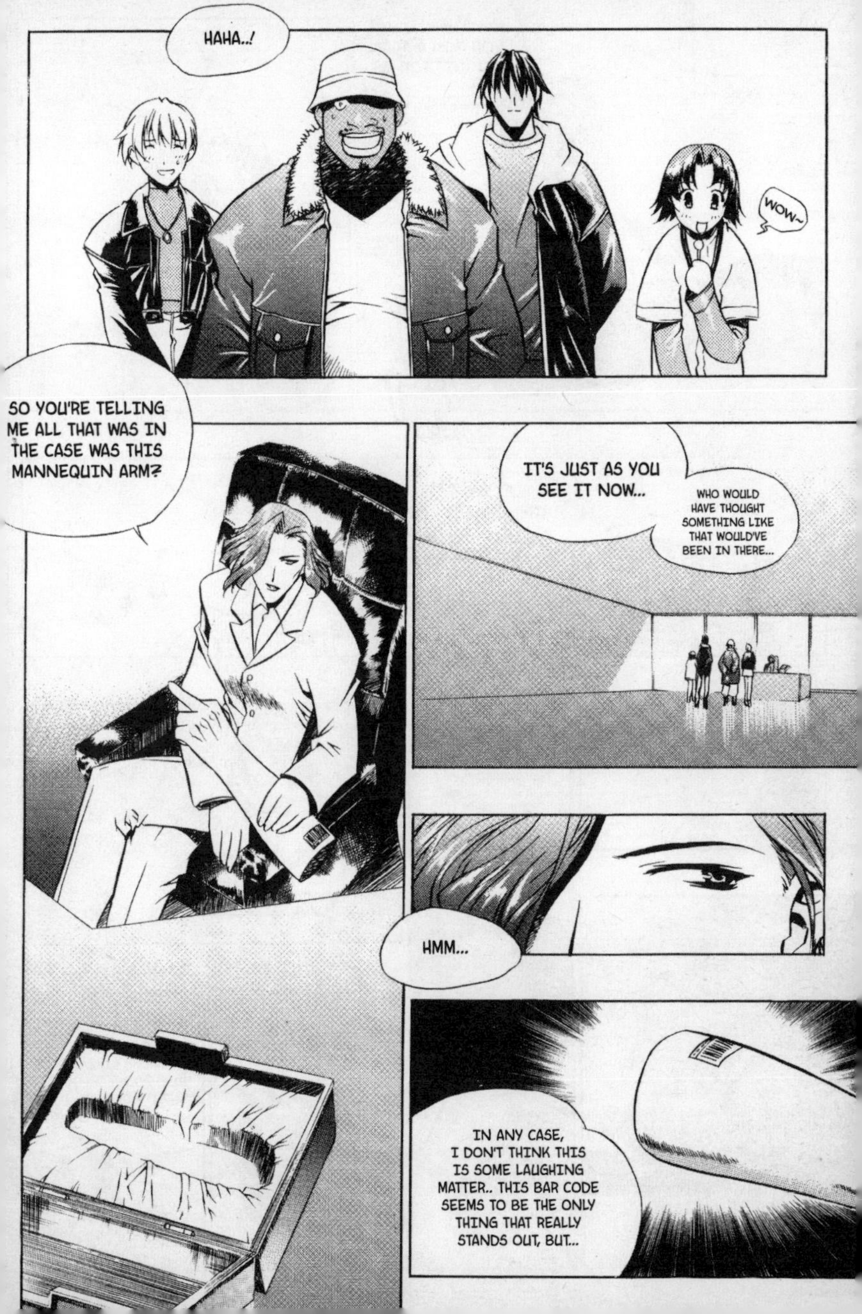
HAHA..!
WOW~
SO YOU'RE TELLING ME ALL THAT WAS IN THE CASE WAS THIS MANNEQUIN ARM?
IT'S JUST AS YOU SEE IT NOW...
WHO WOULD HAVE THOUGHT SOMETHING LIKE THAT WOULD'VE BEEN IN THERE...
HMM...
IN ANY CASE, I DON'T THINK THIS IS SOME LAUGHING MATTER.. THIS BAR CODE SEEMS TO BE THE ONLY THING THAT REALLY STANDS OUT, BUT...

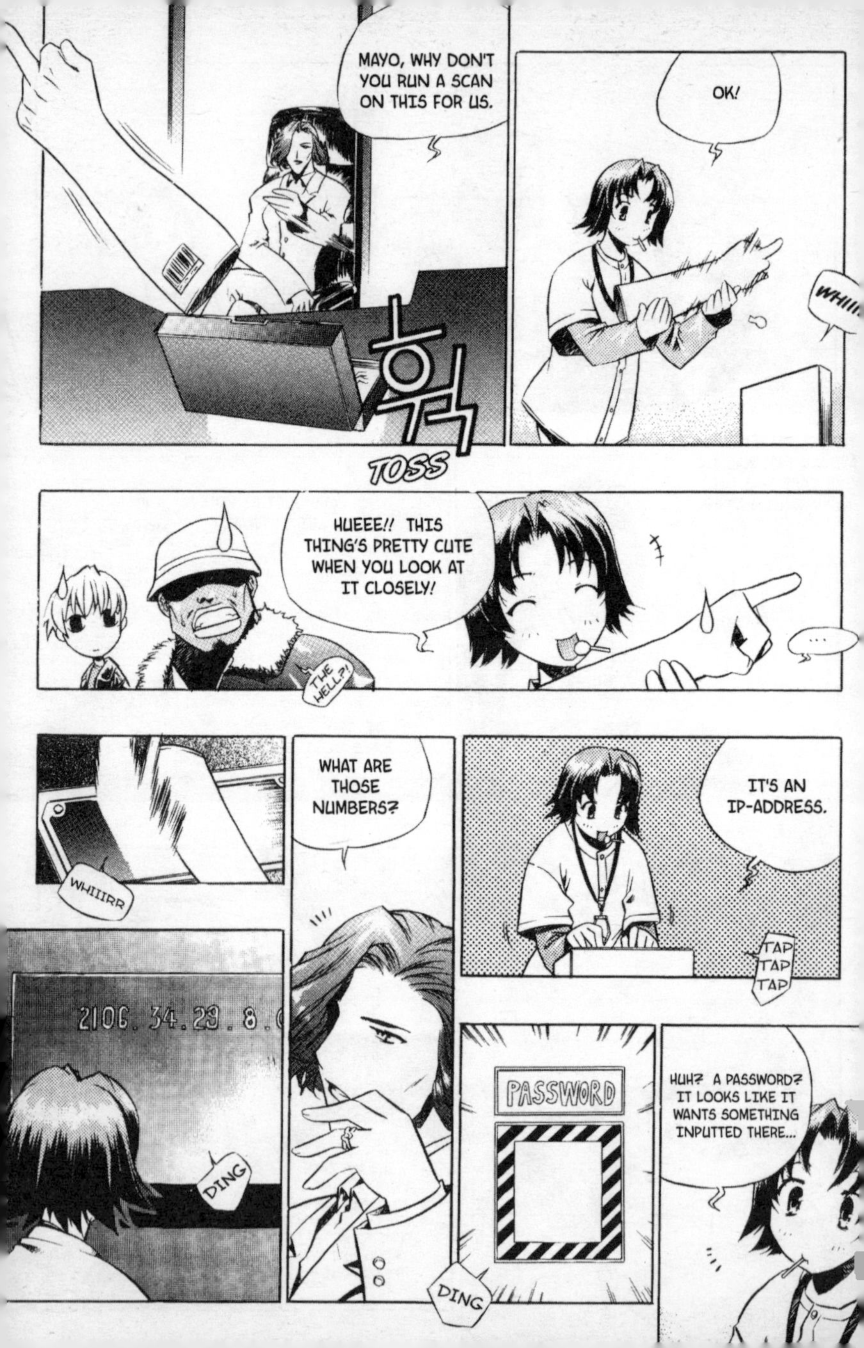
MAYO, WHY DON'T YOU RUN A SCAN ON THIS FOR US.
훅
TOSS
OK!
WHIII
HUEEE!! THIS THING'S PRETTY CUTE WHEN YOU LOOK AT IT CLOSELY!
THE HELL?!
...
WHIIIRR
WHAT ARE THOSE NUMBERS?
IT'S AN IP-ADDRESS.
TAP TAP TAP
2106. 34. 29. 8.
DING
DING
PASSWORD
HUH? A PASSWORD? IT LOOKS LIKE IT WANTS SOMETHING INPUTTED THERE...

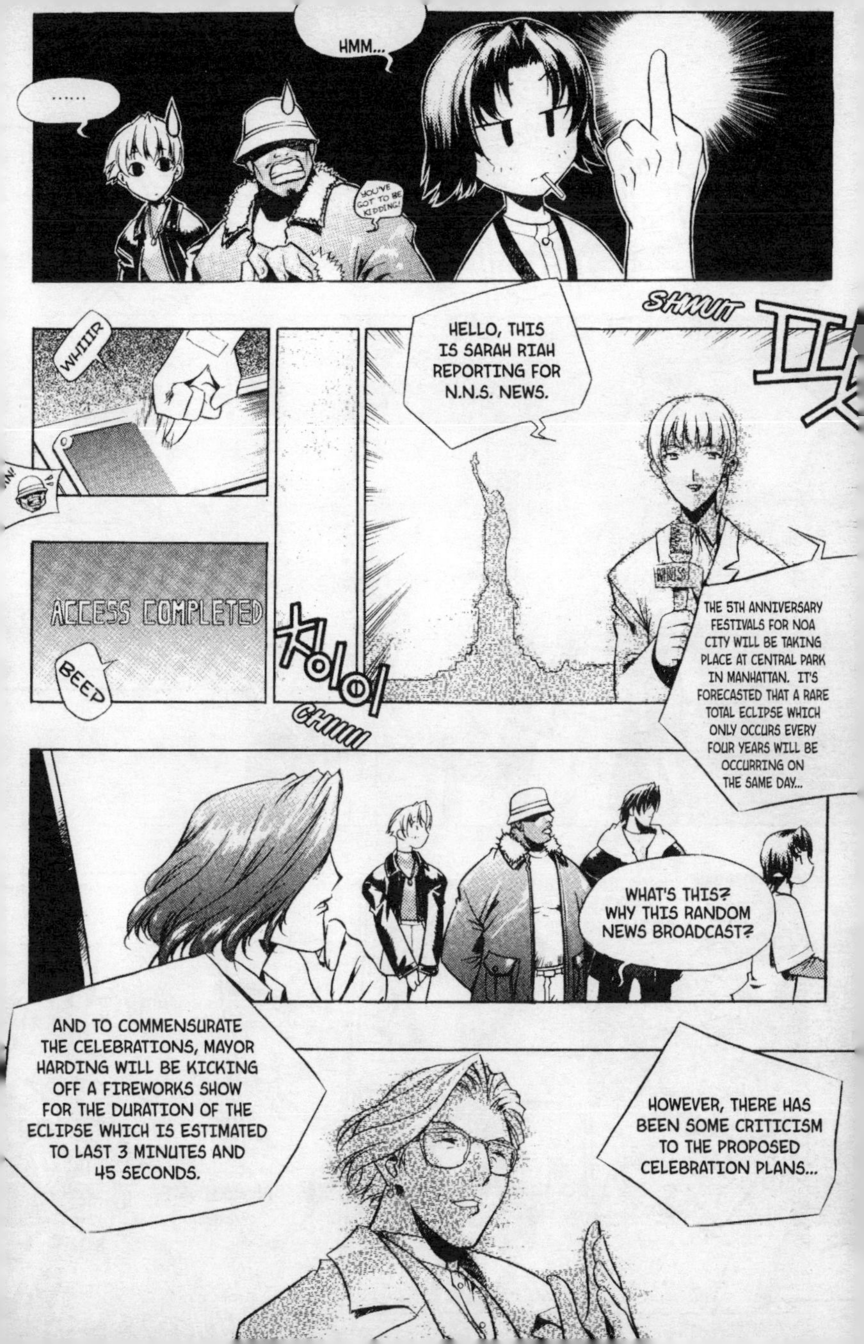

HMM...
......
YOU'VE GOT TO BE KIDDING!
SHWUIT
HELLO, THIS IS SARAH RIAH REPORTING FOR N.N.S. NEWS.
WHIIIR
ACCESS COMPLETED
BEEP
GHIIII
THE 5TH ANNIVERSARY FESTIVALS FOR NOA CITY WILL BE TAKING PLACE AT CENTRAL PARK IN MANHATTAN. IT'S FORECASTED THAT A RARE TOTAL ECLIPSE WHICH ONLY OCCURS EVERY FOUR YEARS WILL BE OCCURRING ON THE SAME DAY...
WHAT'S THIS? WHY THIS RANDOM NEWS BROADCAST?
AND TO COMMENSURATE THE CELEBRATIONS, MAYOR HARDING WILL BE KICKING OFF A FIREWORKS SHOW FOR THE DURATION OF THE ECLIPSE WHICH IS ESTIMATED TO LAST 3 MINUTES AND 45 SECONDS.
HOWEVER, THERE HAS BEEN SOME CRITICISM TO THE PROPOSED CELEBRATION PLANS...

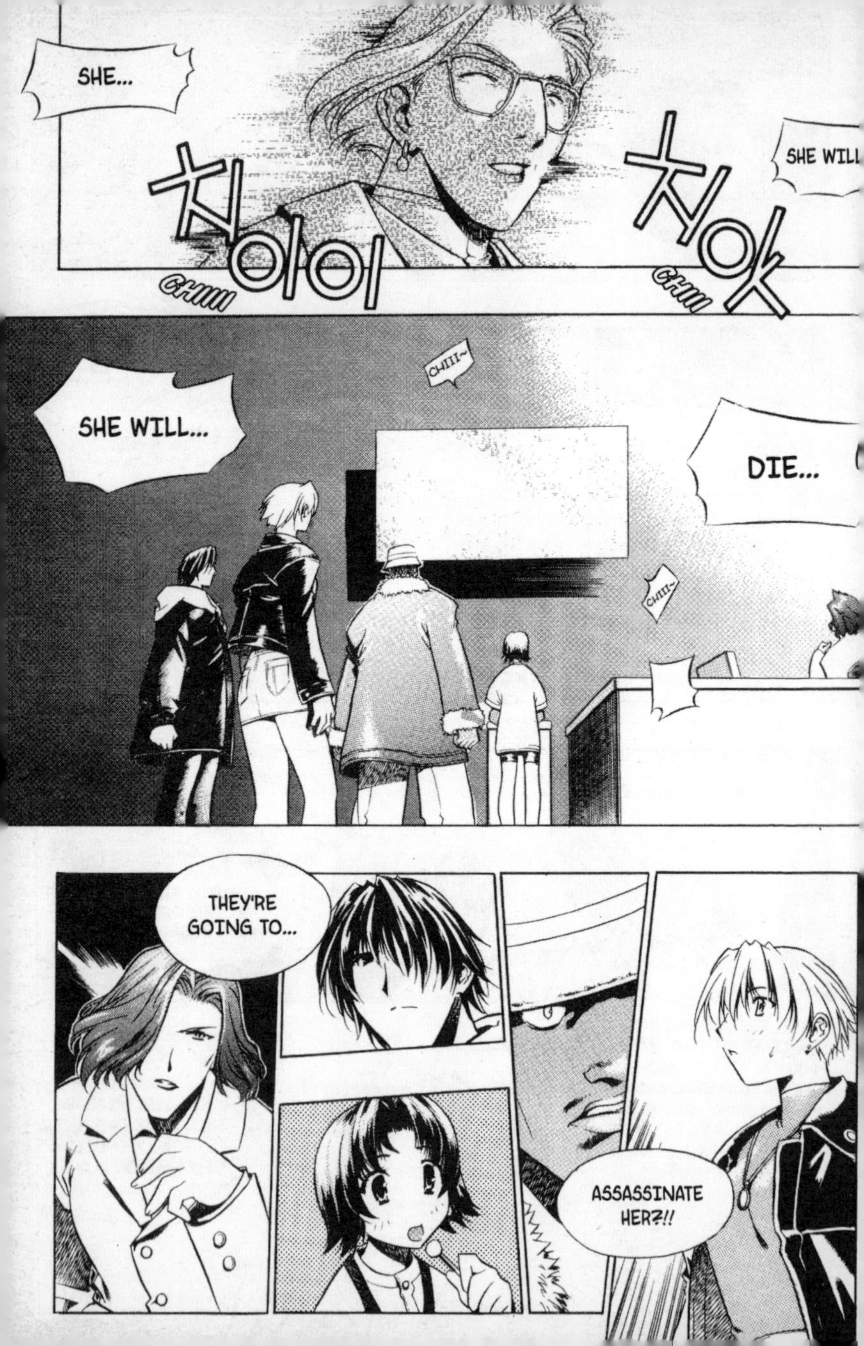
SHE...
SHE WILL
CHIIII
CHIIII
SHE WILL...
CHIII~
DIE...
CHIII~
THEY'RE GOING TO...
ASSASSINATE HER?!!

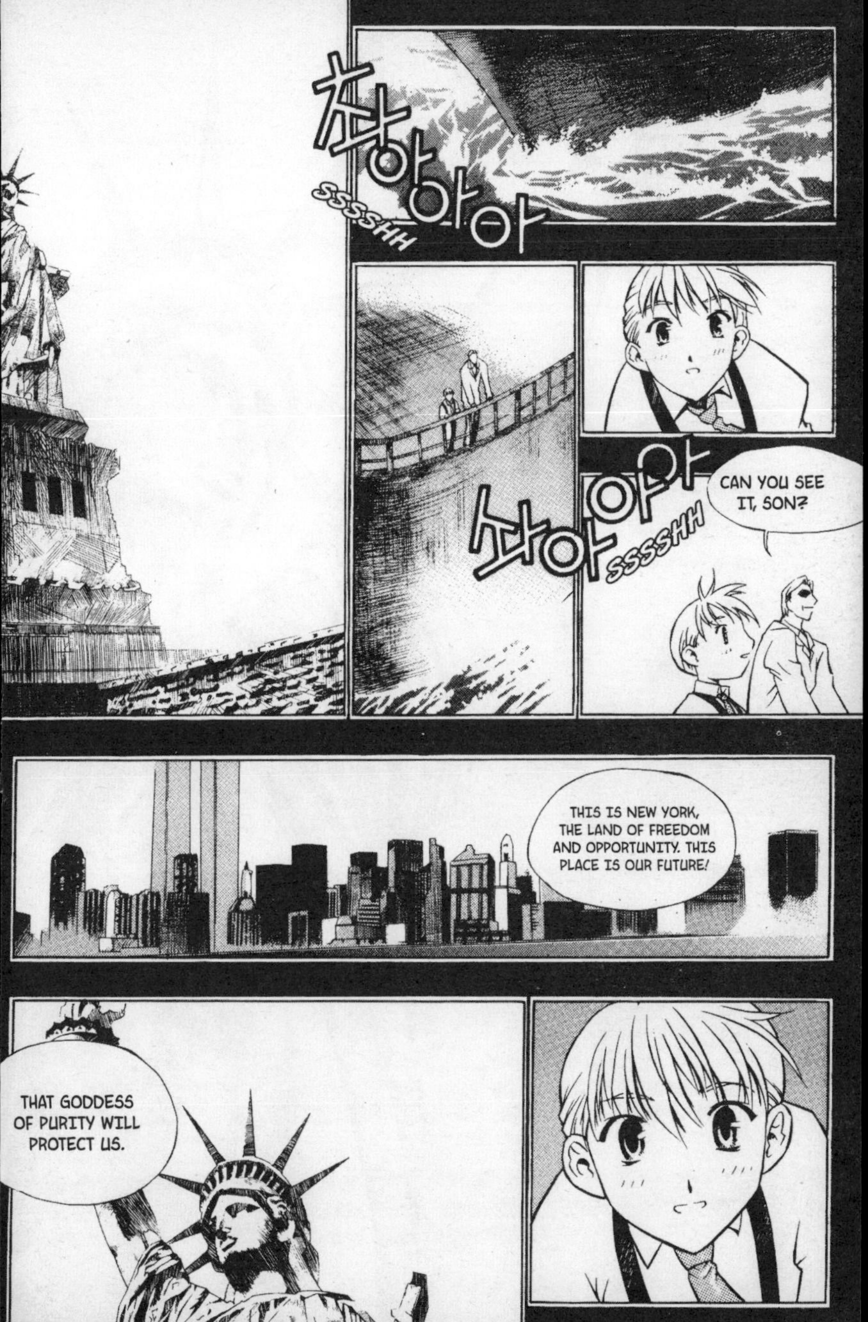
SSSSHH
SSSSHH
CAN YOU SEE IT, SON?
THIS IS NEW YORK, THE LAND OF FREEDOM AND OPPORTUNITY. THIS PLACE IS OUR FUTURE!
THAT GODDESS OF PURITY WILL PROTECT US.

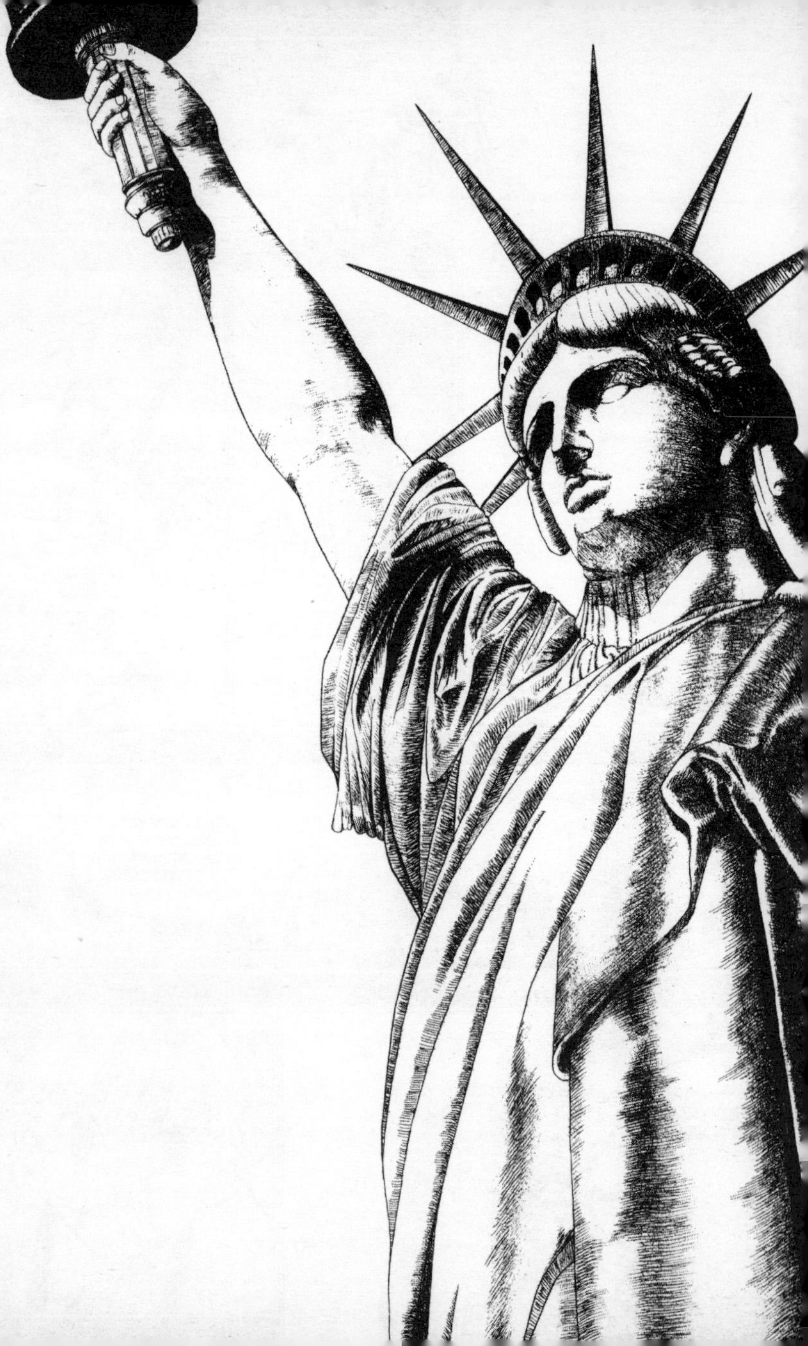

revelation 4 : N.o.A-β

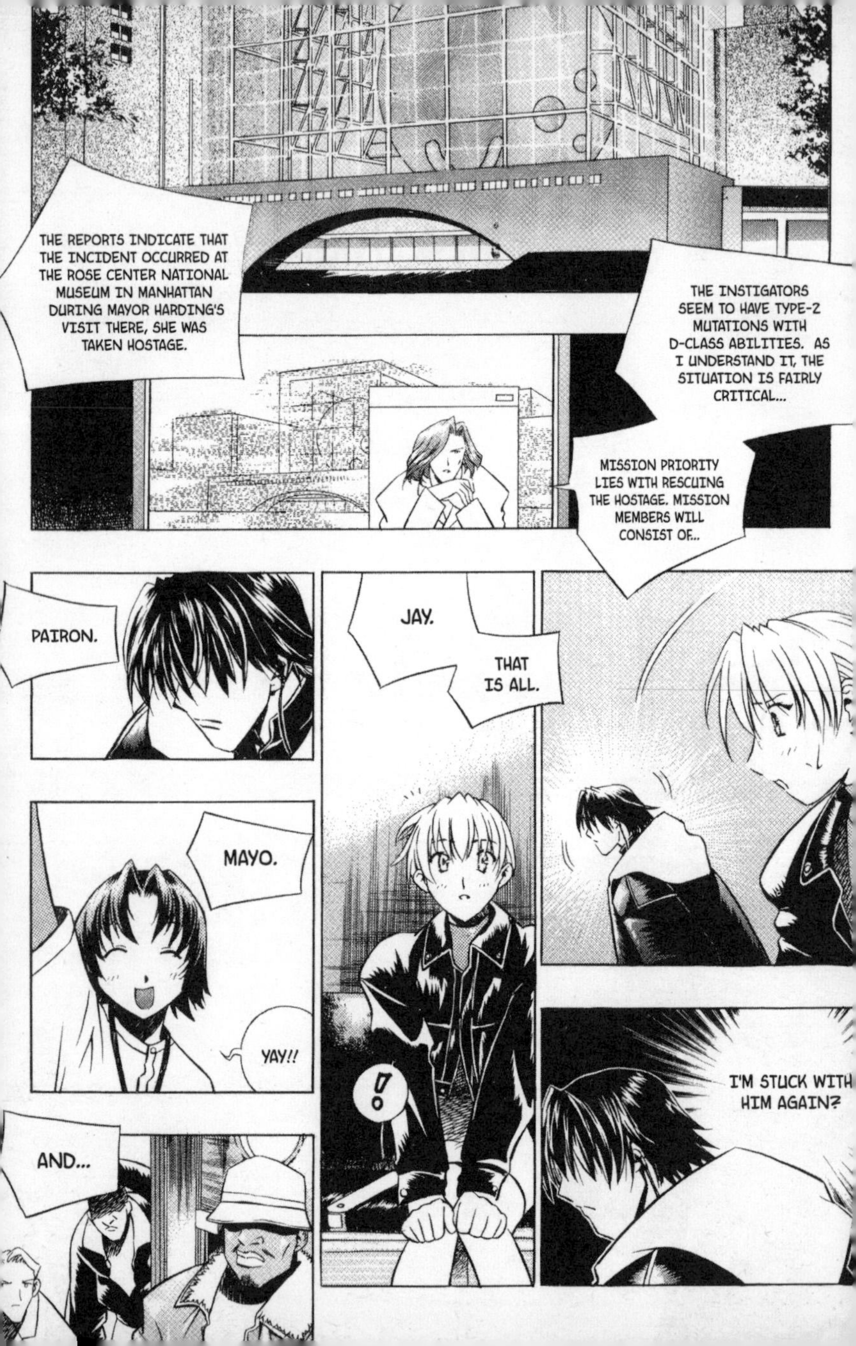
THE REPORTS INDICATE THAT THE INCIDENT OCCURRED AT THE ROSE CENTER NATIONAL MUSEUM IN MANHATTAN DURING MAYOR HARDING'S VISIT THERE, SHE WAS TAKEN HOSTAGE.
THE INSTIGATORS SEEM TO HAVE TYPE-2 MUTATIONS WITH D-CLASS ABILITIES. AS I UNDERSTAND IT, THE SITUATION IS FAIRLY CRITICAL...
MISSION PRIORITY LIES WITH RESCUING THE HOSTAGE. MISSION MEMBERS WILL CONSIST OF...
PAIRON.
MAYO.
YAY!!
AND...
JAY.
THAT IS ALL.
I'M STUCK WITH HIM AGAIN?

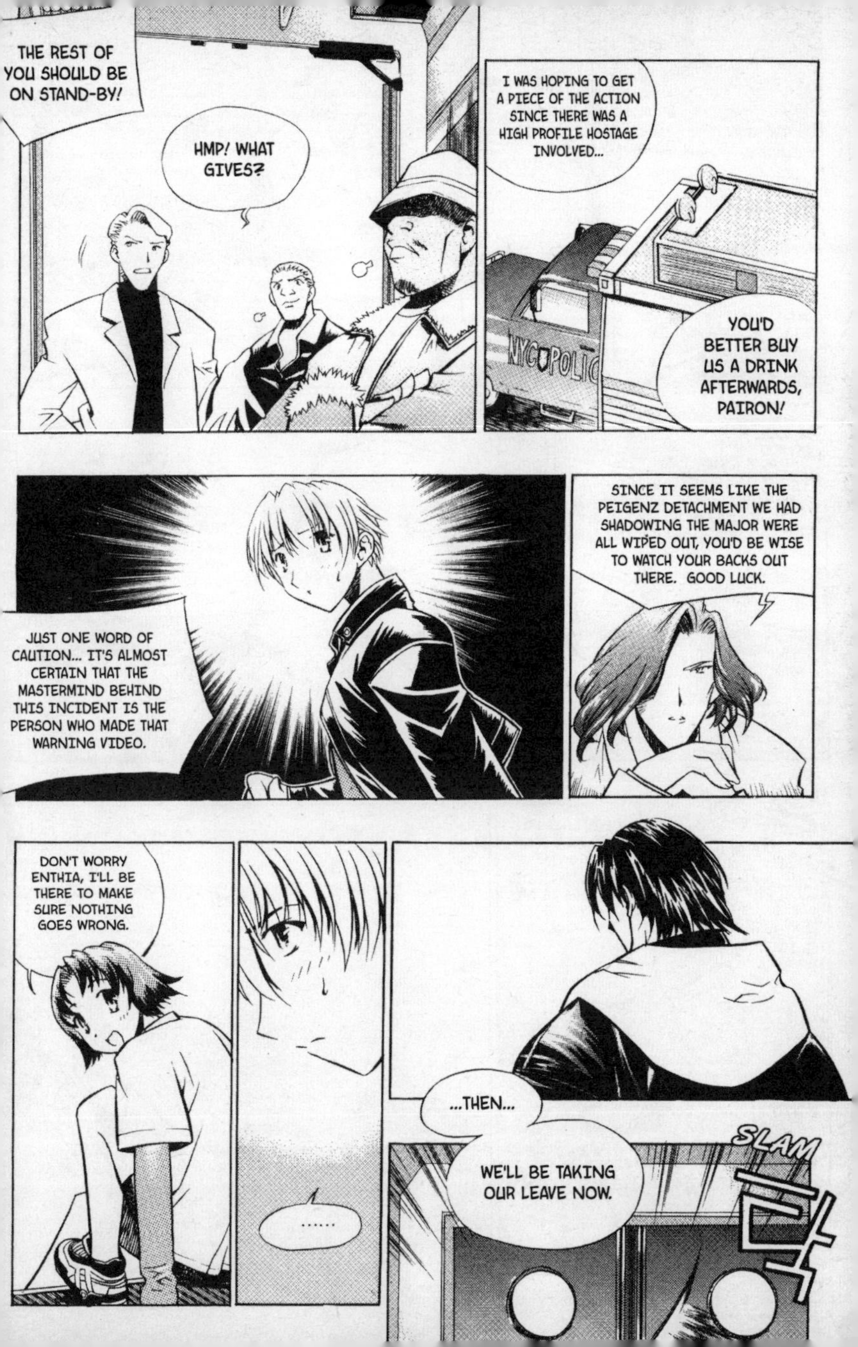
THE REST OF YOU SHOULD BE ON STAND-BY!
HMP! WHAT GIVES?
I WAS HOPING TO GET A PIECE OF THE ACTION SINCE THERE WAS A HIGH PROFILE HOSTAGE INVOLVED...
NYC POLIC
YOU'D BETTER BUY US A DRINK AFTERWARDS, PAIRON!
JUST ONE WORD OF CAUTION... IT'S ALMOST CERTAIN THAT THE MASTERMIND BEHIND THIS INCIDENT IS THE PERSON WHO MADE THAT WARNING VIDEO.
SINCE IT SEEMS LIKE THE PEIGENZ DETACHMENT WE HAD SHADOWING THE MAJOR WERE ALL WIPED OUT, YOU'D BE WISE TO WATCH YOUR BACKS OUT THERE. GOOD LUCK.
DON'T WORRY ENTHIA, I'LL BE THERE TO MAKE SURE NOTHING GOES WRONG.
......
...THEN...
WE'LL BE TAKING OUR LEAVE NOW.
SLAM

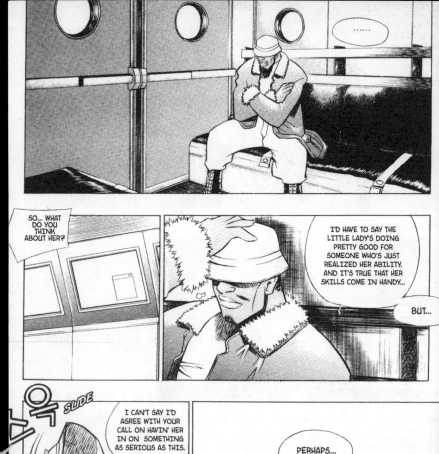

SO... WHAT DO YOU THINK ABOUT HER?

I'D HAVE TO SAY THE LITTLE LADY'S DOING PRETTY GOOD FOR SOMEONE WHO'S JUST REALIZED HER ABILITY. AND IT'S TRUE THAT HER SKILLS COME IN HANDY...

BUT...

SLIDE

I CAN'T SAY I'D AGREE WITH YOUR CALL ON HAVIN' HER IN ON SOMETHING AS SERIOUS AS THIS.

PERHAPS...

HMM...

IN ANY CASE, IS THERE ANY ONE REASON YOU KEEP PAIRING HER UP WITH PAIRON?

I'M SURE YOU'RE ALREADY AWARE THAT THOSE TWO DIDN'T EXACTLY MEET UNDER IDEAL CIRCUMSTANCES, RIGHT?

MY INTENTIONS AREN'T IMPORTANT... I GUESS IT MIGHT BE WHAT SOME PEOPLE CALL, "EXPECTATION."

AND BESIDES, THEY SEEM TO MAKE A GOOD PAIR...

HMP!

DID I EVER TELL YOU THAT YOU'RE A FREAK?

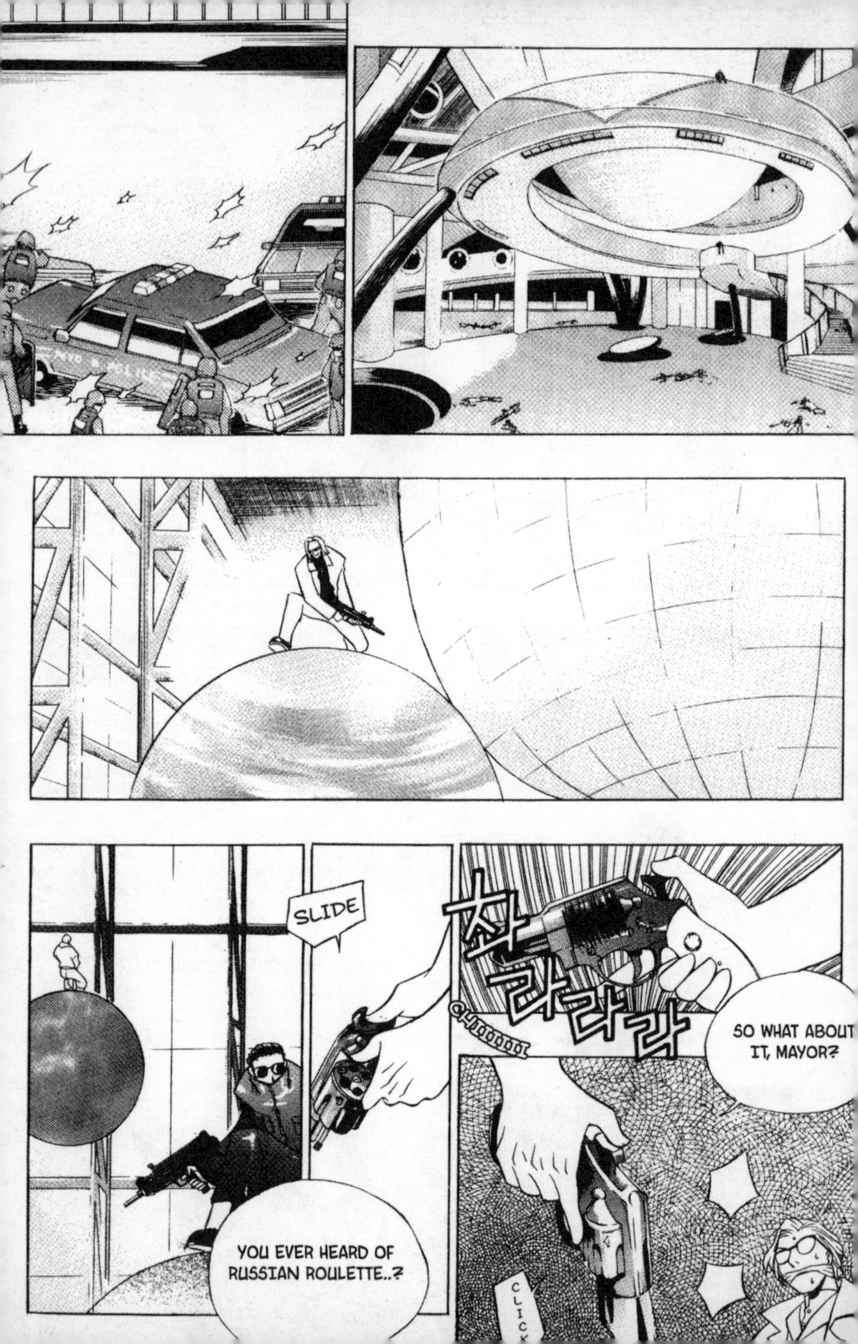
SLIDE
YOU EVER HEARD OF RUSSIAN ROULETTE..?
SO WHAT ABOUT IT, MAYOR?
CLICK

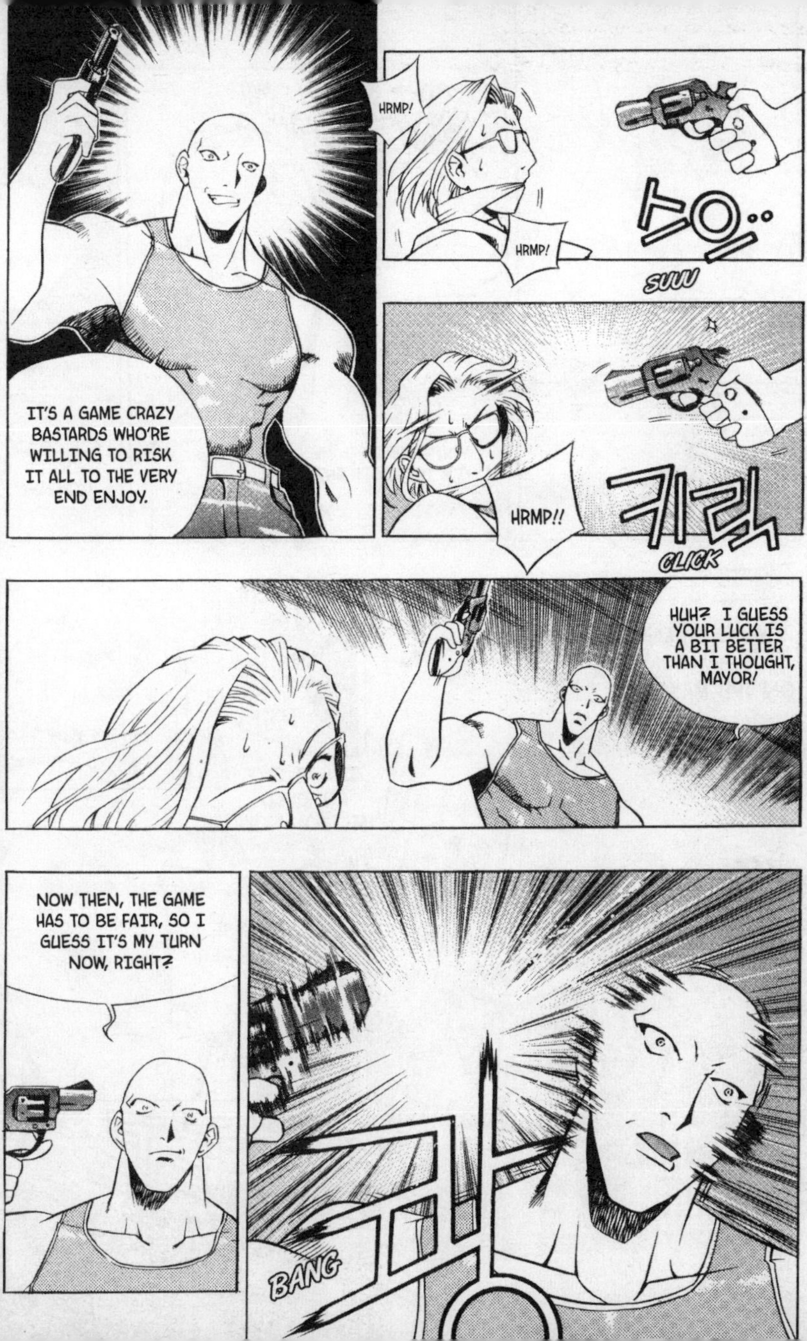

IT'S A GAME CRAZY BASTARDS WHO'RE WILLING TO RISK IT ALL TO THE VERY END ENJOY.
HRMP!
HRMP!
스읍
SUUU
HRMP!!
키릭
CLICK
HUH? I GUESS YOUR LUCK IS A BIT BETTER THAN I THOUGHT, MAYOR!
NOW THEN, THE GAME HAS TO BE FAIR, SO I GUESS IT'S MY TURN NOW, RIGHT?
BANG

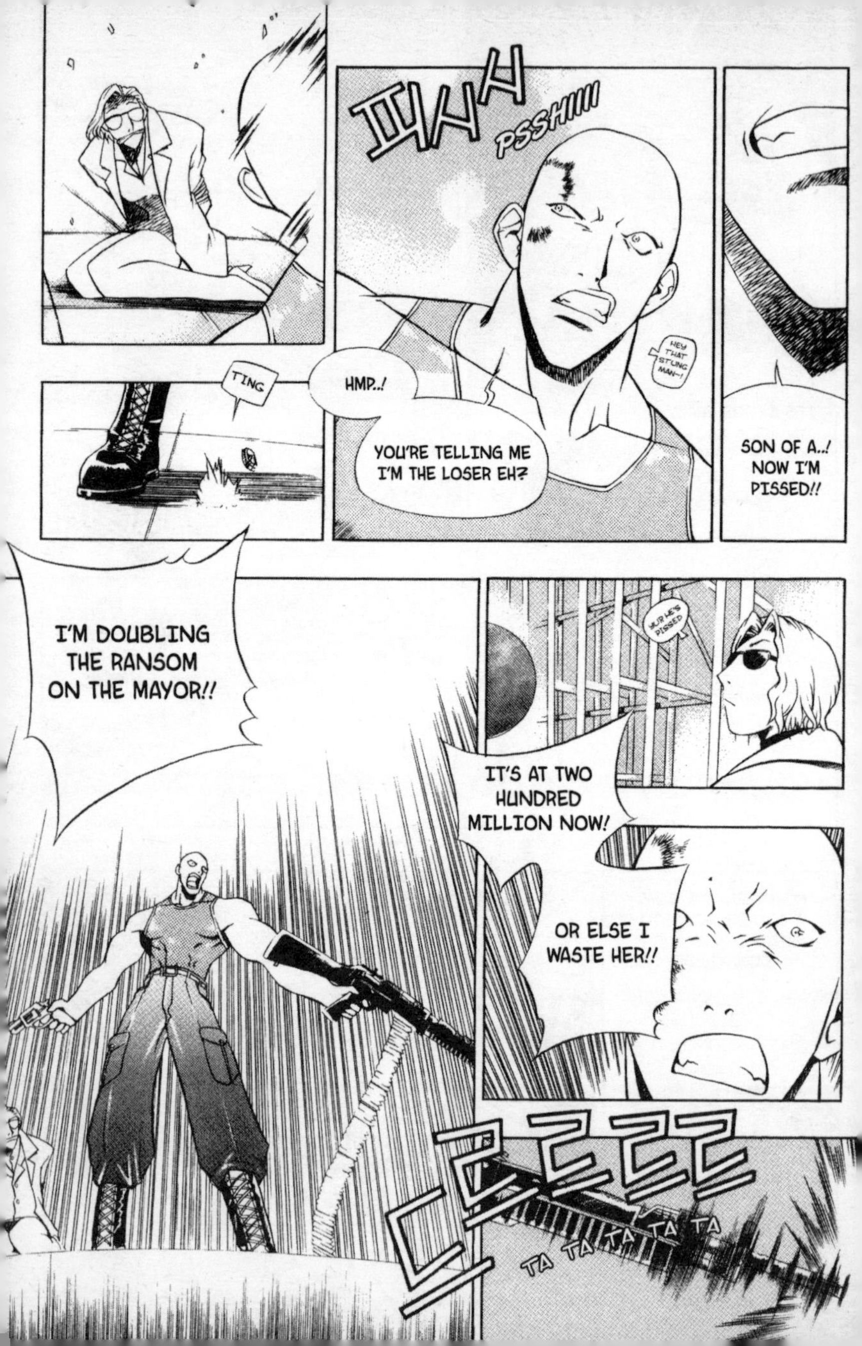
PSSH!!!!
HMP..!
YOU'RE TELLING ME I'M THE LOSER EH?
HEY THAT STUNG MAN~!
TING
SON OF A..! NOW I'M PISSED!!
I'M DOUBLING THE RANSOM ON THE MAYOR!!
YUP HE'S PISSED
IT'S AT TWO HUNDRED MILLION NOW!
OR ELSE I WASTE HER!!
TA TA TA TA TA TA

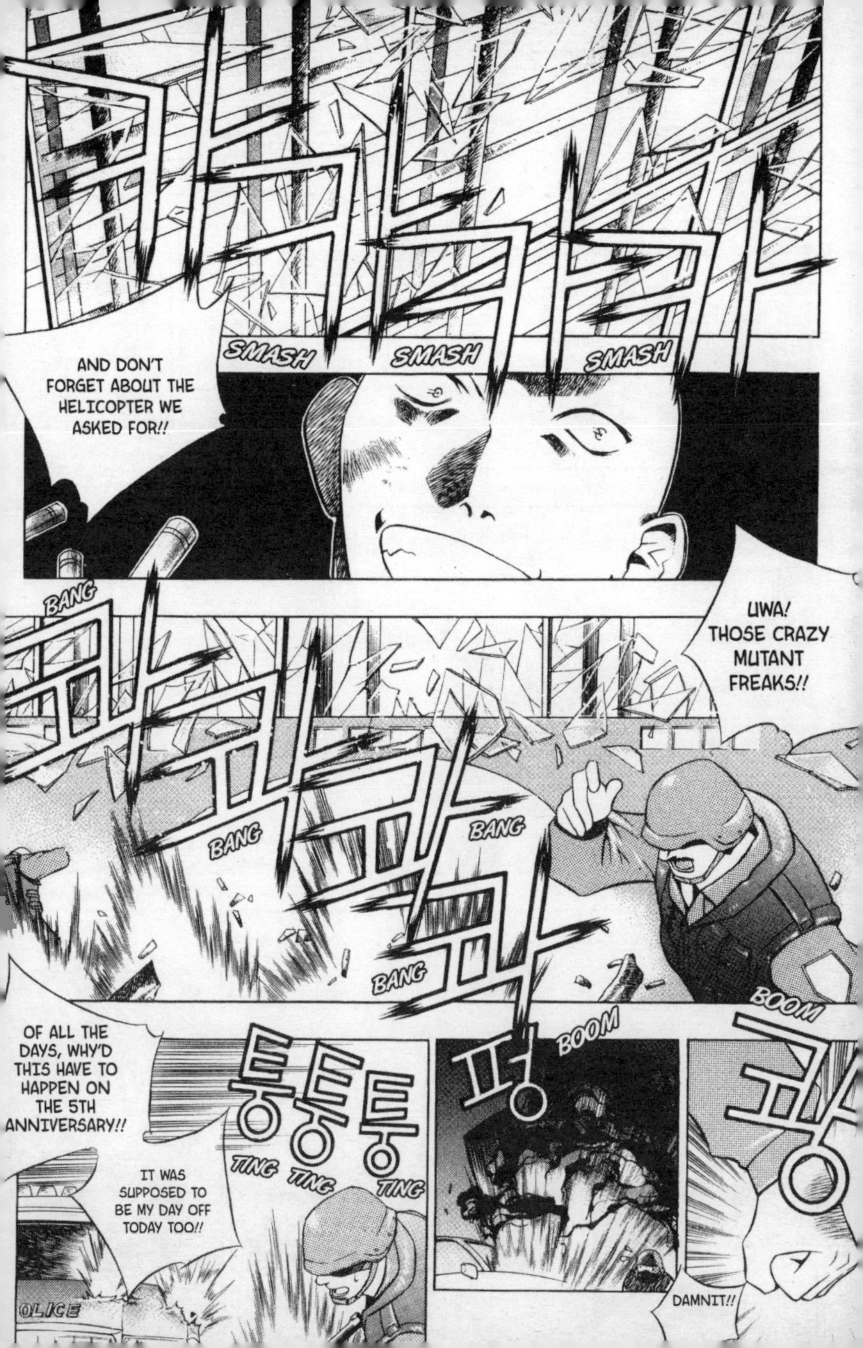
SMASH
SMASH
SMASH
AND DON'T FORGET ABOUT THE HELICOPTER WE ASKED FOR!!
BANG
BANG
BANG
BANG
UWA! THOSE CRAZY MUTANT FREAKS!!
OF ALL THE DAYS, WHY'D THIS HAVE TO HAPPEN ON THE 5TH ANNIVERSARY!!
TING
TING
TING
IT WAS SUPPOSED TO BE MY DAY OFF TODAY TOO!!
OLICE
BOOM
BOOM
DAMNIT!!

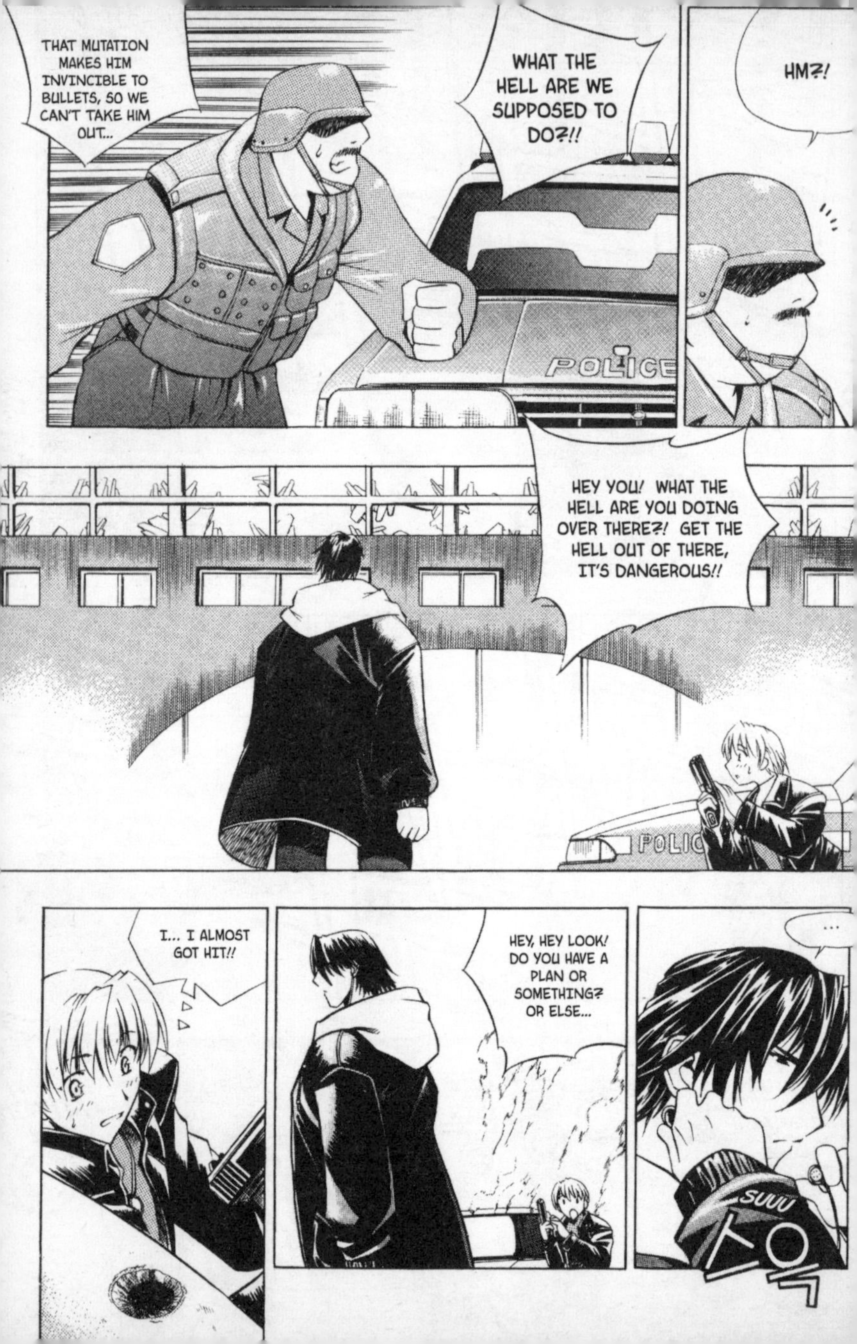
THAT MUTATION MAKES HIM INVINCIBLE TO BULLETS, SO WE CAN'T TAKE HIM OUT...
WHAT THE HELL ARE WE SUPPOSED TO DO?!!
HM?!
HEY YOU! WHAT THE HELL ARE YOU DOING OVER THERE?! GET THE HELL OUT OF THERE, IT'S DANGEROUS!!
POLICE
I... I ALMOST GOT HIT!!
HEY, HEY LOOK! DO YOU HAVE A PLAN OR SOMETHING? OR ELSE...
...
SUUU

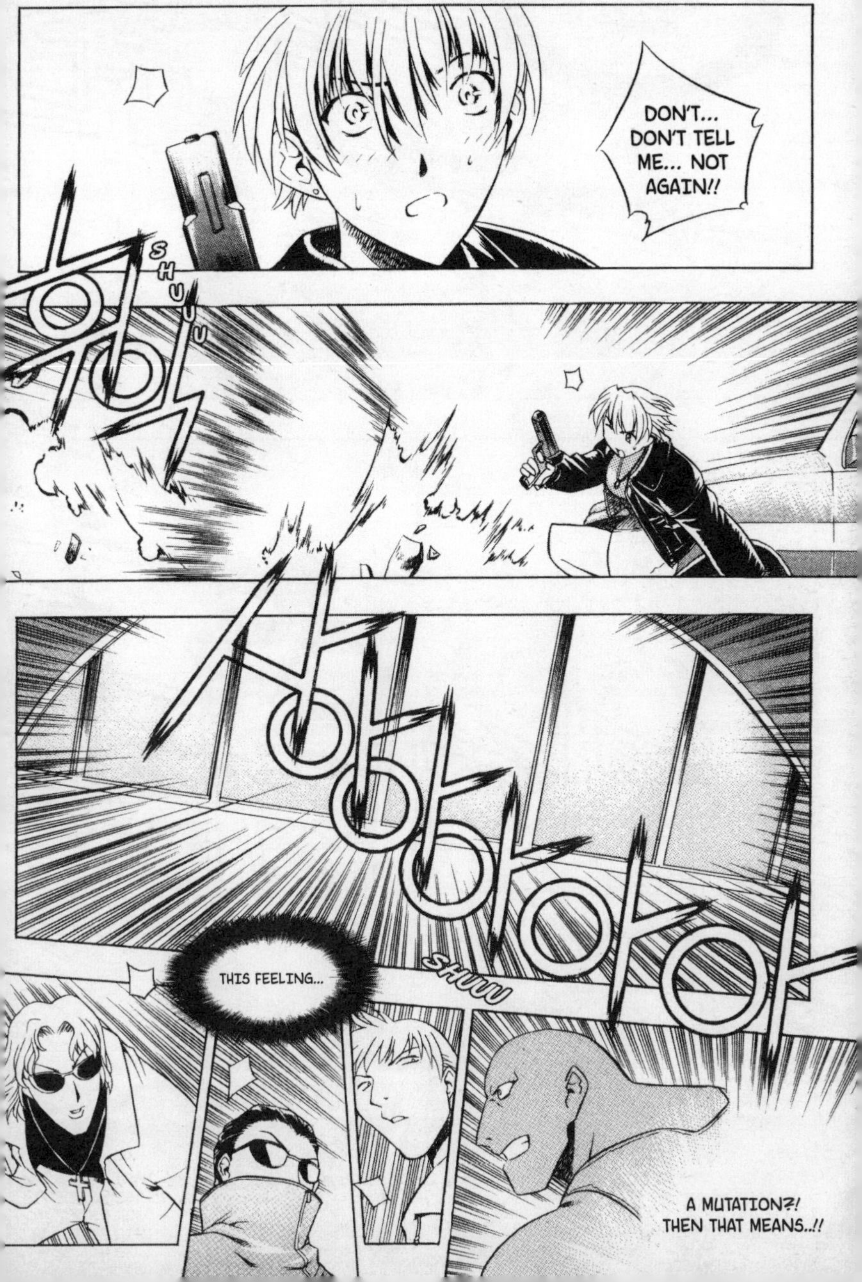
DON'T... DON'T TELL ME... NOT AGAIN!!
SHUUU
THIS FEELING...
SHUUU
A MUTATION?! THEN THAT MEANS..!!

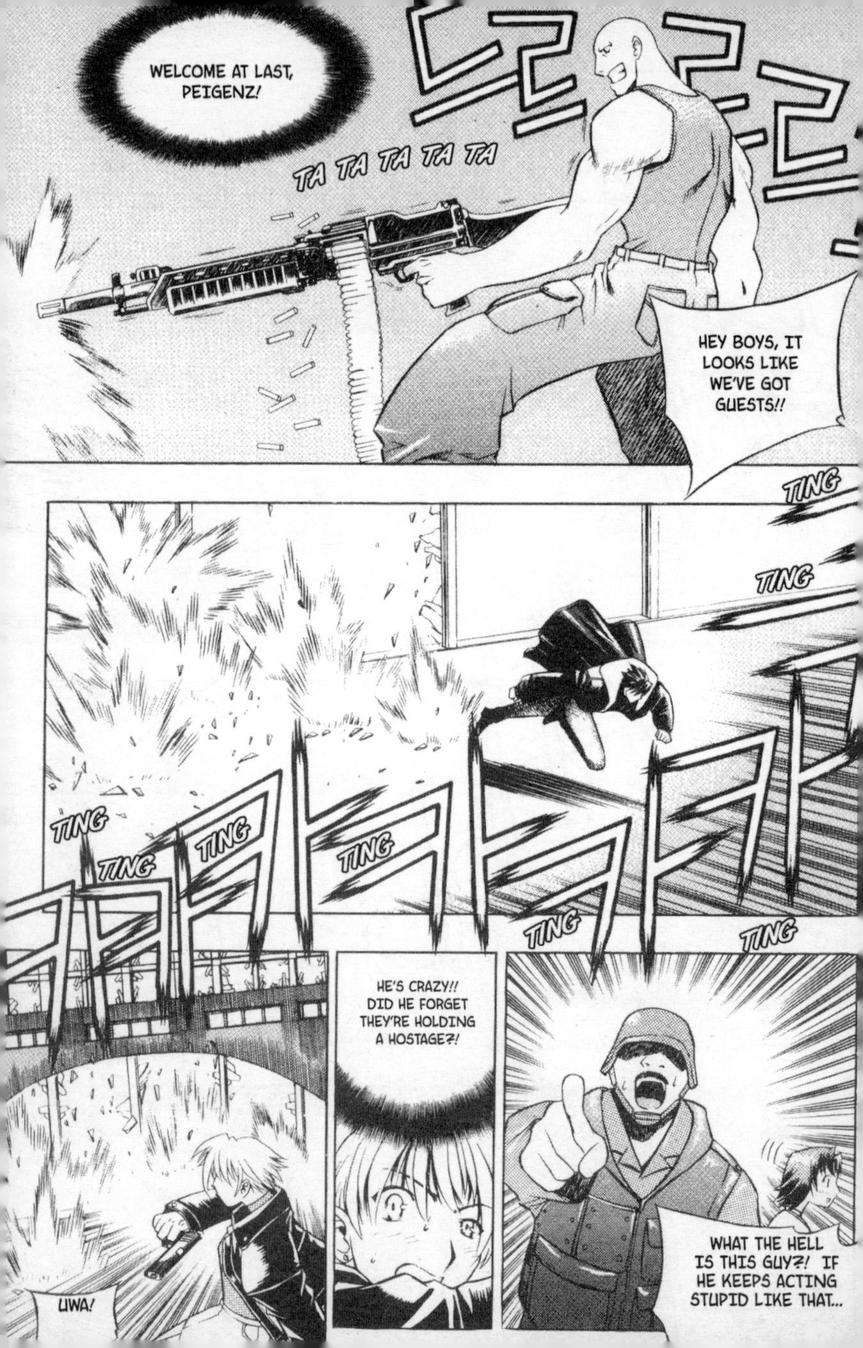
WELCOME AT LAST, PEIGENZ!
TA TA TA TA TA
HEY BOYS, IT LOOKS LIKE WE'VE GOT GUESTS!!
TING
TING
TING
TING
TING
TING
TING
TING
UWA!
HE'S CRAZY!! DID HE FORGET THEY'RE HOLDING A HOSTAGE?!
WHAT THE HELL IS THIS GUY?! IF HE KEEPS ACTING STUPID LIKE THAT...

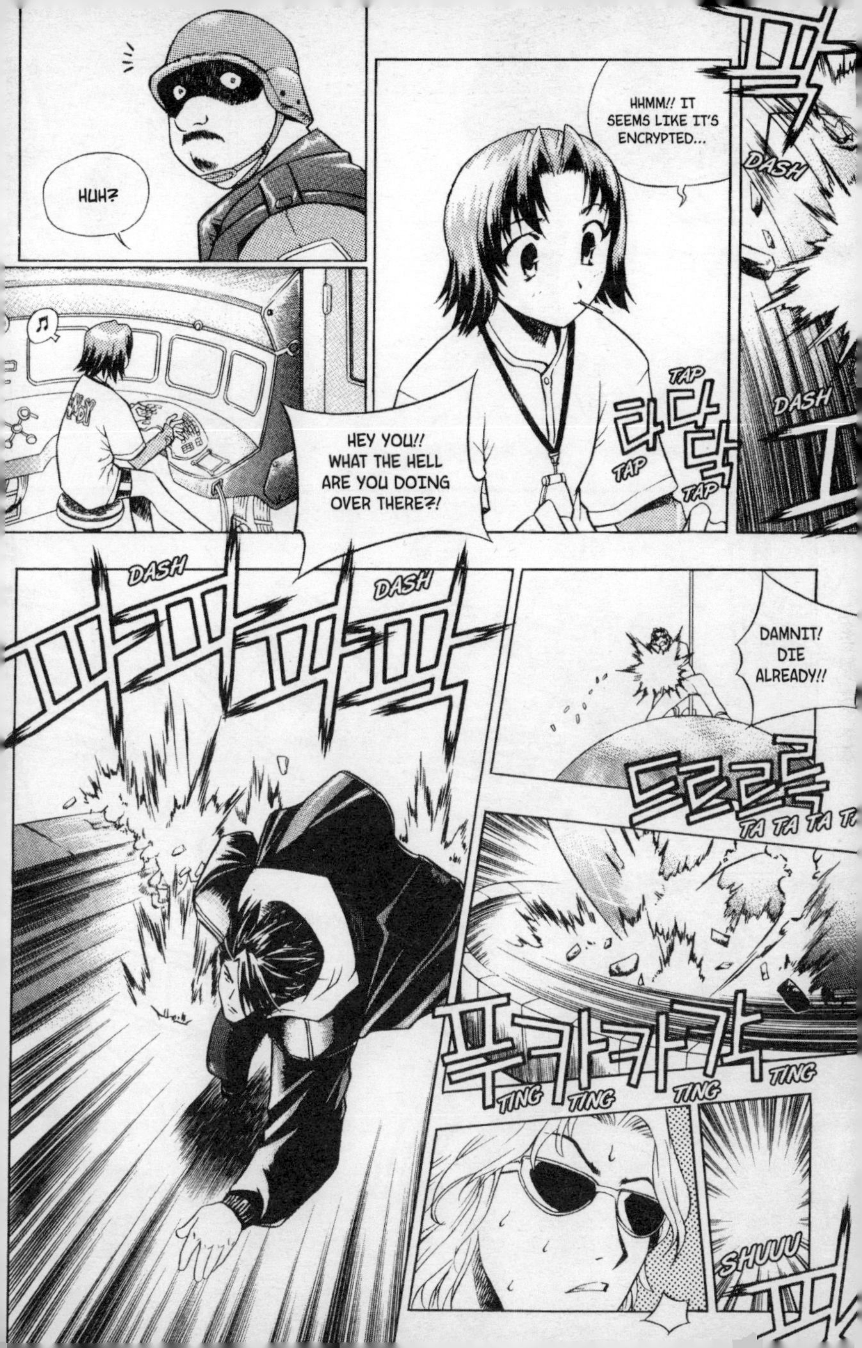
HHMM!! IT SEEMS LIKE IT'S ENCRYPTED...
DASH
HUH?
TAP
TAP
TAP
DASH
HEY YOU!! WHAT THE HELL ARE YOU DOING OVER THERE?!
DASH
DASH
DAMNIT! DIE ALREADY!!
TA TA TA TA
TING
TING
TING
TING
SHUUU

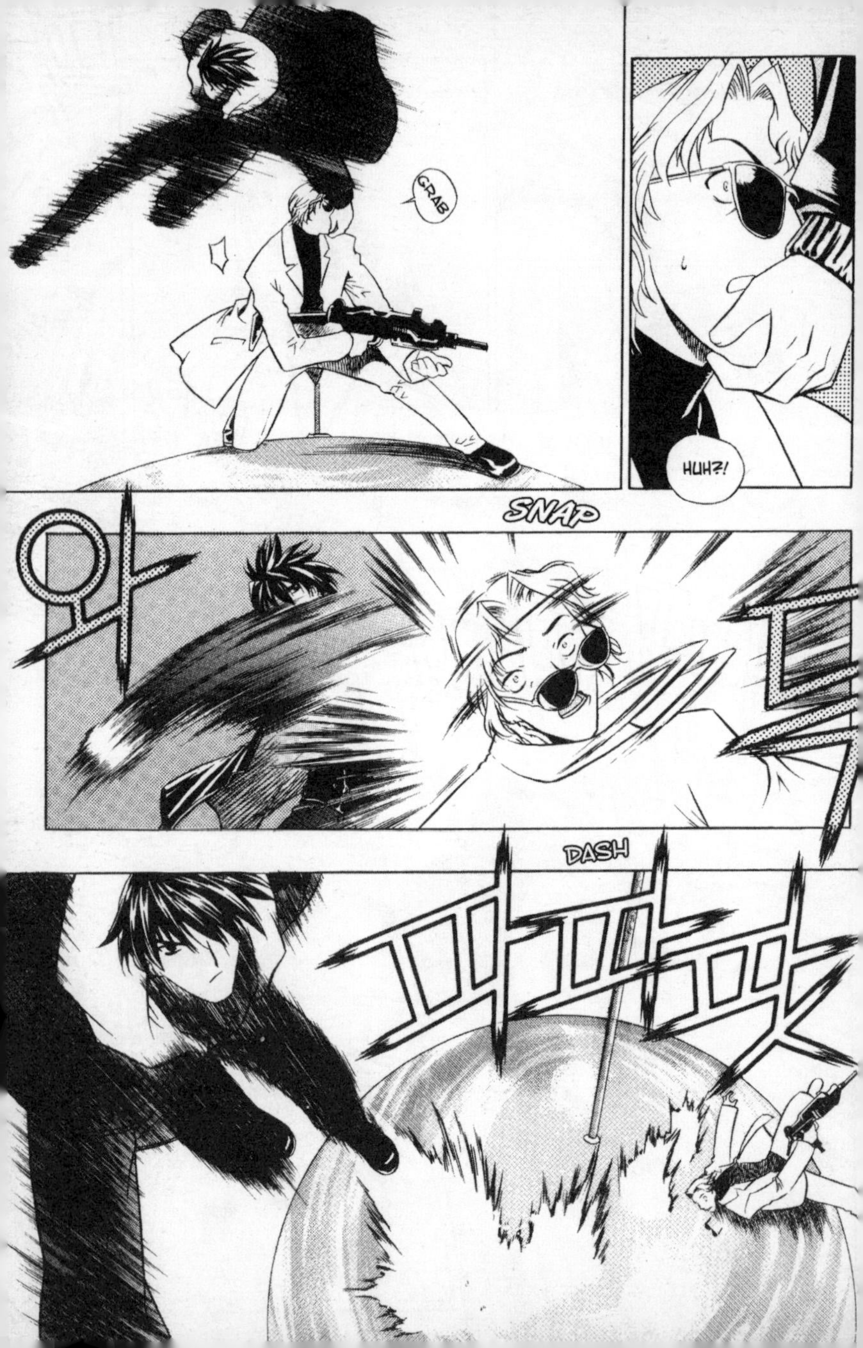
GRAB
HUH?!
SNAP
DASH

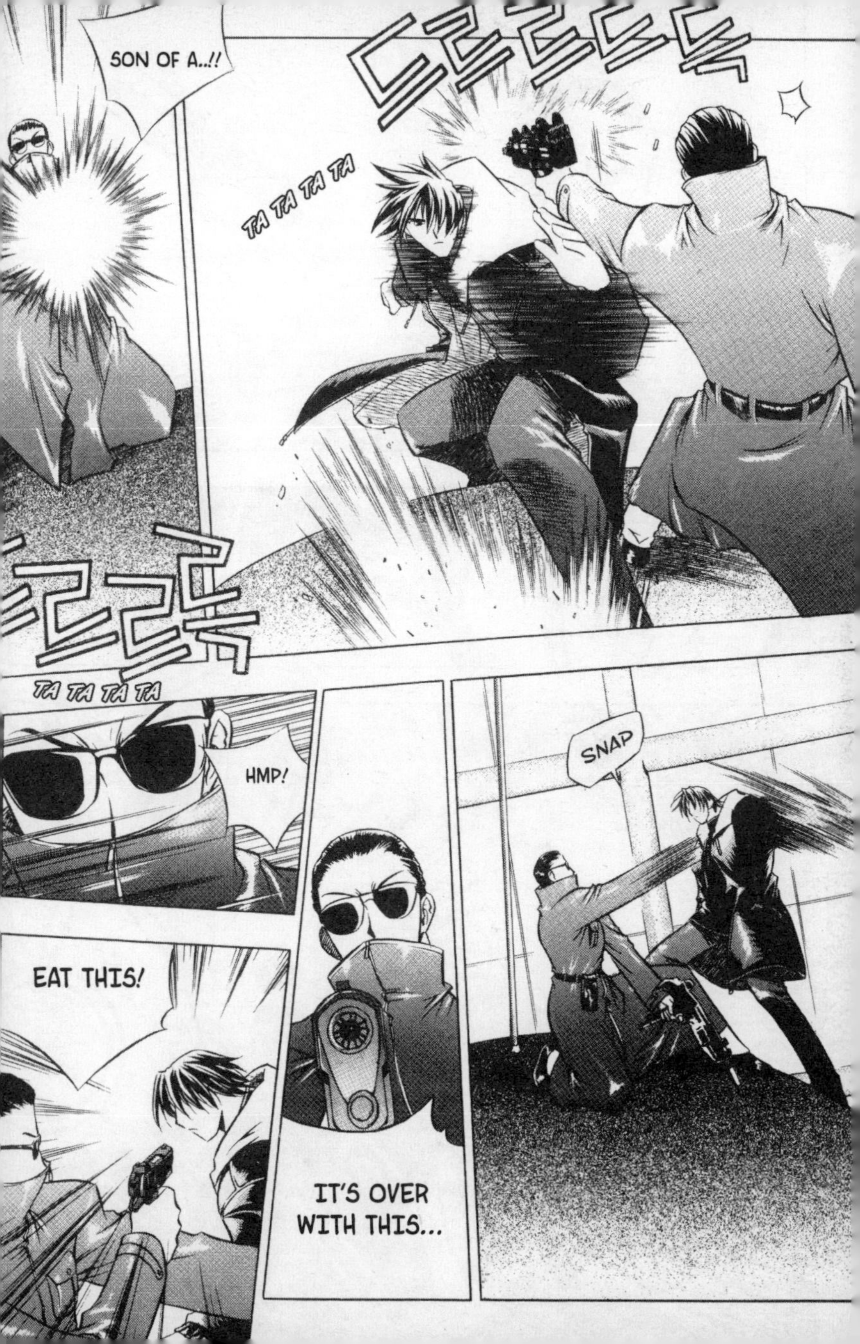
SON OF A..!!
TA TA TA TA
TA TA TA TA
HMP!
EAT THIS!
IT'S OVER WITH THIS...
SNAP

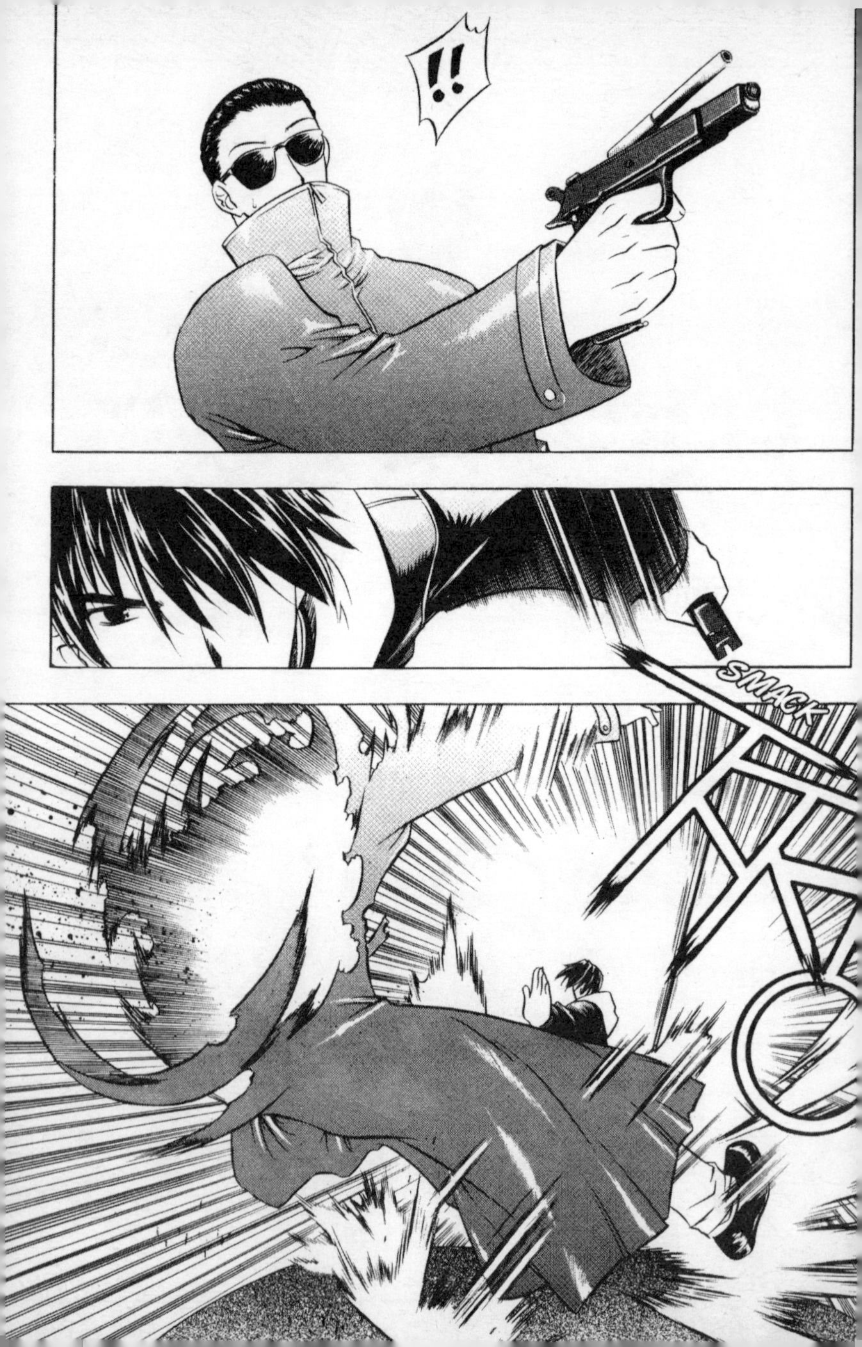
!!
SMACK

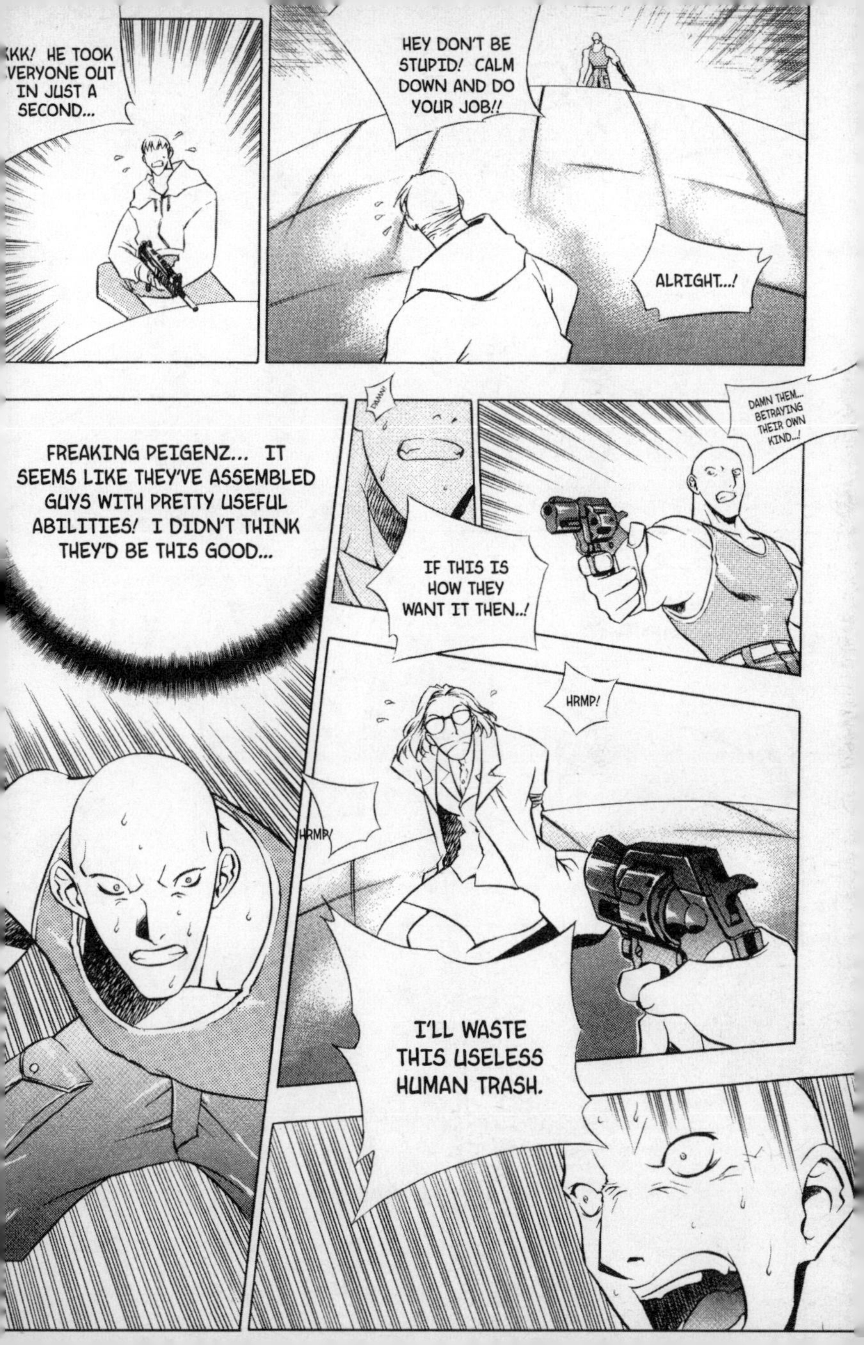
KKK! HE TOOK EVERYONE OUT IN JUST A SECOND...
HEY DON'T BE STUPID! CALM DOWN AND DO YOUR JOB!!
ALRIGHT...!
FREAKING PEIGENZ... IT SEEMS LIKE THEY'VE ASSEMBLED GUYS WITH PRETTY USEFUL ABILITIES! I DIDN'T THINK THEY'D BE THIS GOOD...
DAMN!
DAMN THEM... BETRAYING THEIR OWN KIND...!
IF THIS IS HOW THEY WANT IT THEN..!
HRMP!
HRMP!
I'LL WASTE THIS USELESS HUMAN TRASH.

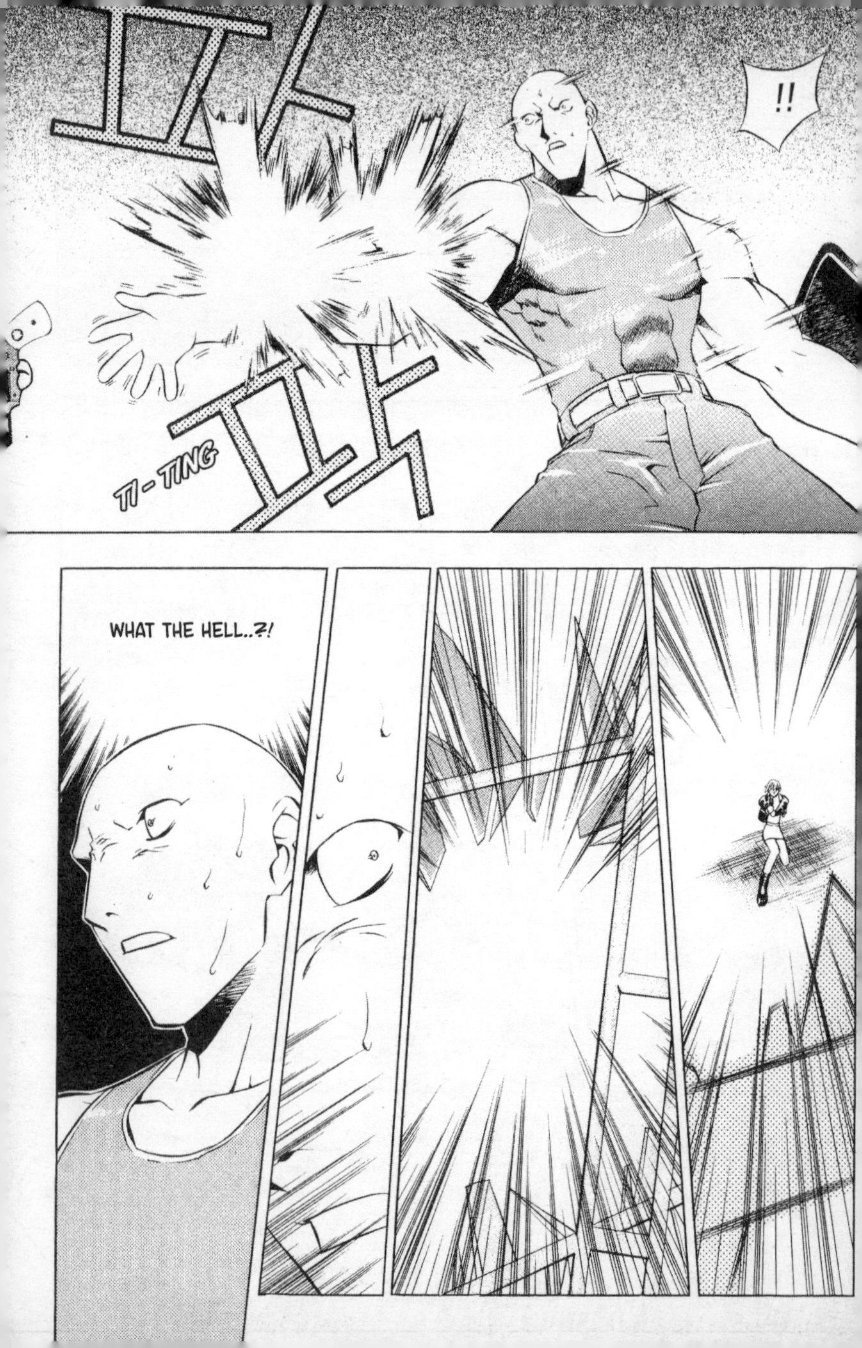
!!
TI - TING
WHAT THE HELL..?!

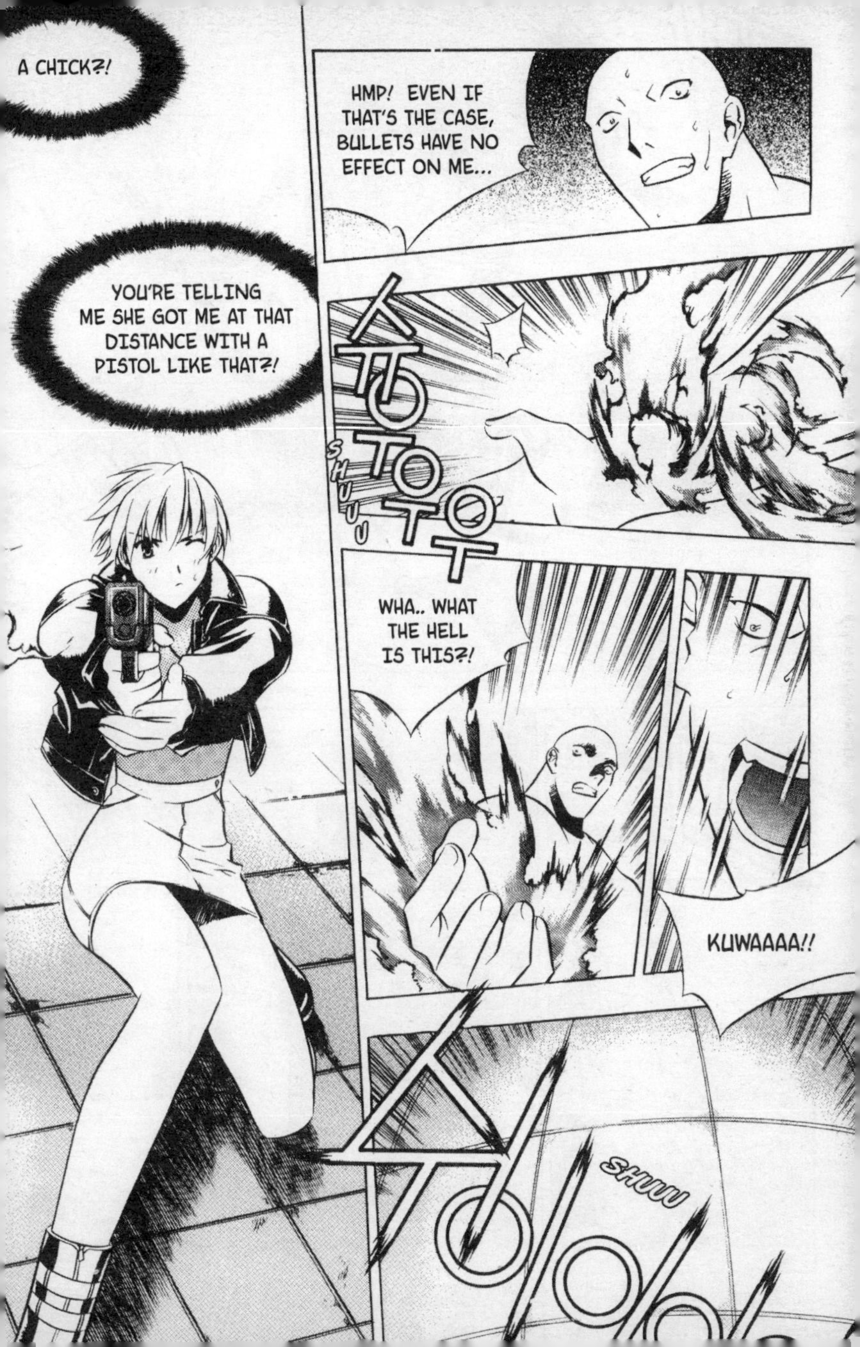
A CHICK?!
YOU'RE TELLING ME SHE GOT ME AT THAT DISTANCE WITH A PISTOL LIKE THAT?!
HMP! EVEN IF THAT'S THE CASE, BULLETS HAVE NO EFFECT ON ME...
SHUUU
WHA.. WHAT THE HELL IS THIS?!
KUWAAAA!!
SHUUU

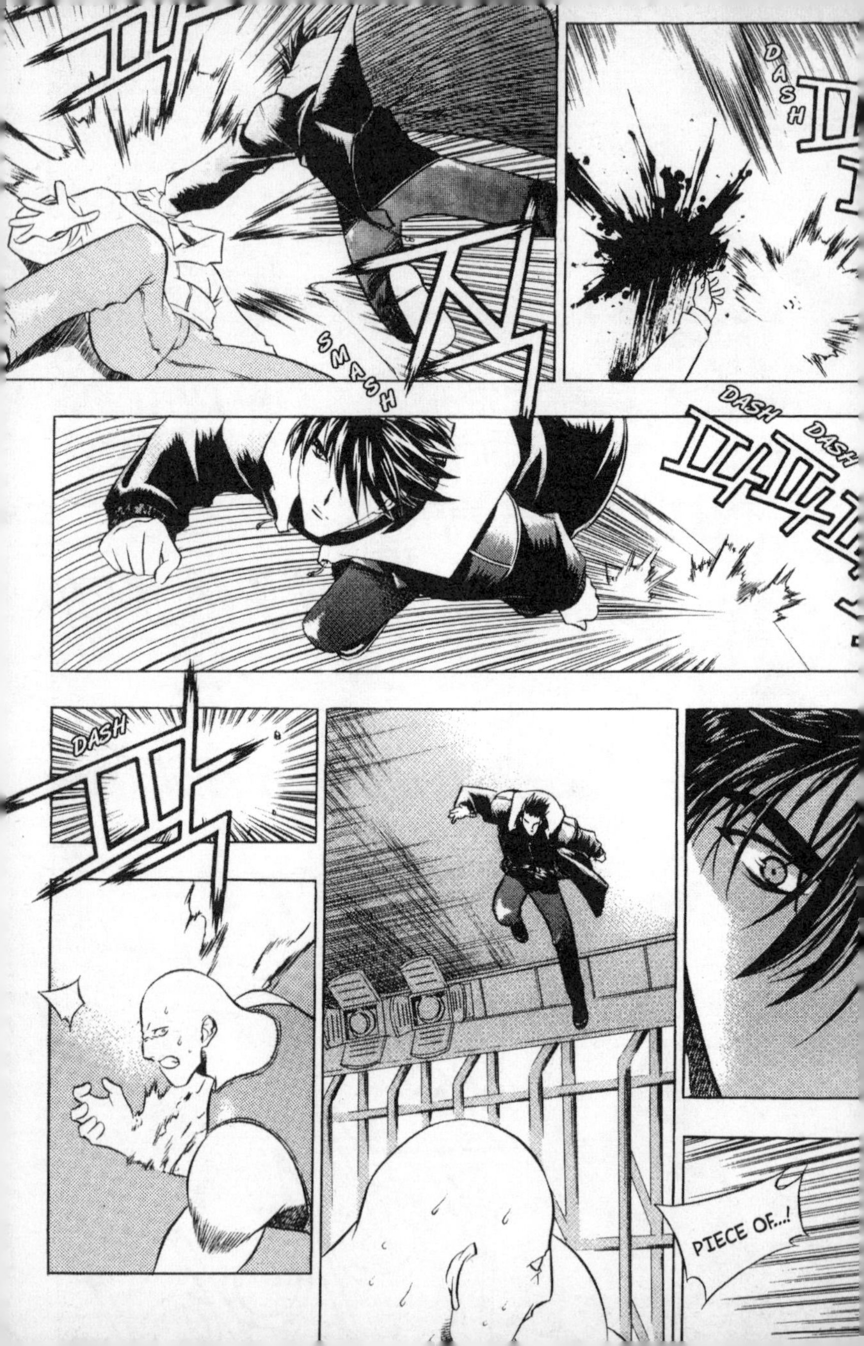
SMASH
DASH
DASH
DASH
DASH
PIECE OF...!

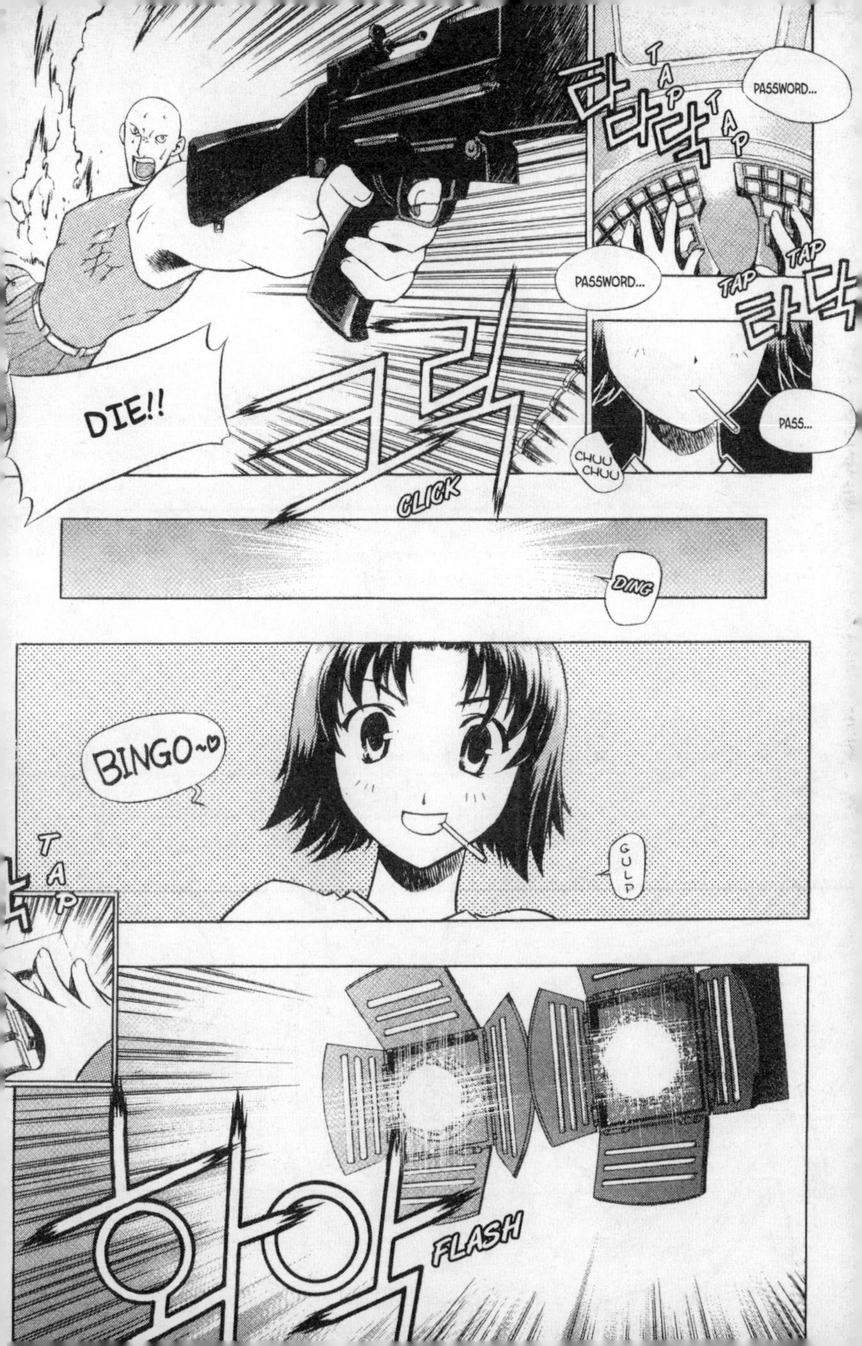
DIE!!
CLICK
TAP TAP
PASSWORD...
PASSWORD...
TAP TAP
PASS...
CHUU CHUU
DING
BINGO~♡
GULP
TAP
FLASH

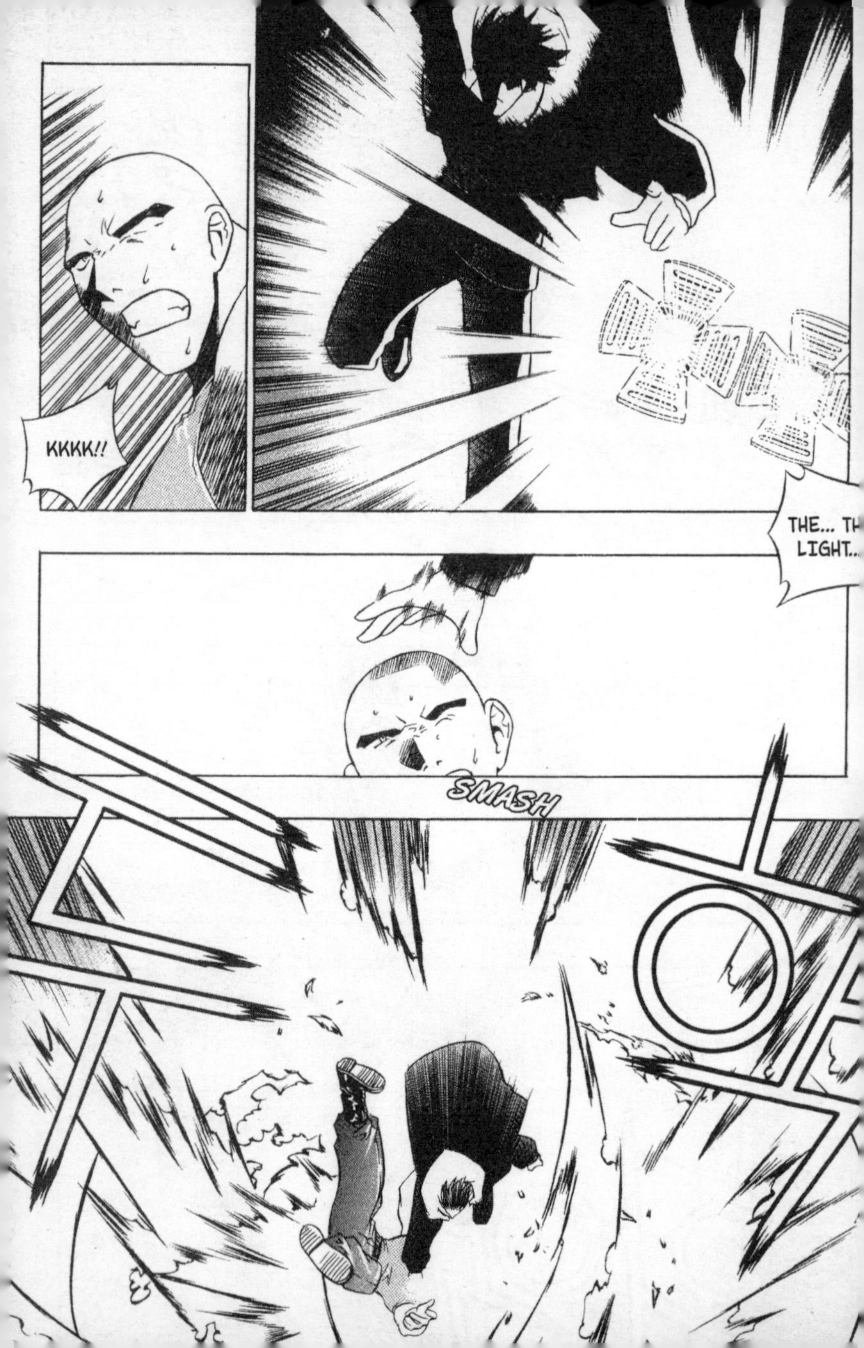
KKKK!!
THE... TH
LIGHT...
SMASH

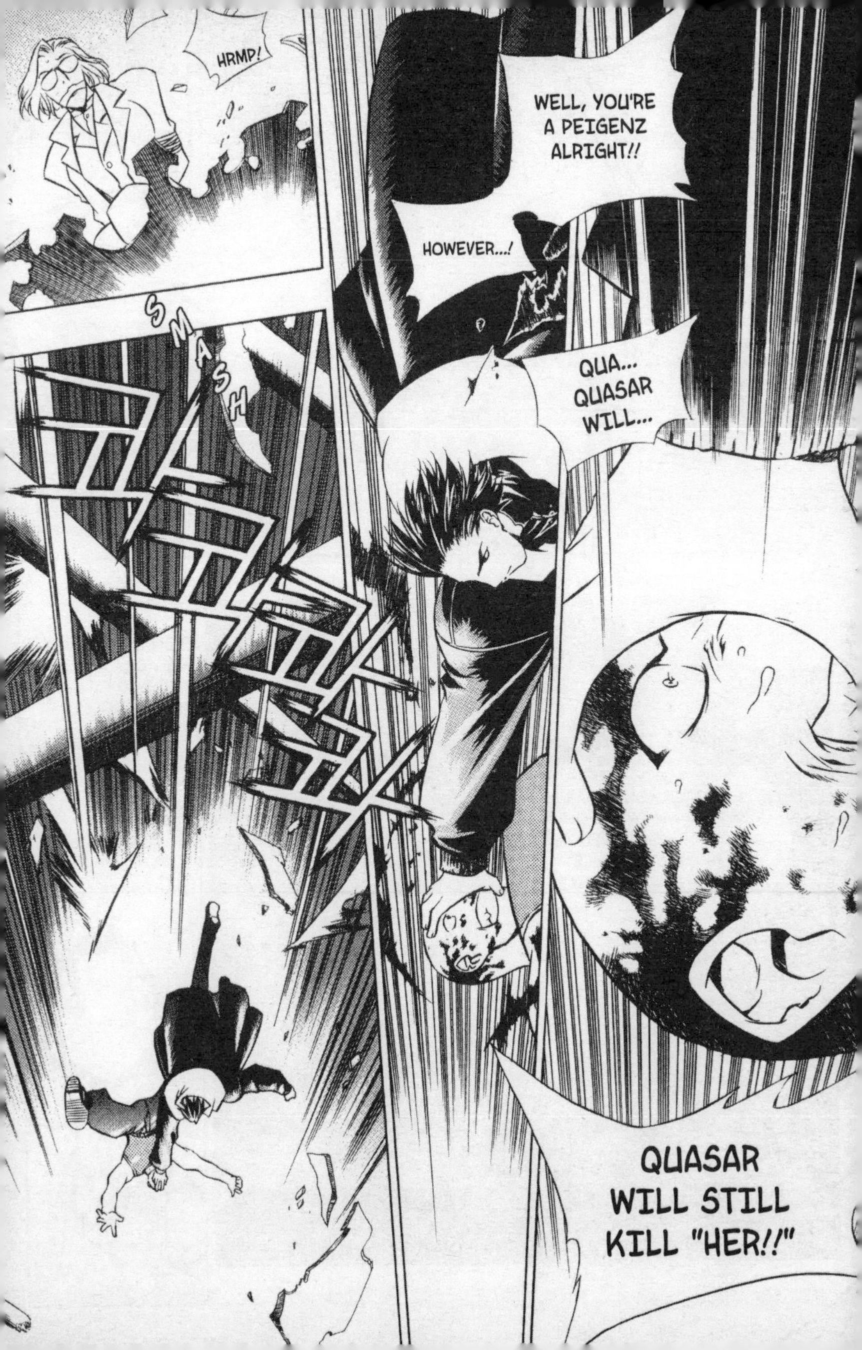
HRMP!
SMASH
WELL, YOU'RE A PEIGENZ ALRIGHT!!
HOWEVER...!
QUA... QUASAR WILL...
QUASAR WILL STILL KILL "HER!!"

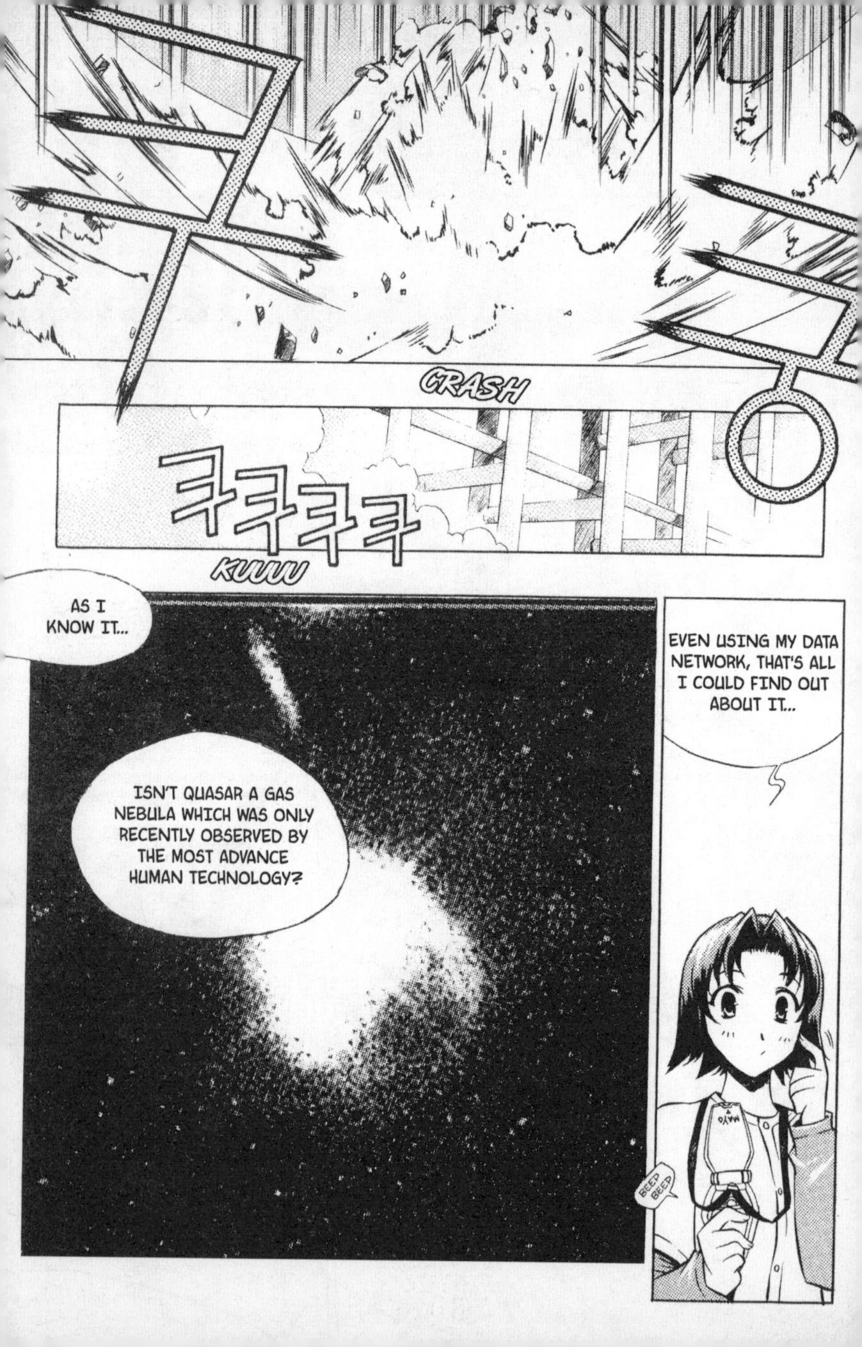
CRASH
쿠쿠쿠쿠
KUUUU
AS I KNOW IT...
ISN'T QUASAR A GAS NEBULA WHICH WAS ONLY RECENTLY OBSERVED BY THE MOST ADVANCE HUMAN TECHNOLOGY?
EVEN USING MY DATA NETWORK, THAT'S ALL I COULD FIND OUT ABOUT IT...
BEEP BEEP

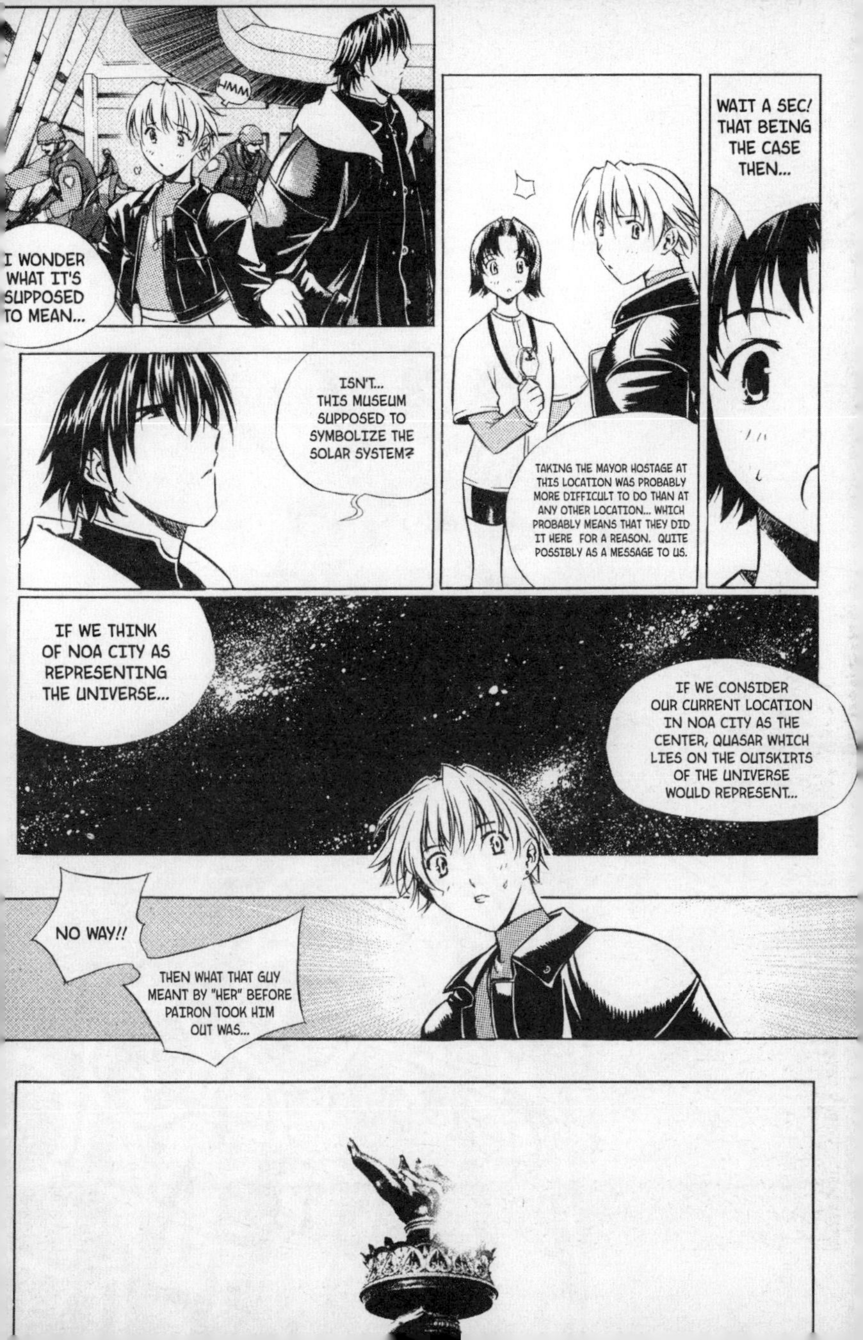
HMM
I WONDER WHAT IT'S SUPPOSED TO MEAN...
WAIT A SEC! THAT BEING THE CASE THEN...
ISN'T... THIS MUSEUM SUPPOSED TO SYMBOLIZE THE SOLAR SYSTEM?
TAKING THE MAYOR HOSTAGE AT THIS LOCATION WAS PROBABLY MORE DIFFICULT TO DO THAN AT ANY OTHER LOCATION... WHICH PROBABLY MEANS THAT THEY DID IT HERE FOR A REASON. QUITE POSSIBLY AS A MESSAGE TO US.
IF WE THINK OF NOA CITY AS REPRESENTING THE UNIVERSE...
IF WE CONSIDER OUR CURRENT LOCATION IN NOA CITY AS THE CENTER, QUASAR WHICH LIES ON THE OUTSKIRTS OF THE UNIVERSE WOULD REPRESENT...
NO WAY!!
THEN WHAT THAT GUY MEANT BY "HER" BEFORE PAIRON TOOK HIM OUT WAS...

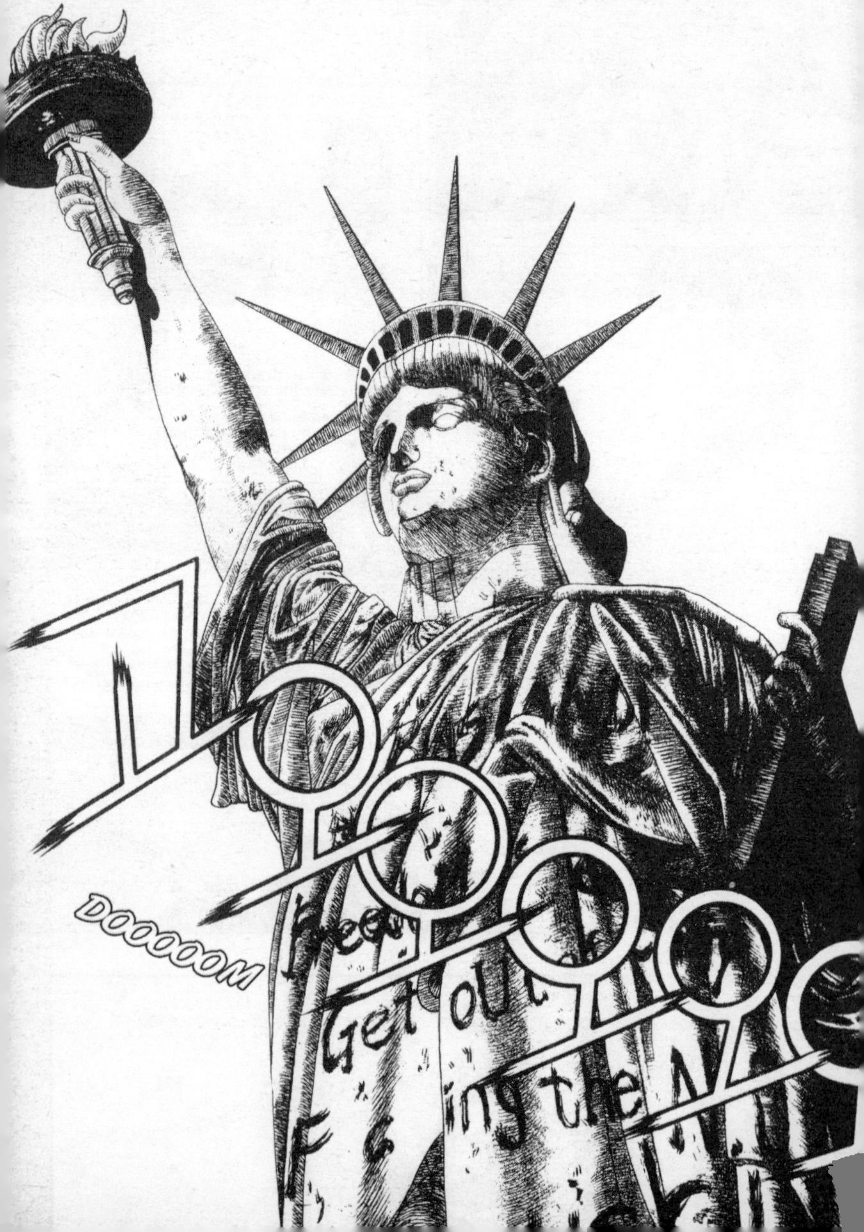
DOOOOOM
Get out
ing the

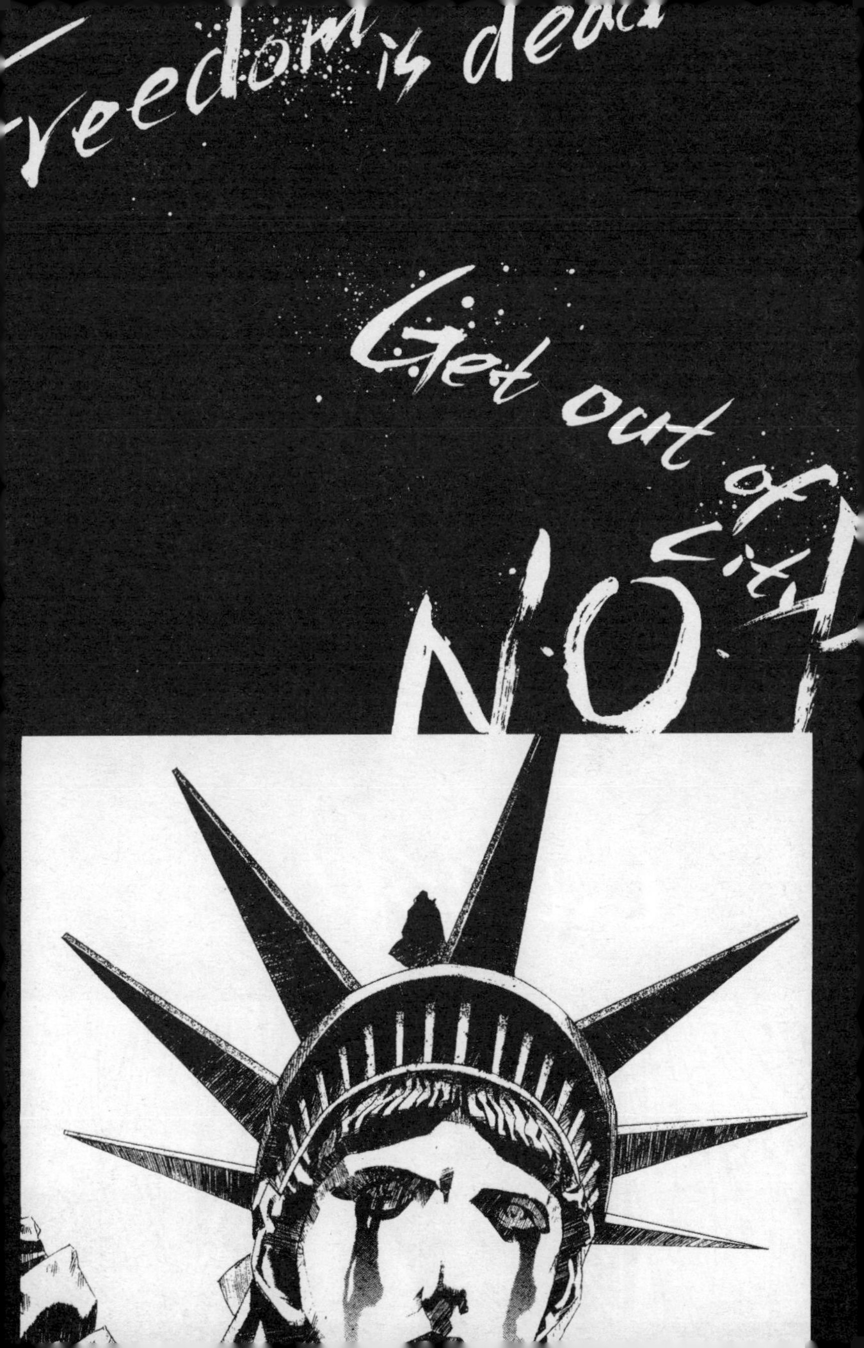
Freedom is dea
Get out of city
NO

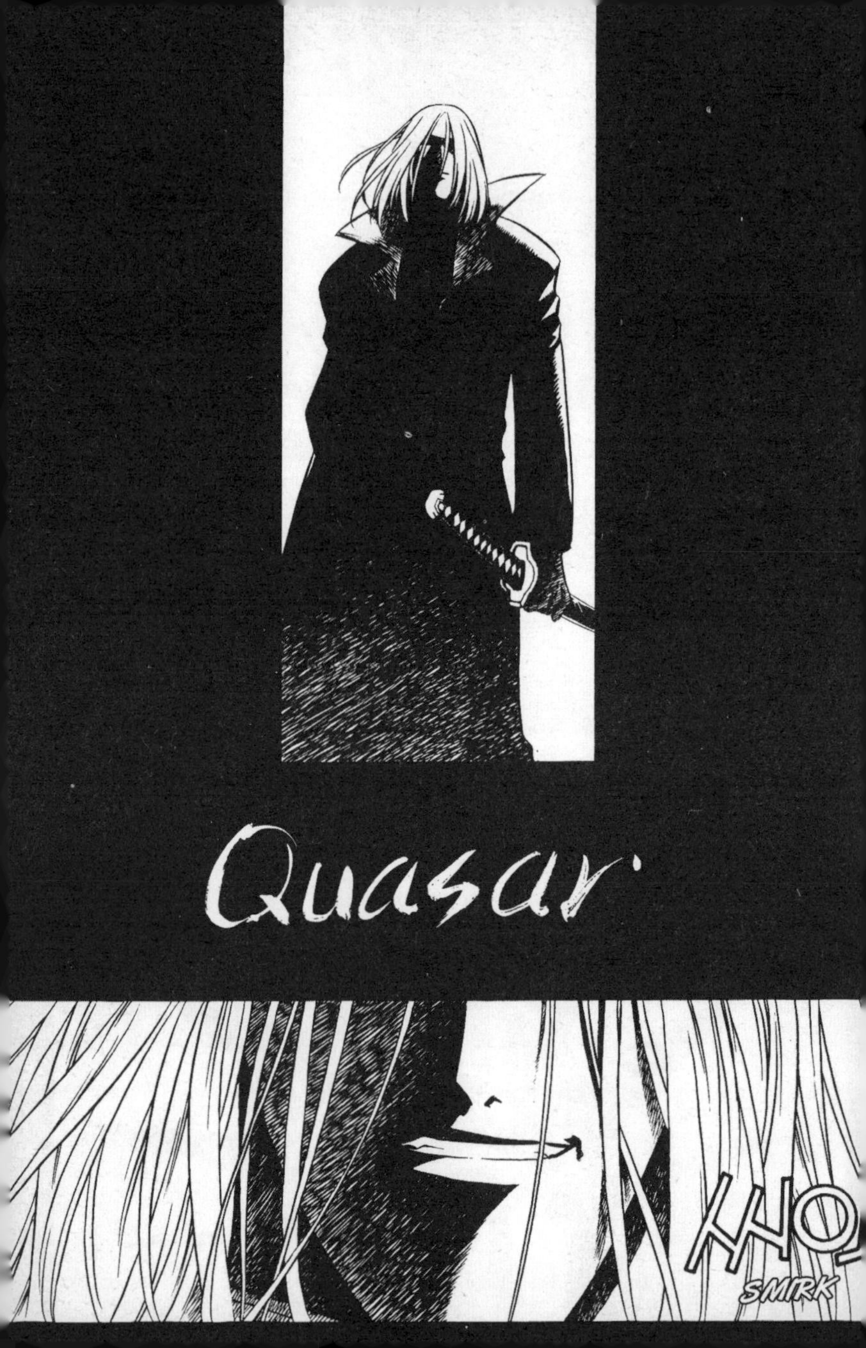
Quasar
SMIRK

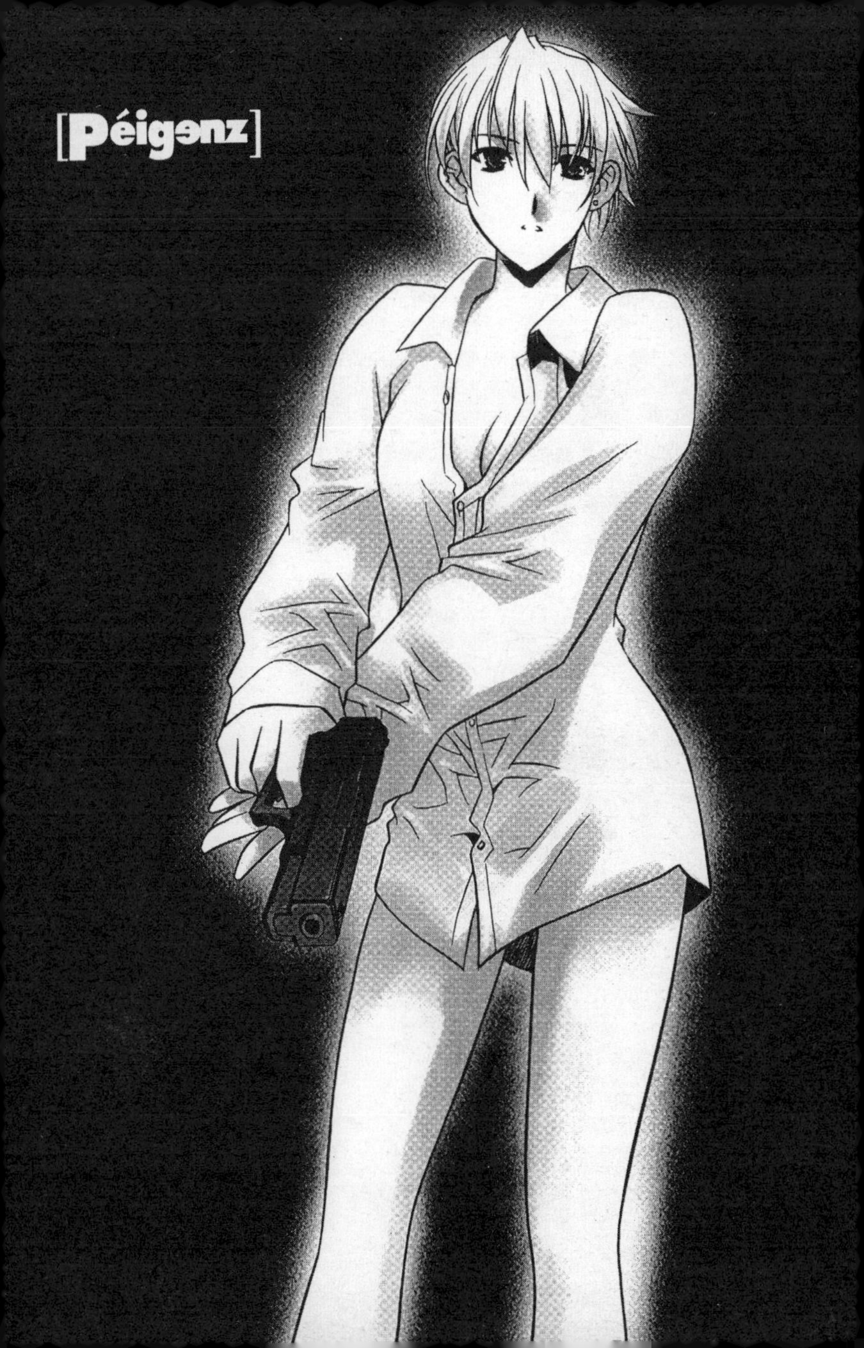
[Péigenz]

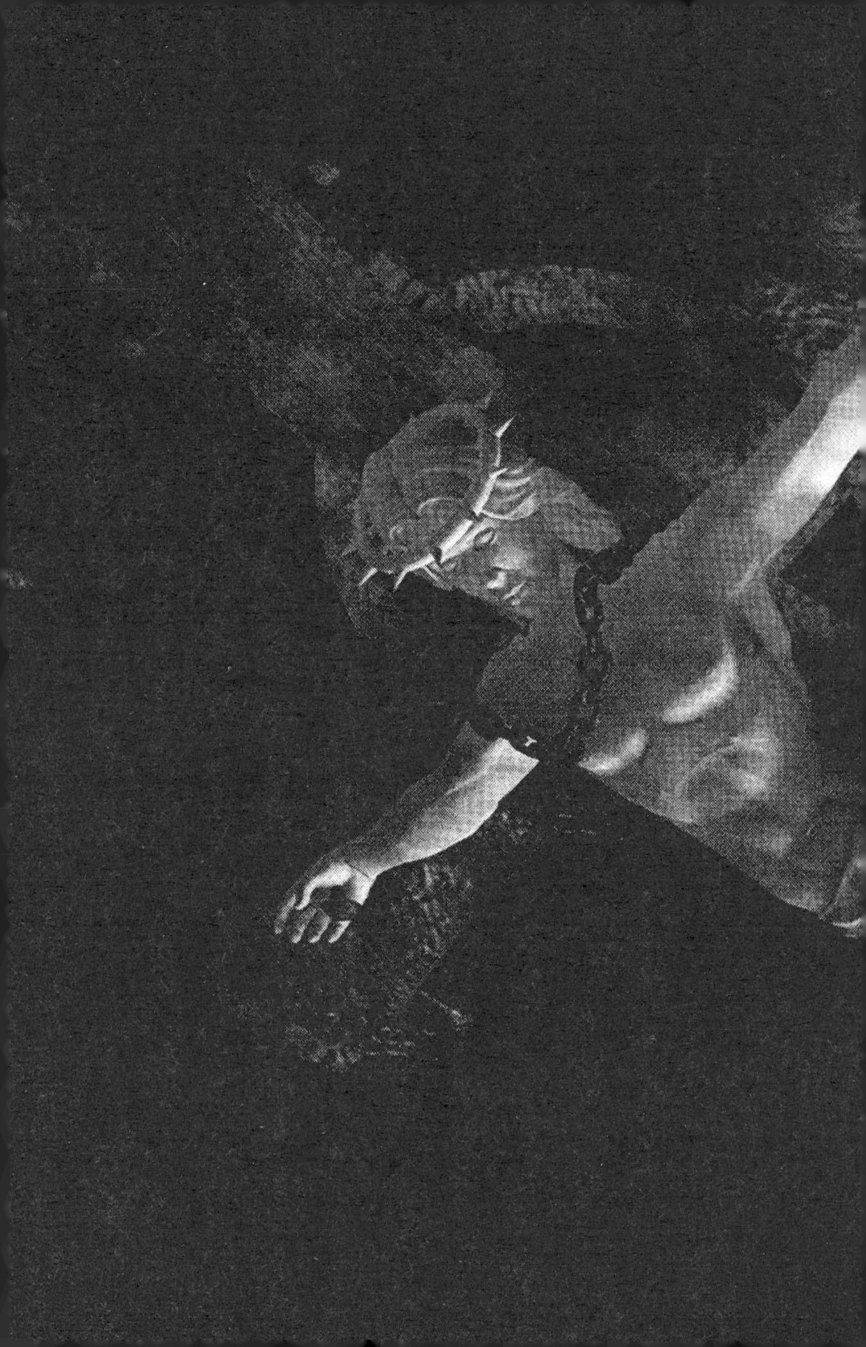

revelation 5 : Quasar-α

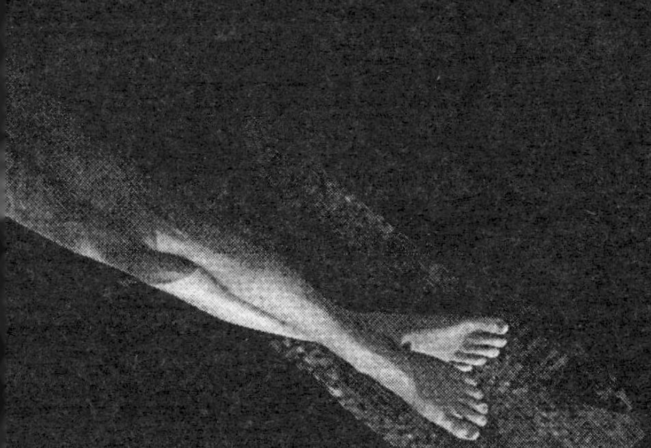

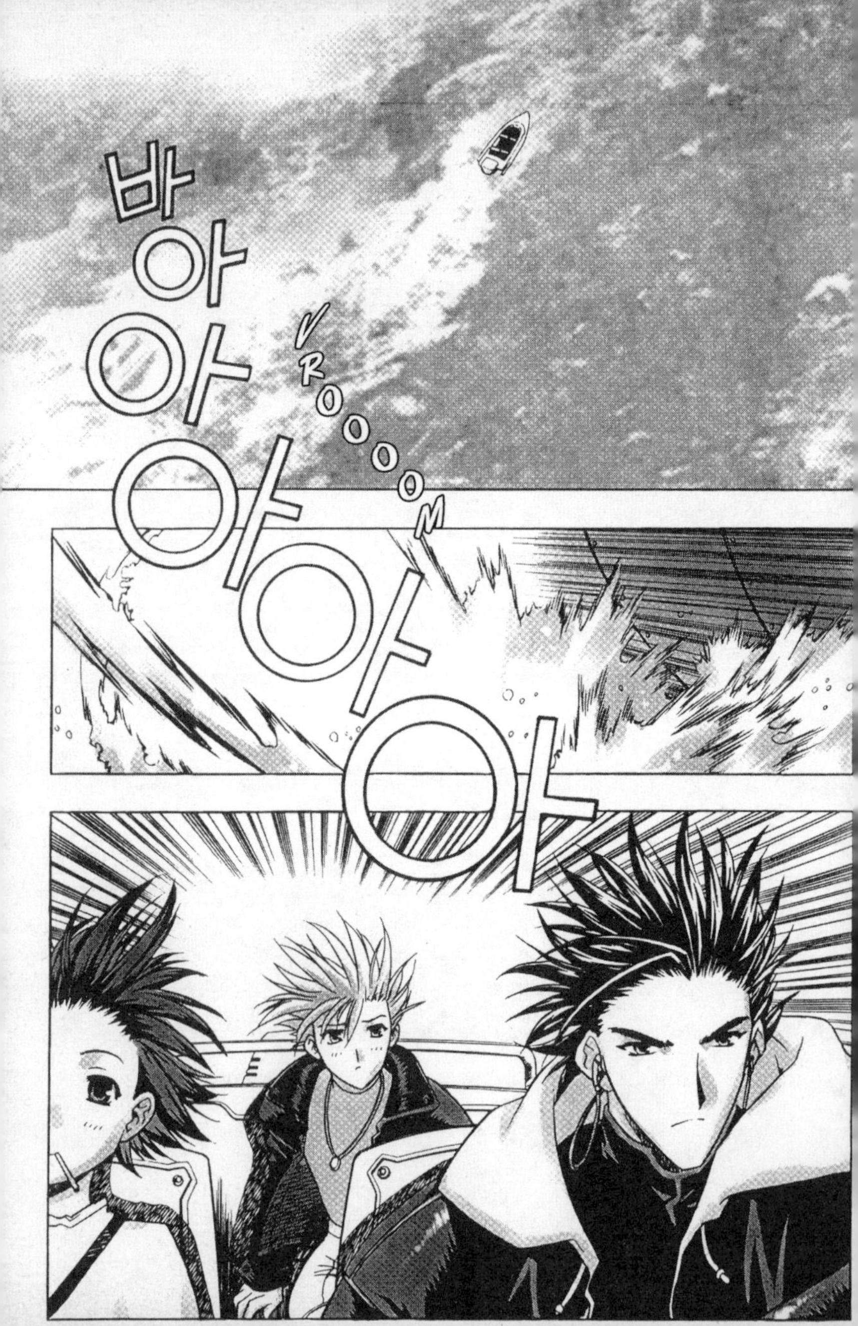

바아아아아
VROOOOOM

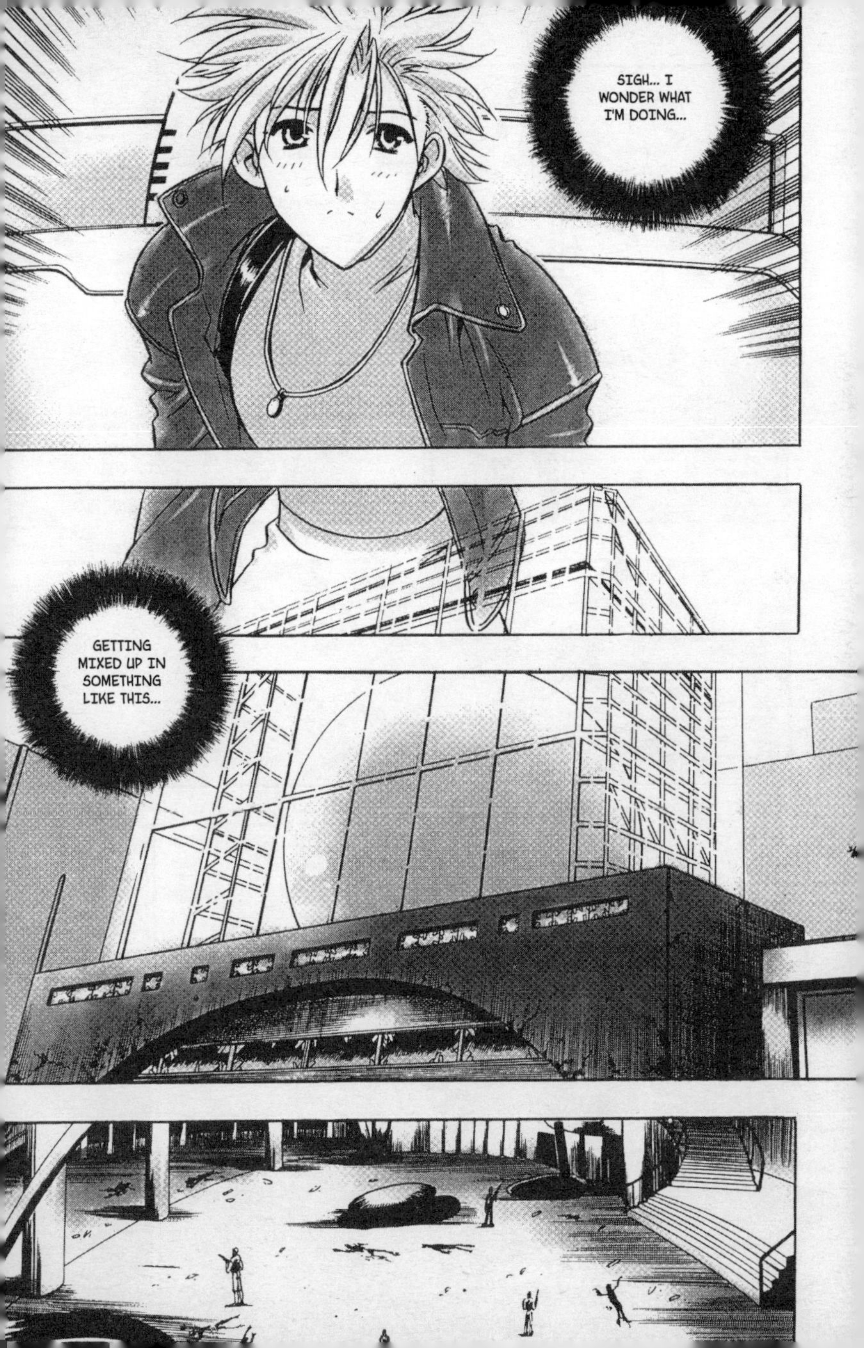
SIGH... I WONDER WHAT I'M DOING...
GETTING MIXED UP IN SOMETHING LIKE THIS...

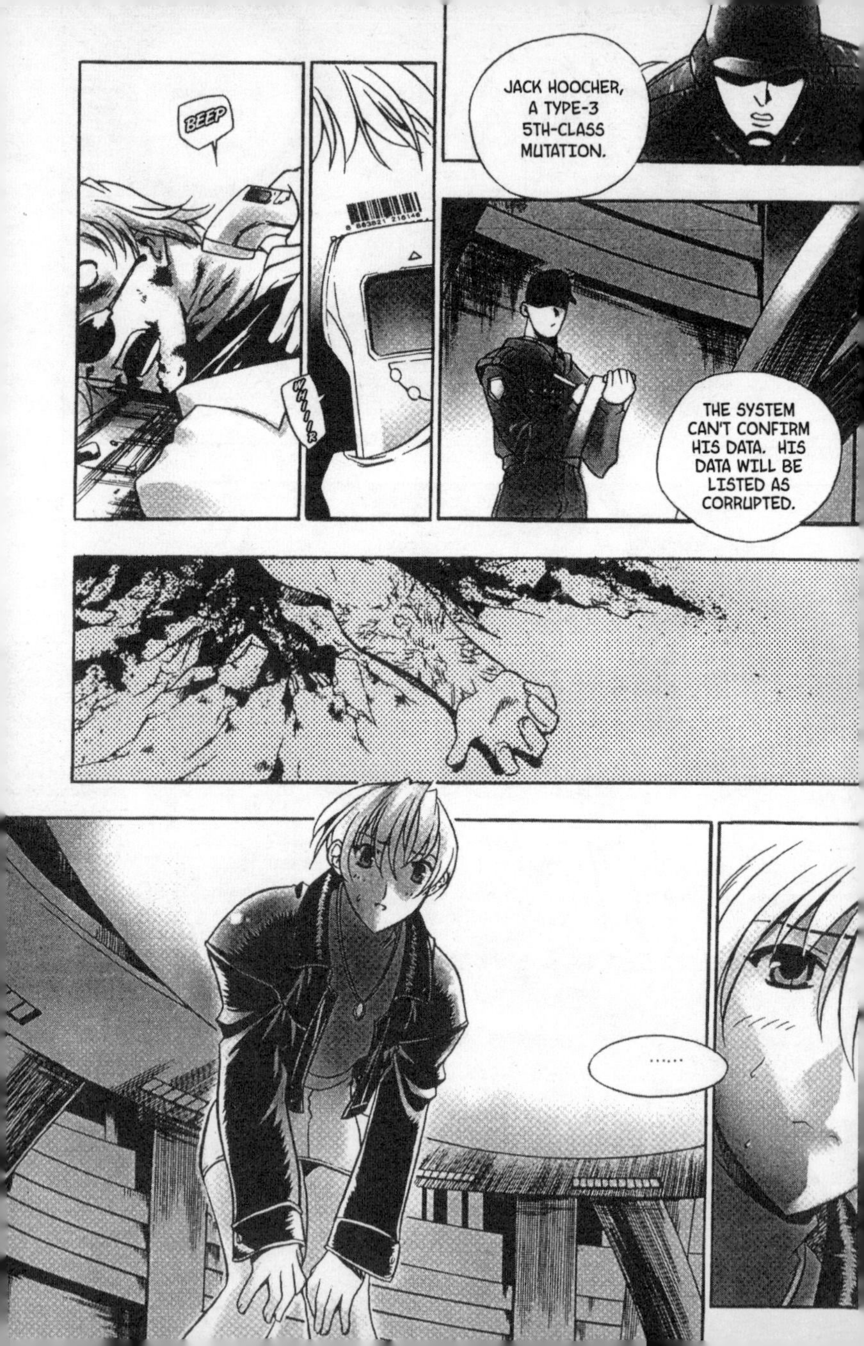
BEEP
WHIIIR
JACK HOOCHER, A TYPE-3 5TH-CLASS MUTATION.
THE SYSTEM CAN'T CONFIRM HIS DATA. HIS DATA WILL BE LISTED AS CORRUPTED.
......

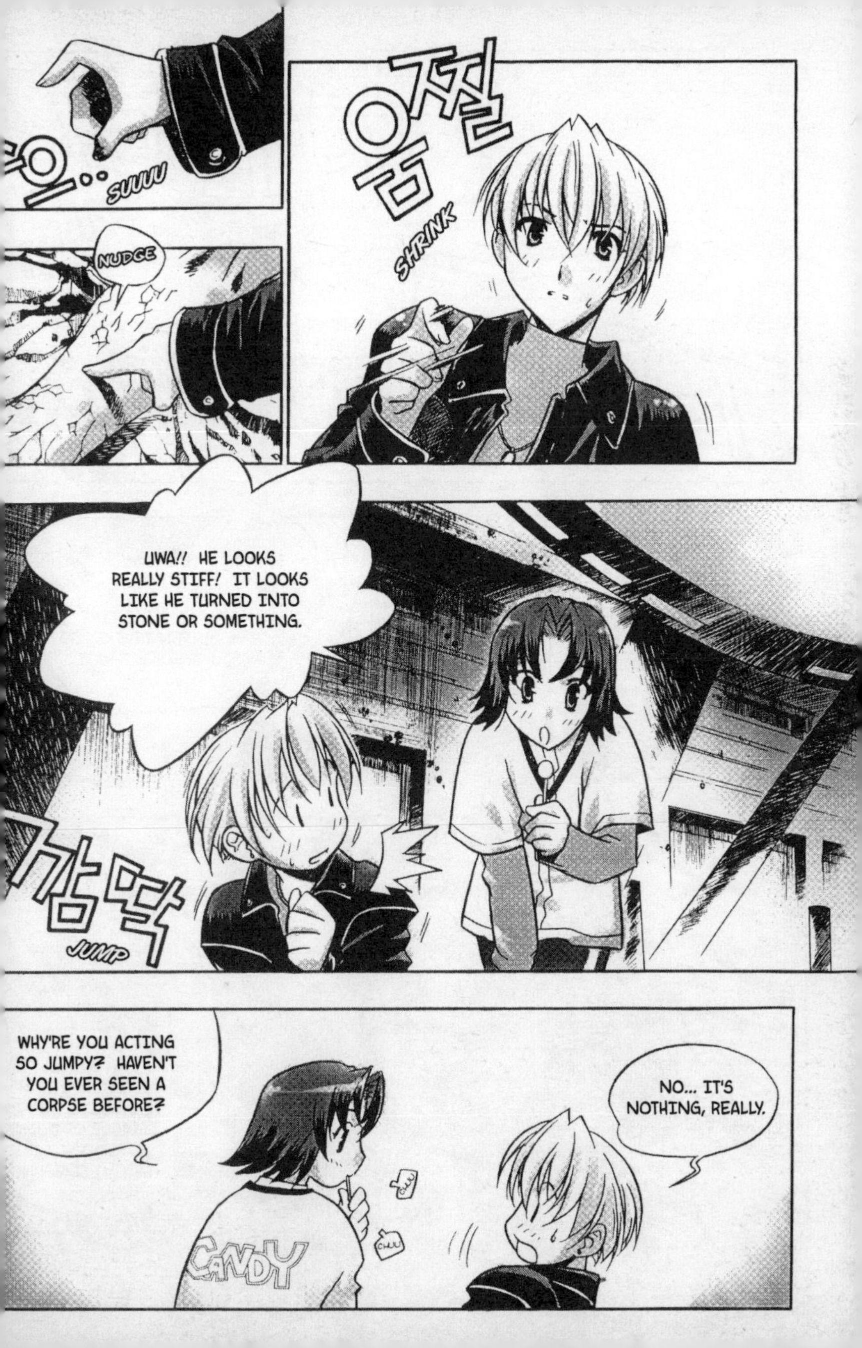
오..
SUUUU
NUDGE
움찔
SHRINK
UWA!! HE LOOKS REALLY STIFF! IT LOOKS LIKE HE TURNED INTO STONE OR SOMETHING.
깜딱
JUMP
WHY'RE YOU ACTING SO JUMPY? HAVEN'T YOU EVER SEEN A CORPSE BEFORE?
CHUU
CHUU
CANDY
NO... IT'S NOTHING, REALLY.

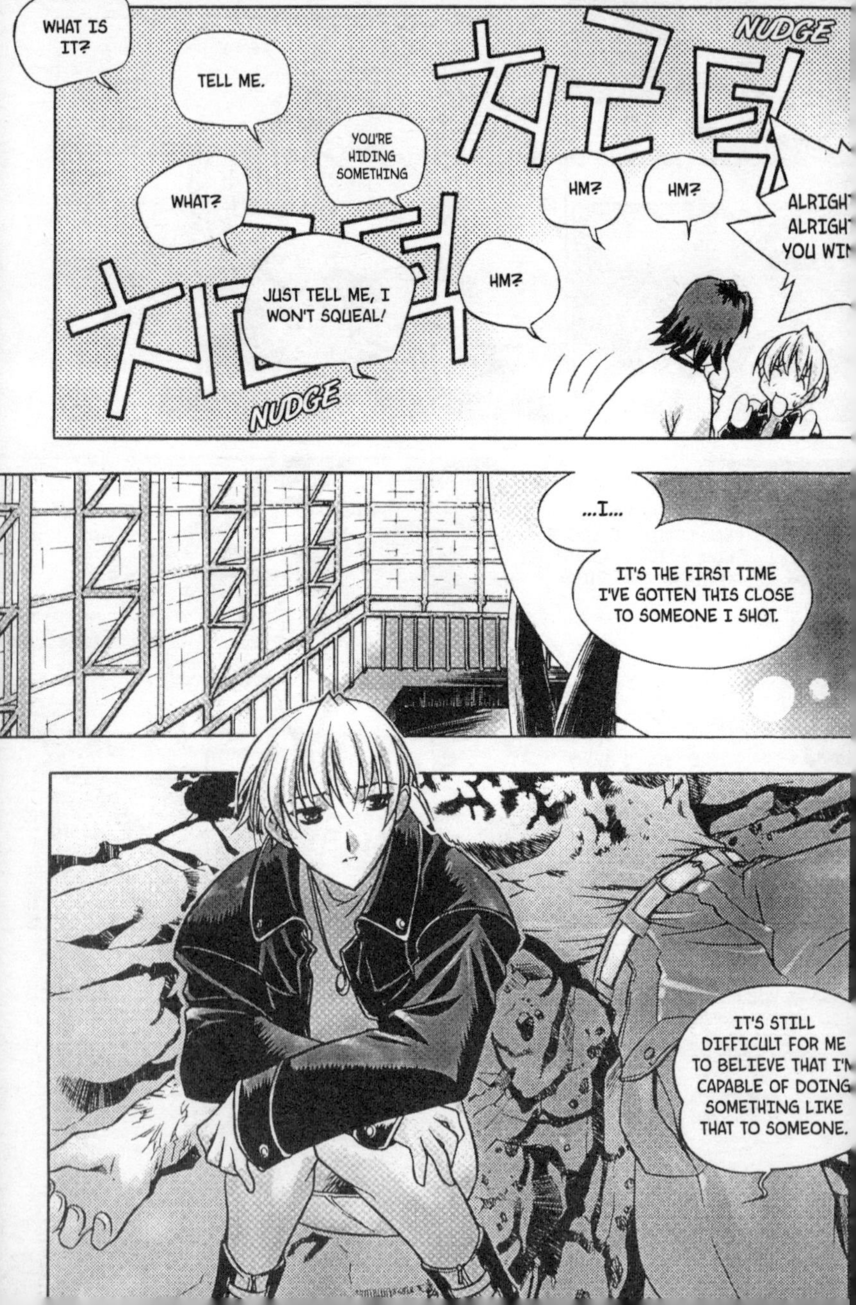
WHAT IS IT?
TELL ME.
YOU'RE HIDING SOMETHING
NUDGE
WHAT?
HM?
HM?
ALRIGH ALRIGH YOU WI
JUST TELL ME, I WON'T SQUEAL!
HM?
NUDGE
...I...
IT'S THE FIRST TIME I'VE GOTTEN THIS CLOSE TO SOMEONE I SHOT.
IT'S STILL DIFFICULT FOR ME TO BELIEVE THAT I' CAPABLE OF DOING SOMETHING LIKE THAT TO SOMEONE.

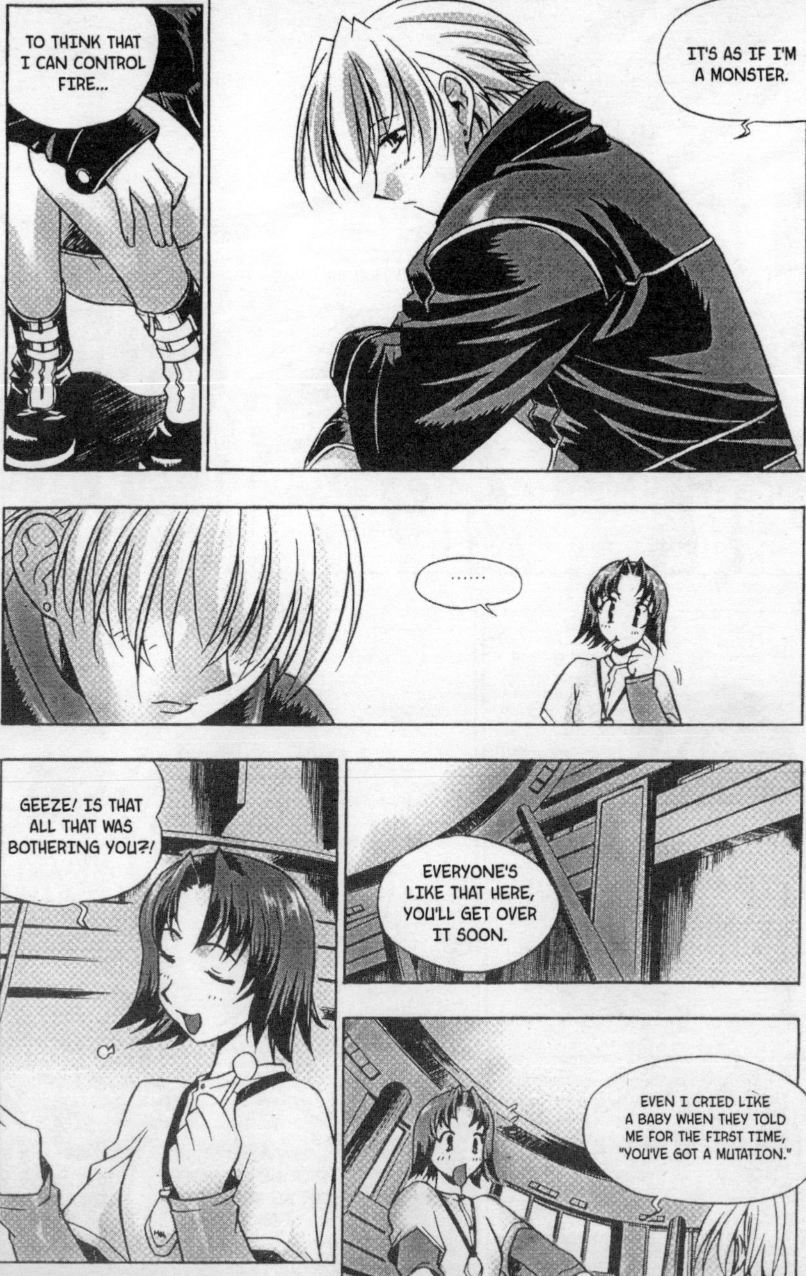
TO THINK THAT I CAN CONTROL FIRE...
IT'S AS IF I'M A MONSTER.
......
GEEZE! IS THAT ALL THAT WAS BOTHERING YOU?!
EVERYONE'S LIKE THAT HERE, YOU'LL GET OVER IT SOON.
EVEN I CRIED LIKE A BABY WHEN THEY TOLD ME FOR THE FIRST TIME, "YOU'VE GOT A MUTATION."

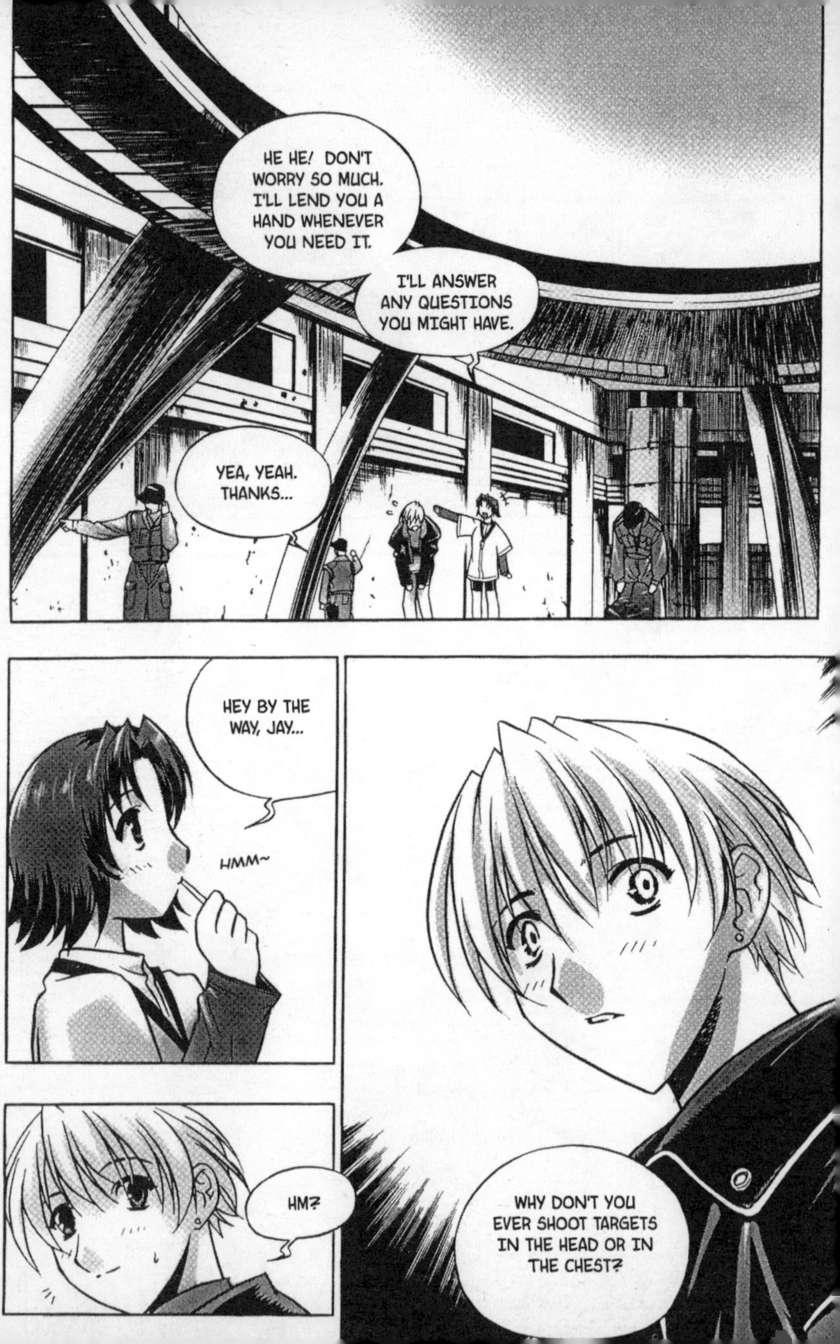
HE HE! DON'T WORRY SO MUCH. I'LL LEND YOU A HAND WHENEVER YOU NEED IT.
I'LL ANSWER ANY QUESTIONS YOU MIGHT HAVE.
YEA, YEAH. THANKS...
HEY BY THE WAY, JAY...
HMM~
HM?
WHY DON'T YOU EVER SHOOT TARGETS IN THE HEAD OR IN THE CHEST?

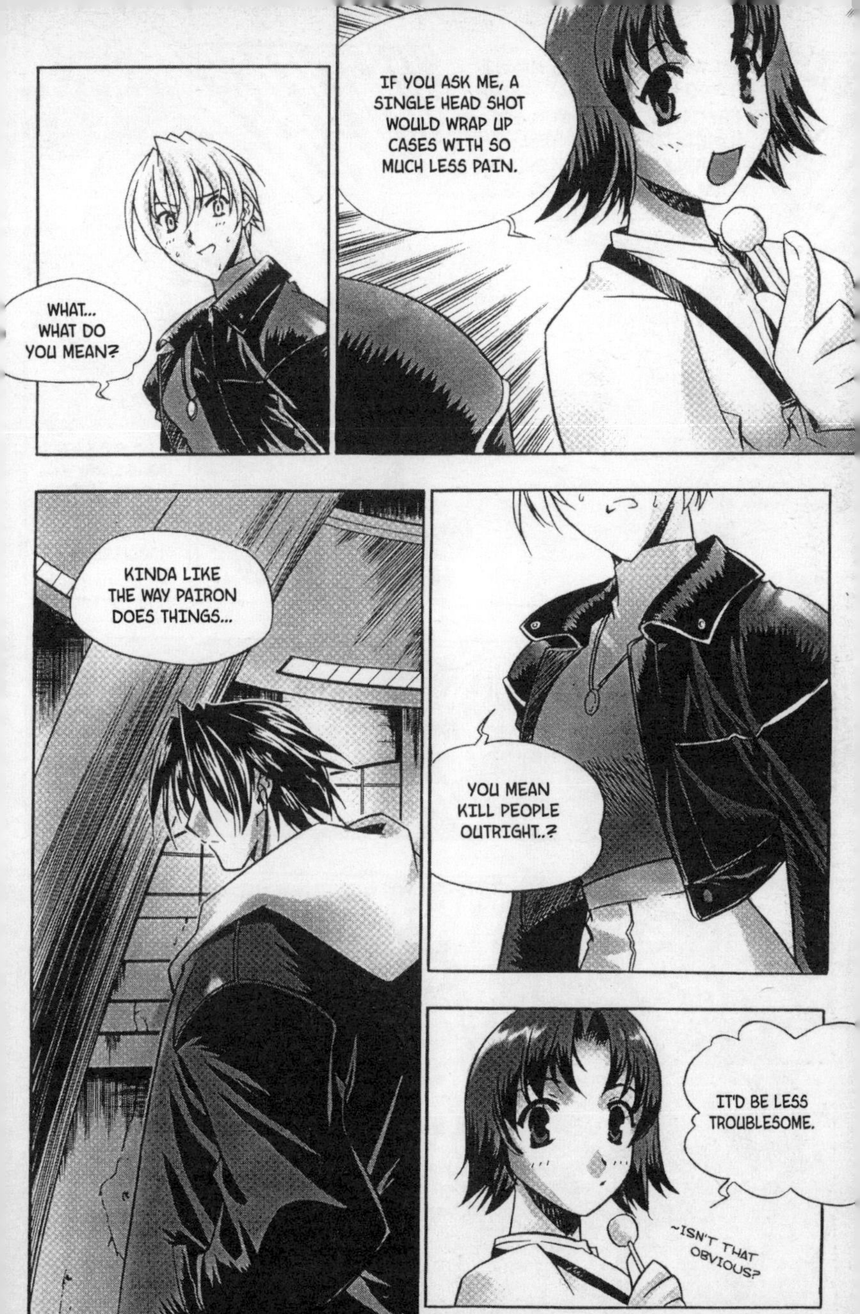
WHAT... WHAT DO YOU MEAN?
IF YOU ASK ME, A SINGLE HEAD SHOT WOULD WRAP UP CASES WITH SO MUCH LESS PAIN.
KINDA LIKE THE WAY PAIRON DOES THINGS...
YOU MEAN KILL PEOPLE OUTRIGHT..?
IT'D BE LESS TROUBLESOME.
~ISN'T THAT OBVIOUS?

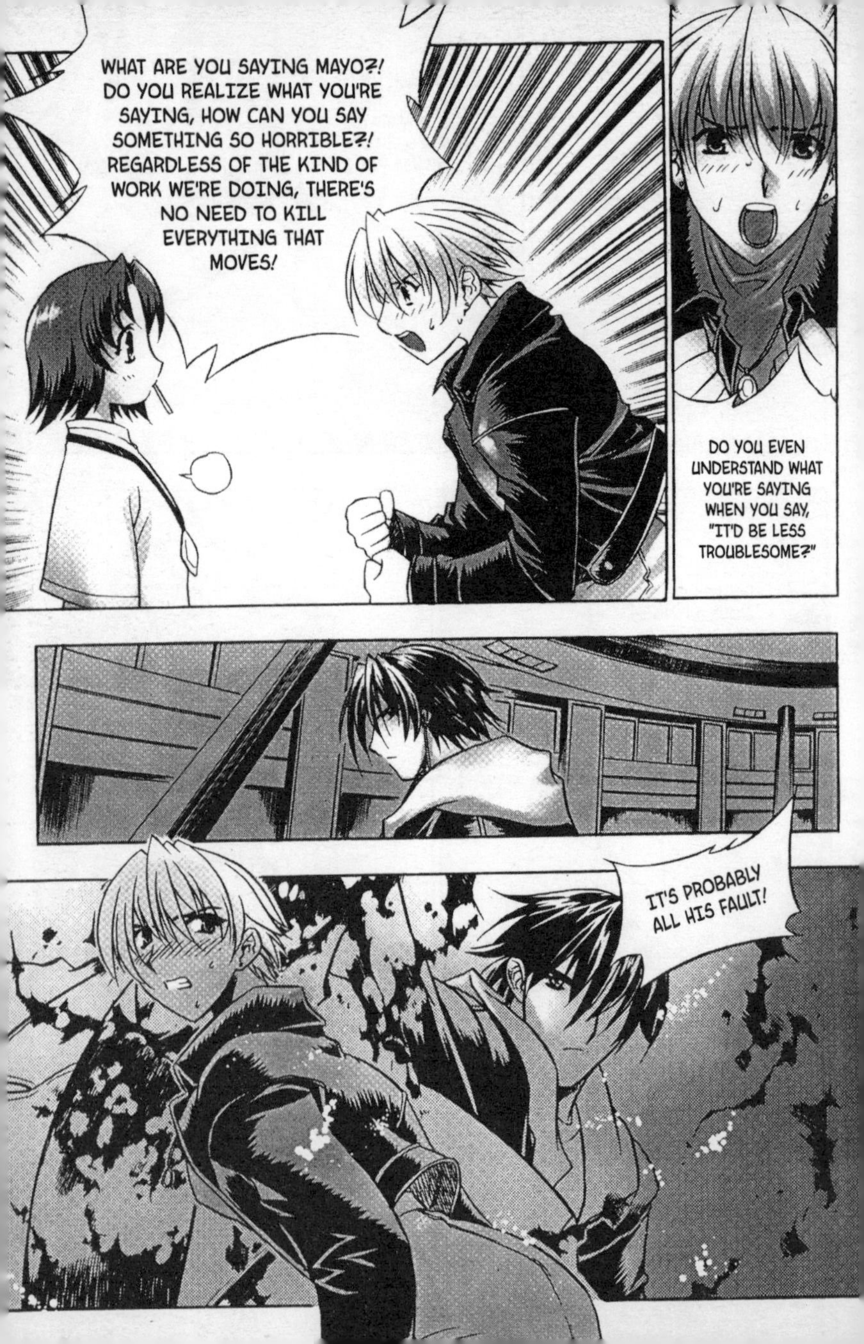
WHAT ARE YOU SAYING MAYO⁈! DO YOU REALIZE WHAT YOU'RE SAYING, HOW CAN YOU SAY SOMETHING SO HORRIBLE⁈! REGARDLESS OF THE KIND OF WORK WE'RE DOING, THERE'S NO NEED TO KILL EVERYTHING THAT MOVES!
DO YOU EVEN UNDERSTAND WHAT YOU'RE SAYING WHEN YOU SAY, "IT'D BE LESS TROUBLESOME⁈"
IT'S PROBABLY ALL HIS FAULT!

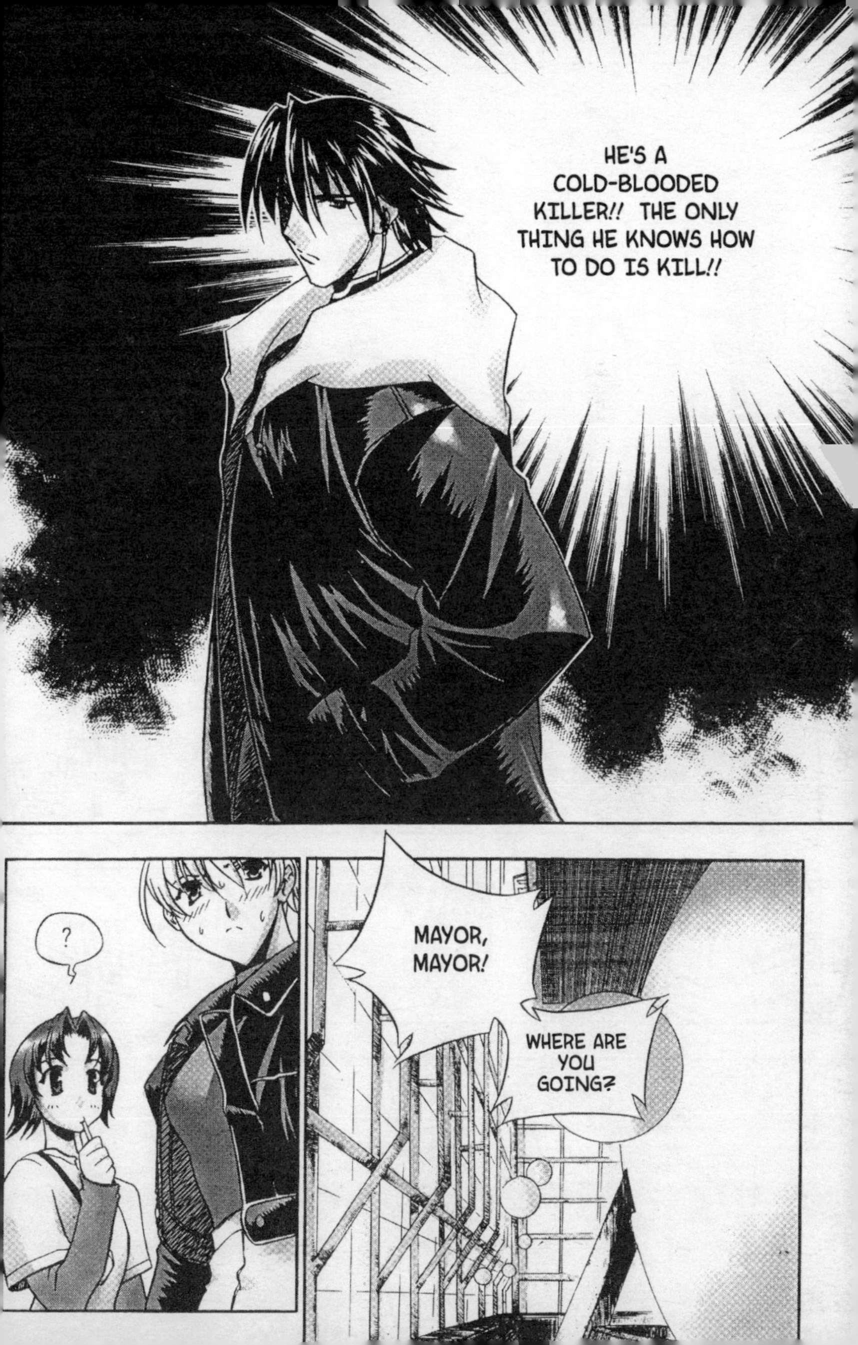
HE'S A COLD-BLOODED KILLER!! THE ONLY THING HE KNOWS HOW TO DO IS KILL!!
?
MAYOR, MAYOR!
WHERE ARE YOU GOING?

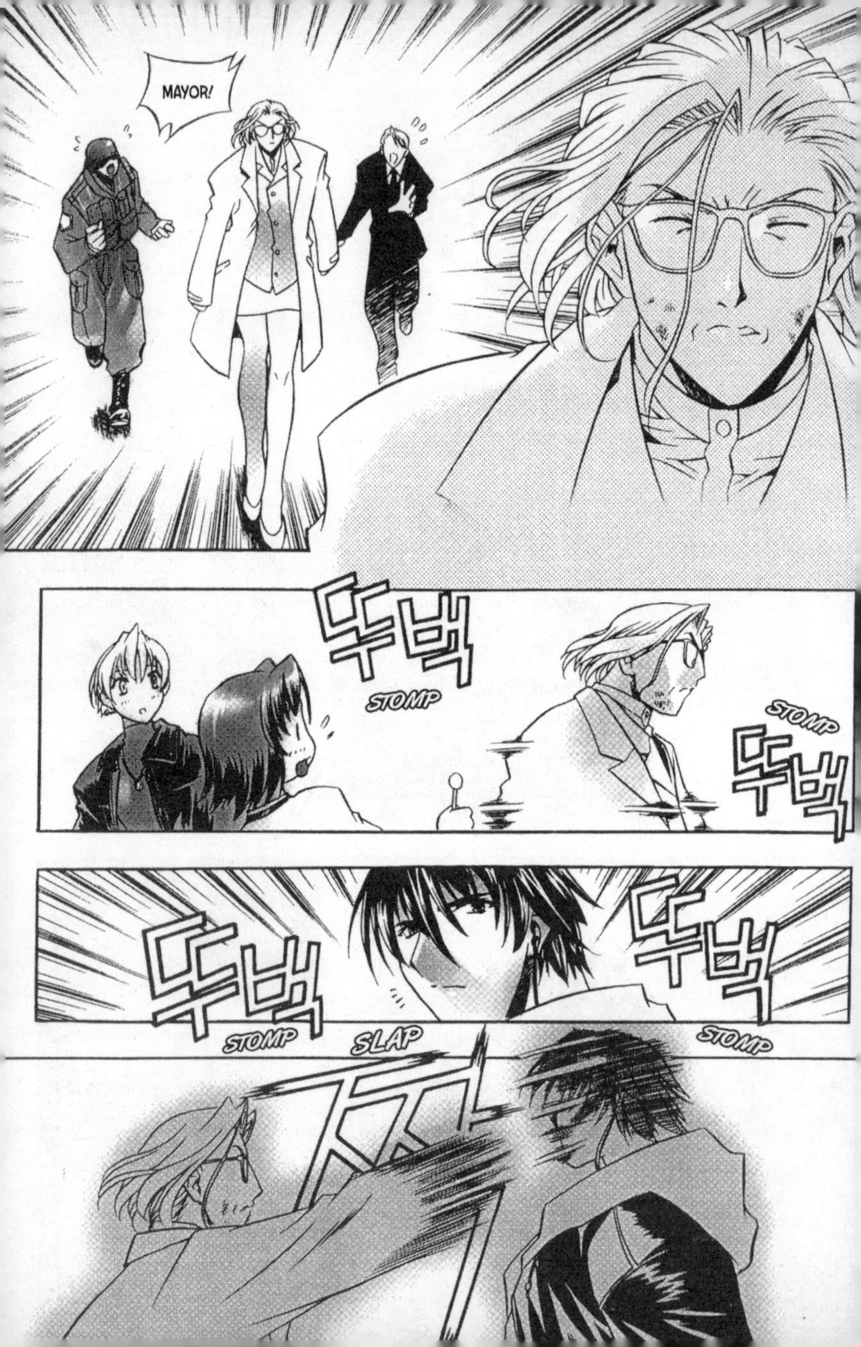

MAYOR!
뚜벅
STOMP
STOMP
뚜벅
뚜벅
STOMP
뚜벅
STOMP
SLAP
짝

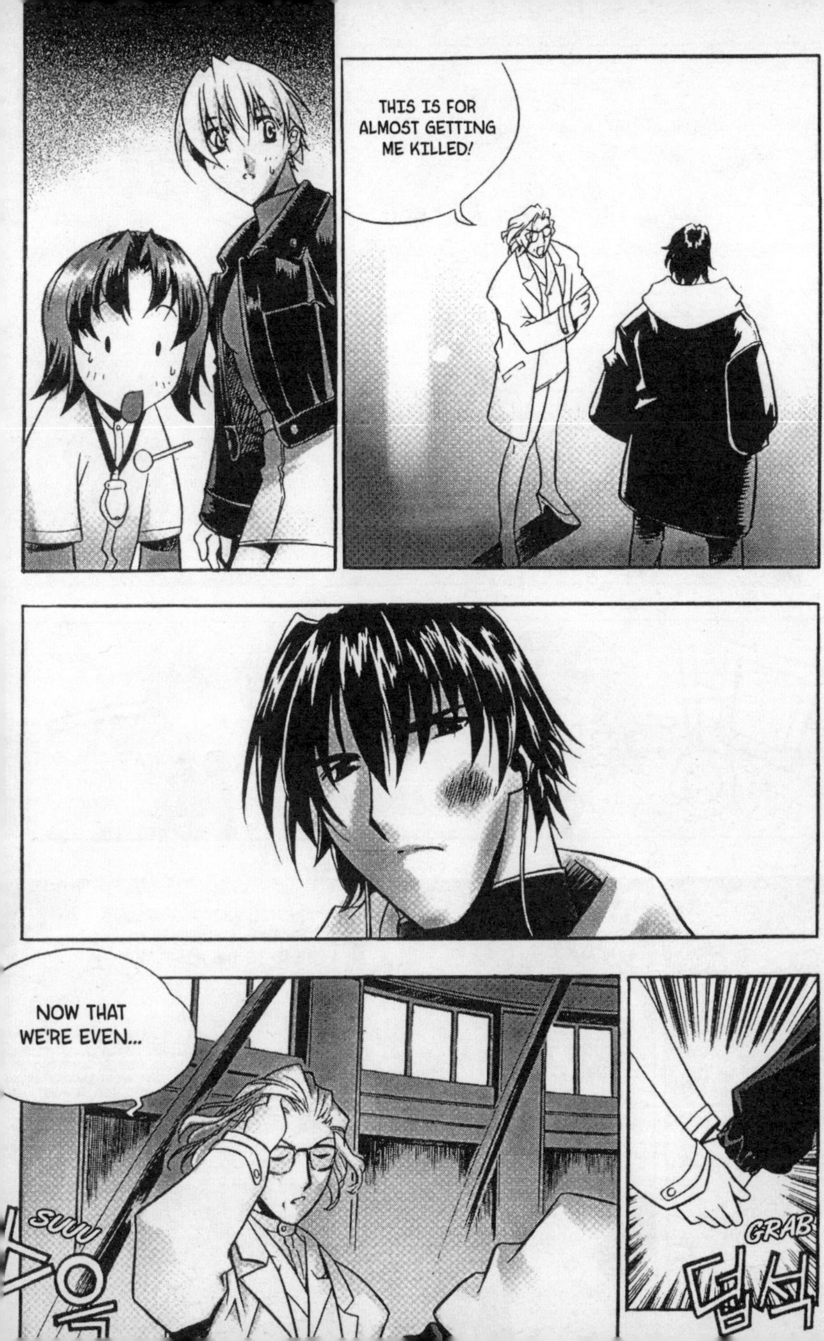
THIS IS FOR ALMOST GETTING ME KILLED!
NOW THAT WE'RE EVEN...
SUUU
GRAB
덥석

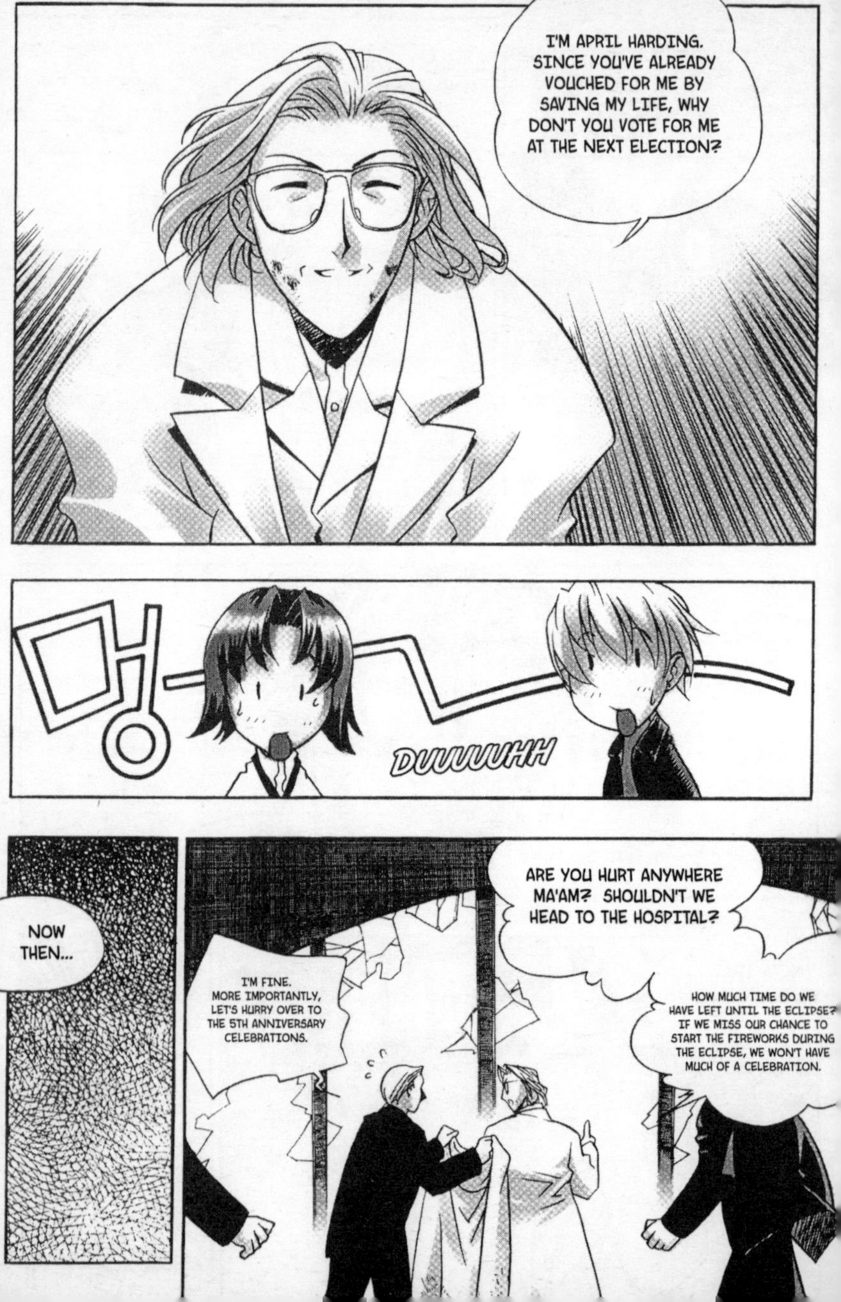
I'M APRIL HARDING. SINCE YOU'VE ALREADY VOUCHED FOR ME BY SAVING MY LIFE, WHY DON'T YOU VOTE FOR ME AT THE NEXT ELECTION?
DUUUUUHH
NOW THEN...
ARE YOU HURT ANYWHERE MA'AM? SHOULDN'T WE HEAD TO THE HOSPITAL?
I'M FINE. MORE IMPORTANTLY, LET'S HURRY OVER TO THE 5TH ANNIVERSARY CELEBRATIONS.
HOW MUCH TIME DO WE HAVE LEFT UNTIL THE ECLIPSE? IF WE MISS OUR CHANCE TO START THE FIREWORKS DURING THE ECLIPSE, WE WON'T HAVE MUCH OF A CELEBRATION.

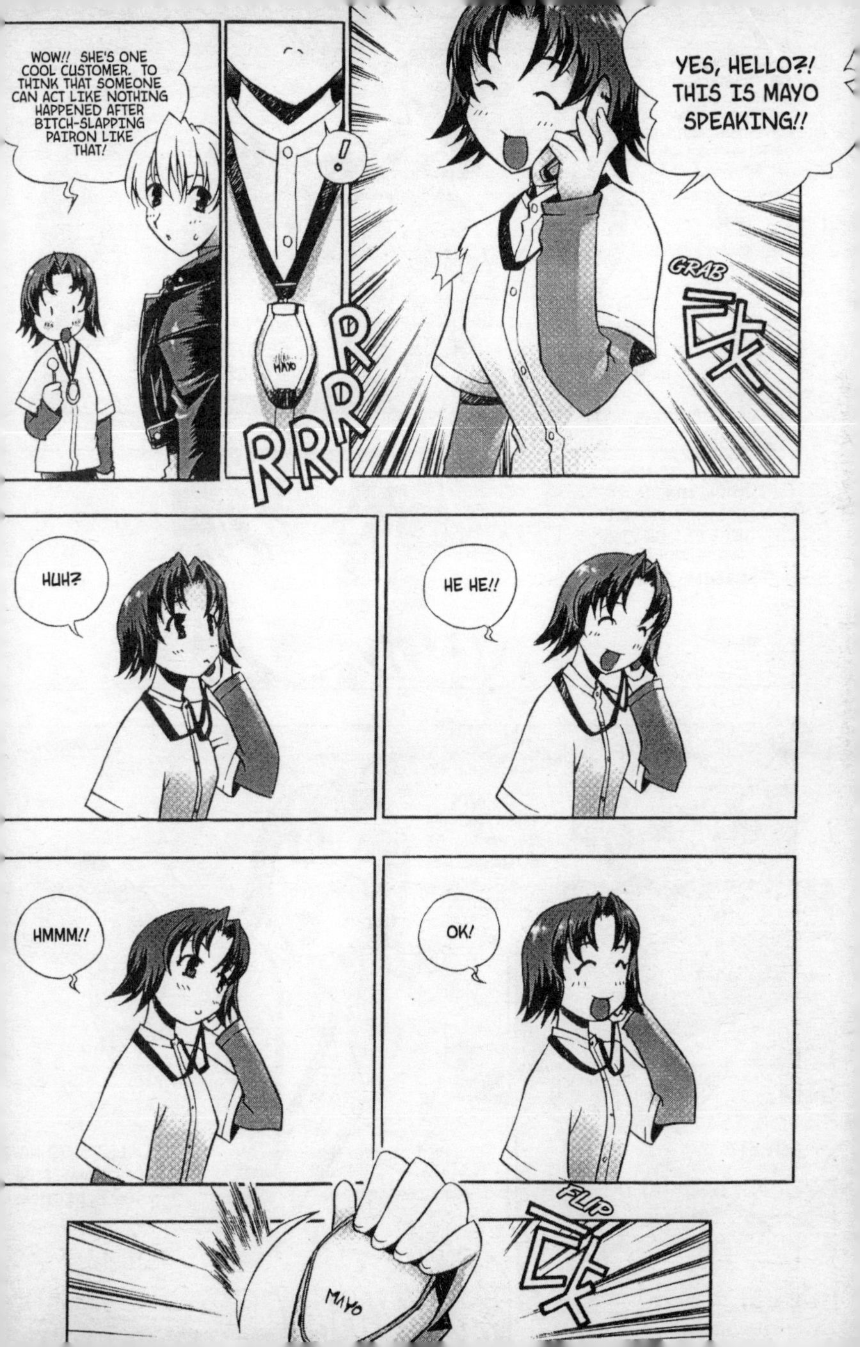
WOW!! SHE'S ONE COOL CUSTOMER. TO THINK THAT SOMEONE CAN ACT LIKE NOTHING HAPPENED AFTER BITCH-SLAPPING PAIRON LIKE THAT!
!
MAYO
RRRR
YES, HELLO?! THIS IS MAYO SPEAKING!!
GRAB
HUH?
HE HE!!
HMMM!!
OK!
MAYO
FLIP

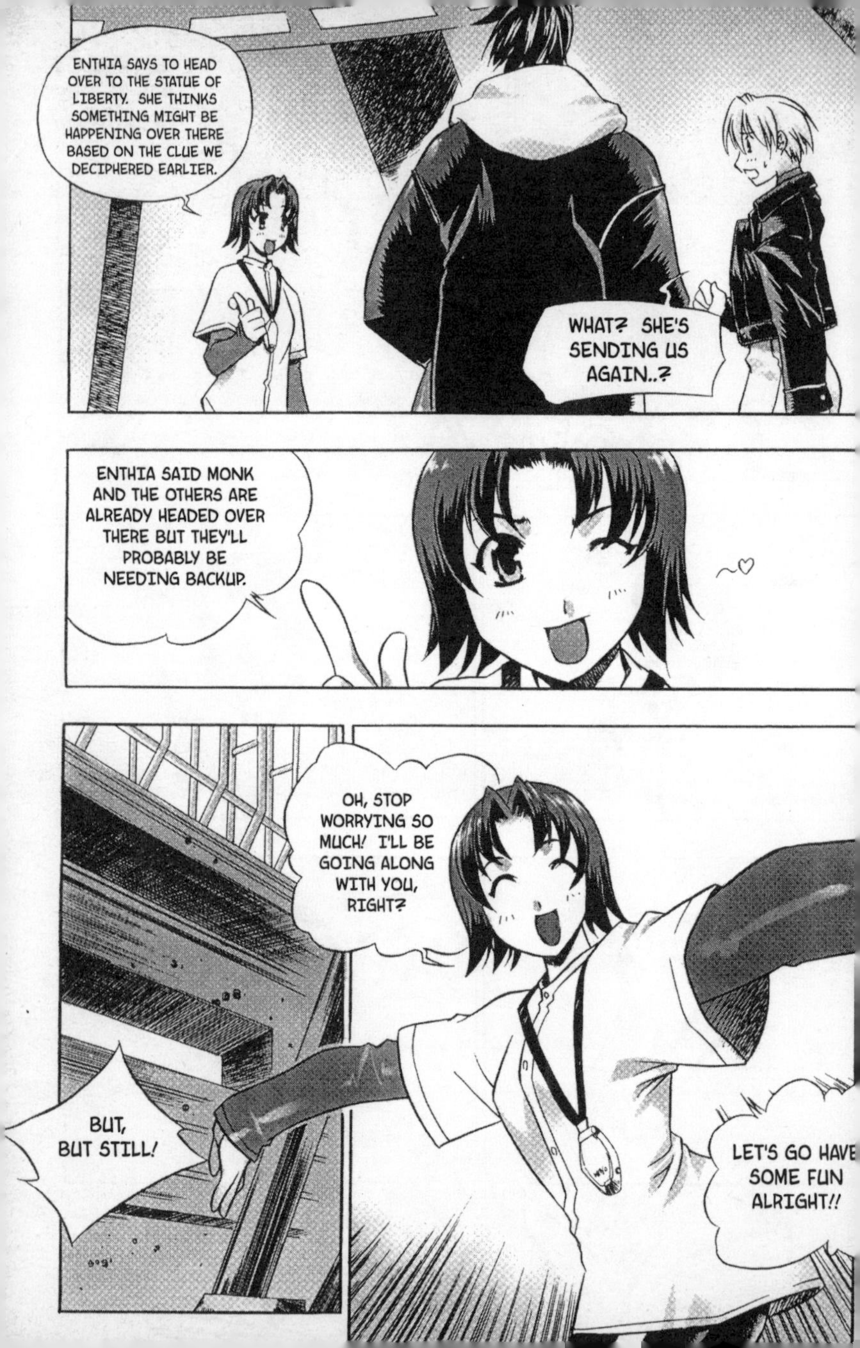
ENTHIA SAYS TO HEAD OVER TO THE STATUE OF LIBERTY. SHE THINKS SOMETHING MIGHT BE HAPPENING OVER THERE BASED ON THE CLUE WE DECIPHERED EARLIER.
WHAT? SHE'S SENDING US AGAIN..?
ENTHIA SAID MONK AND THE OTHERS ARE ALREADY HEADED OVER THERE BUT THEY'LL PROBABLY BE NEEDING BACKUP.
BUT, BUT STILL!
OH, STOP WORRYING SO MUCH! I'LL BE GOING ALONG WITH YOU, RIGHT?
LET'S GO HAVE SOME FUN ALRIGHT!!

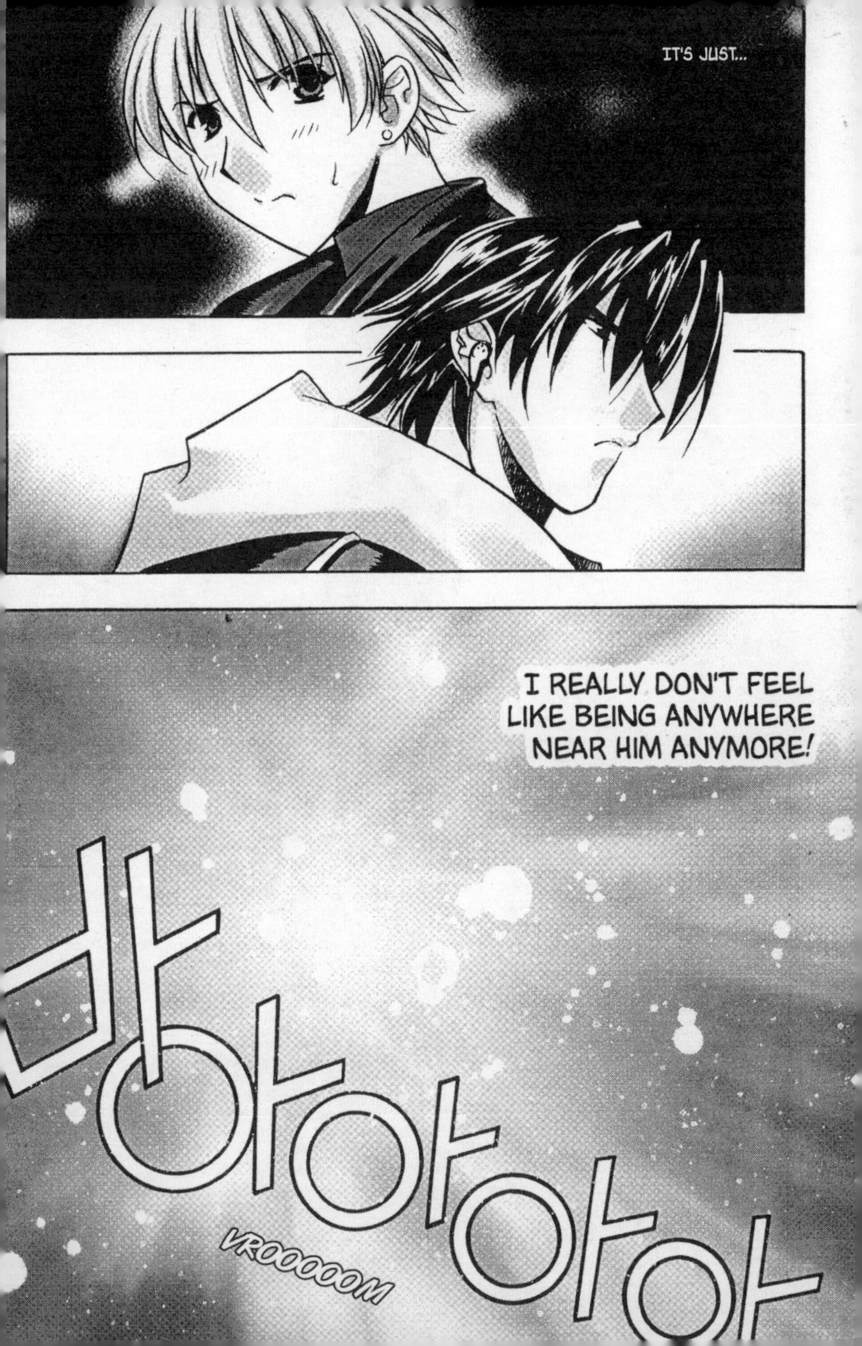
IT'S JUST...
I REALLY DON'T FEEL LIKE BEING ANYWHERE NEAR HIM ANYMORE!
VROOOOOOM

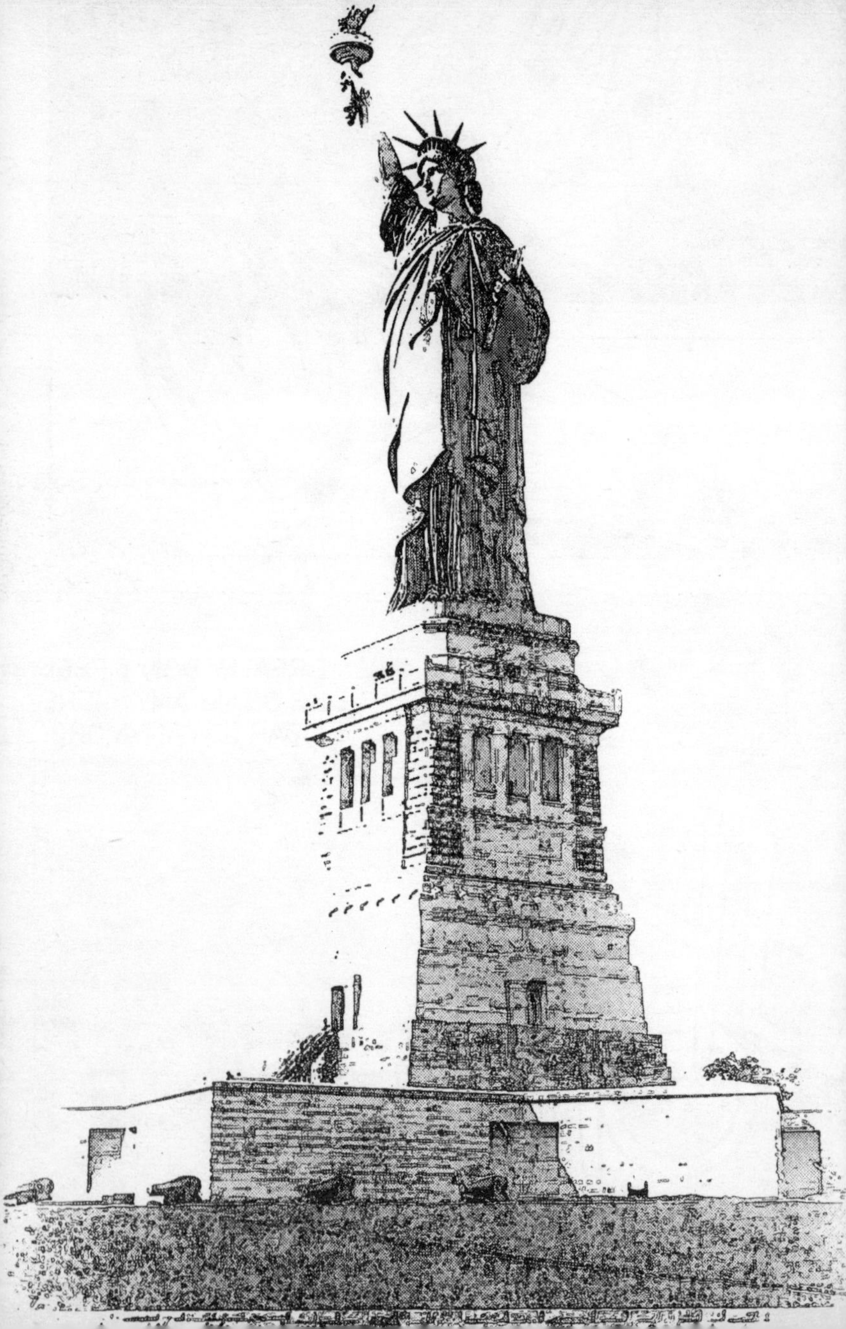

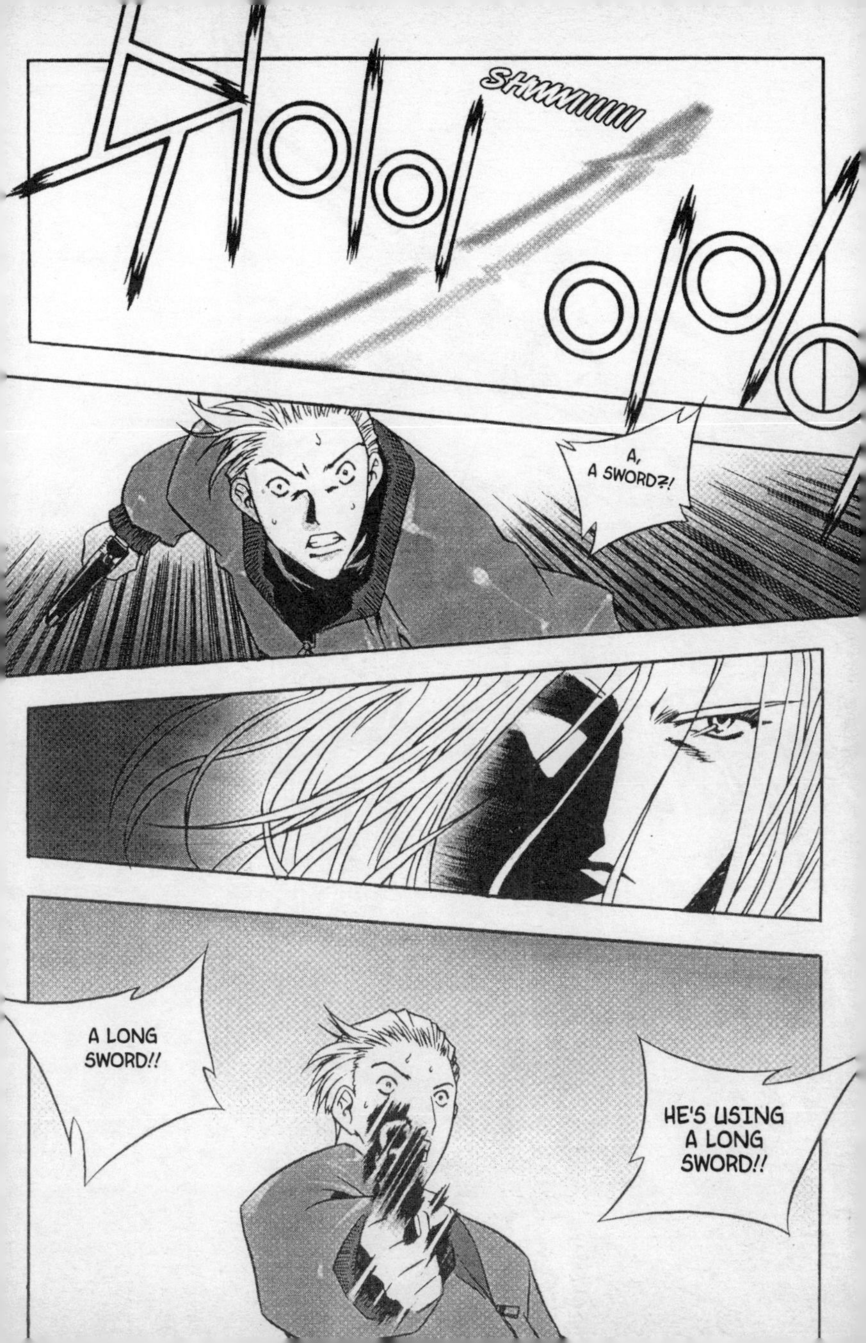
SHWWIIIIIII
A, A SWORD?!
A LONG SWORD!!
HE'S USING A LONG SWORD!!

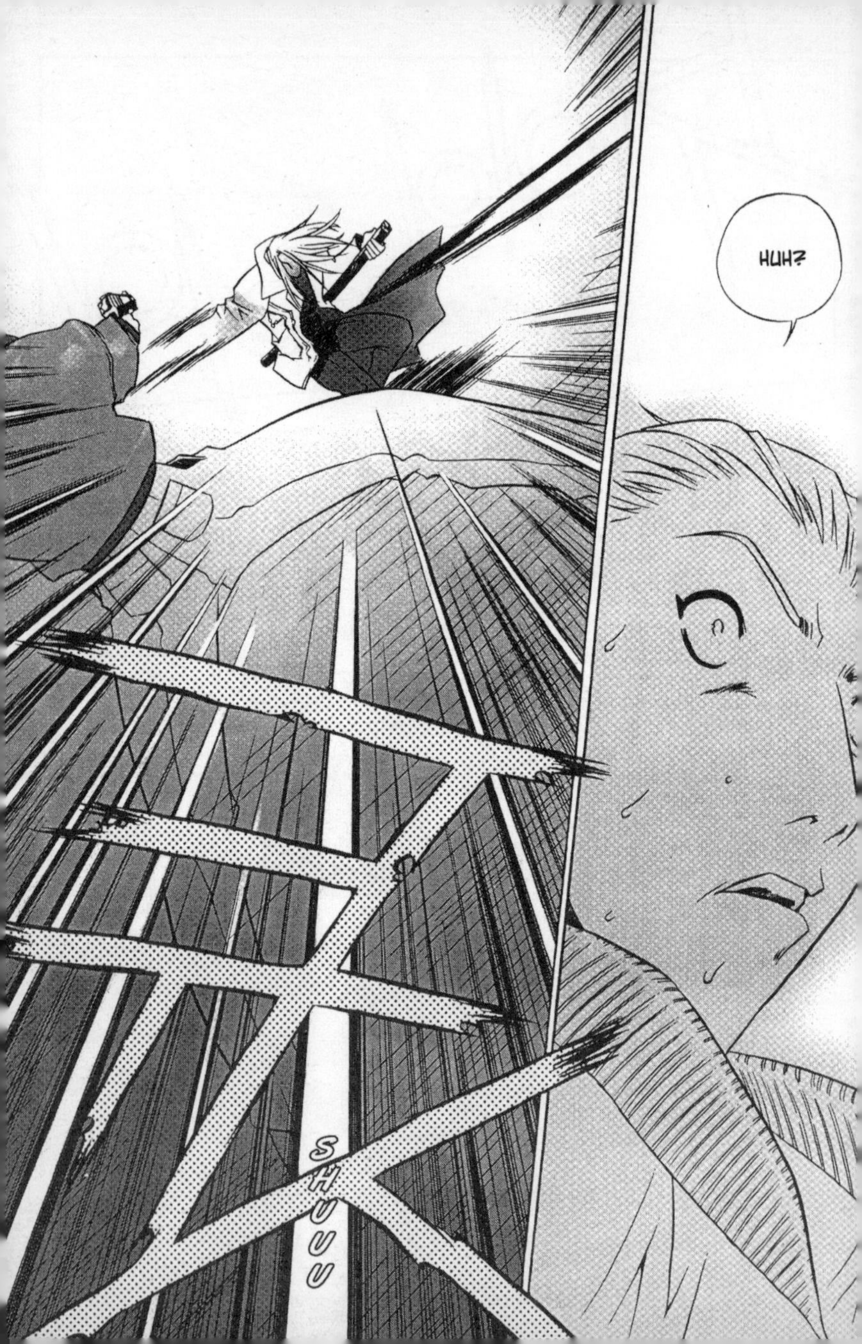
HUH?
SHUUU

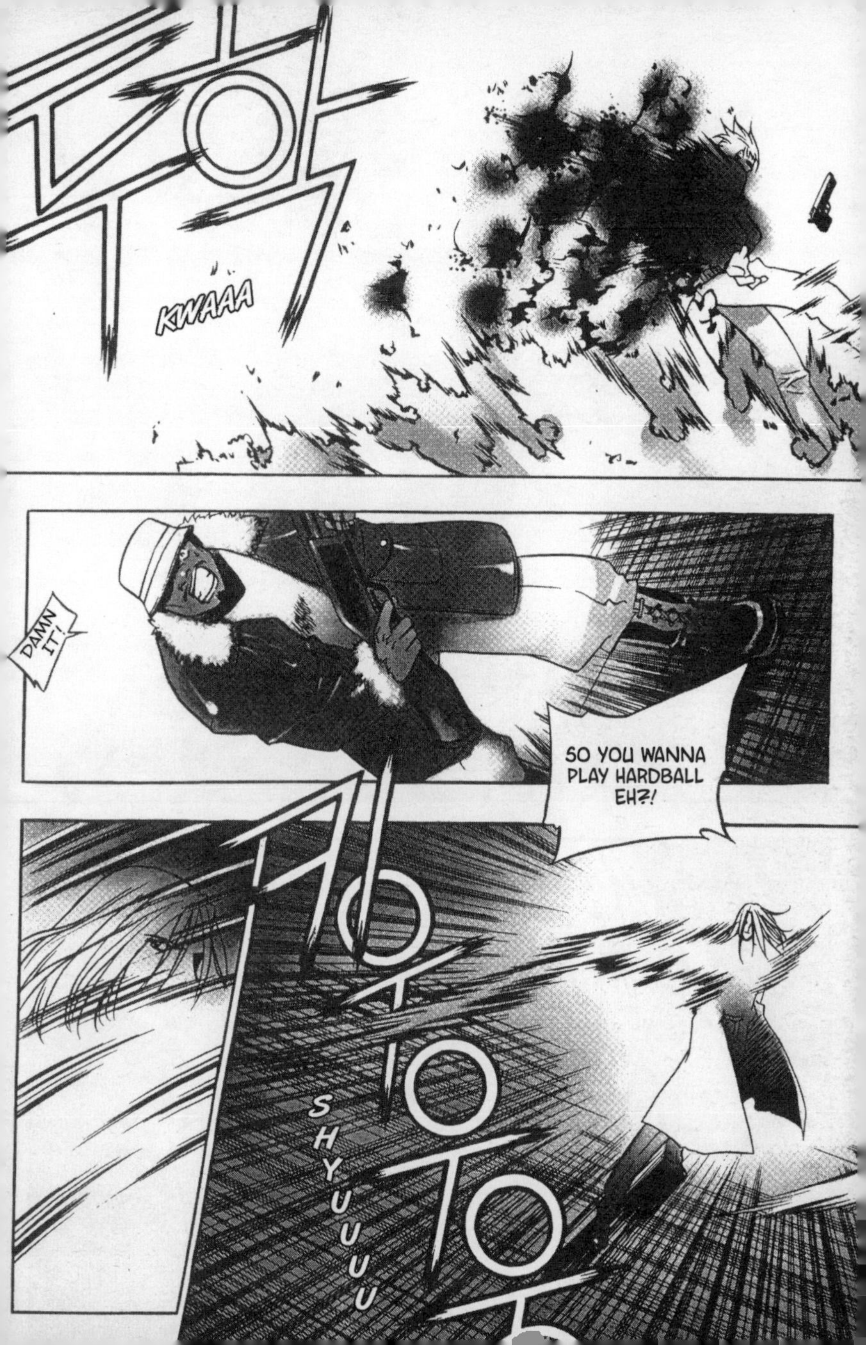
KWAAA
DAMN IT!
SO YOU WANNA PLAY HARDBALL EH?!
SHYUUUU

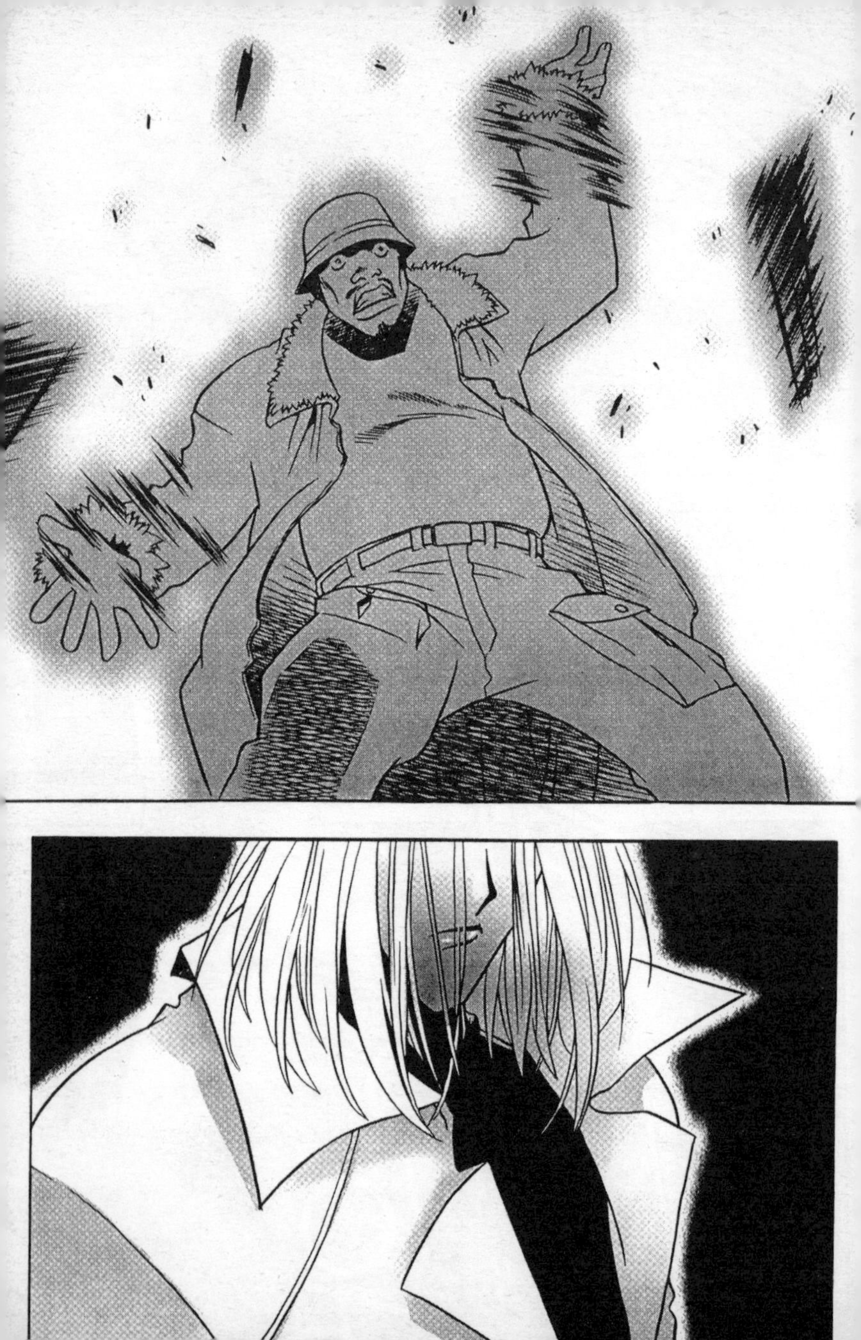

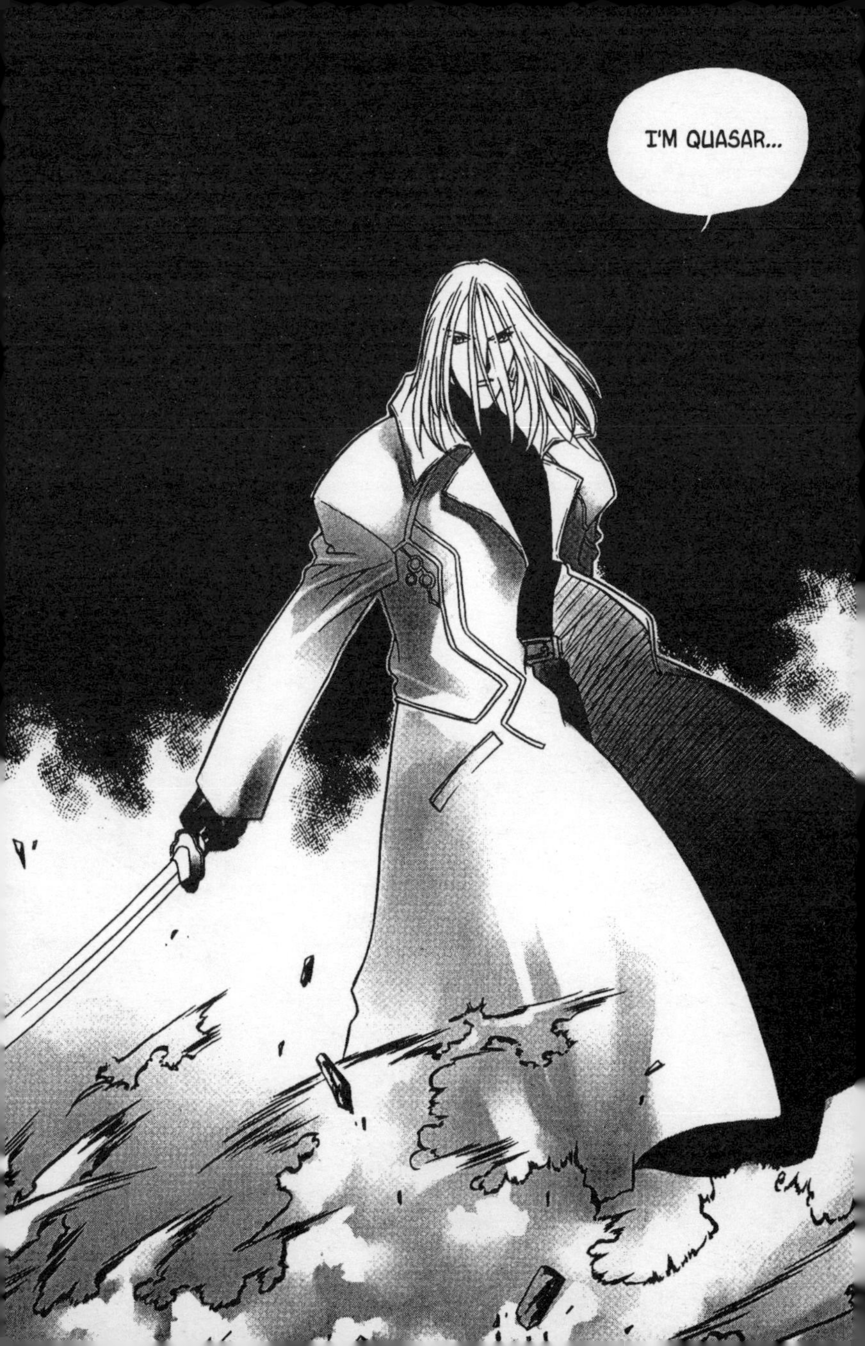
I'M QUASAR...

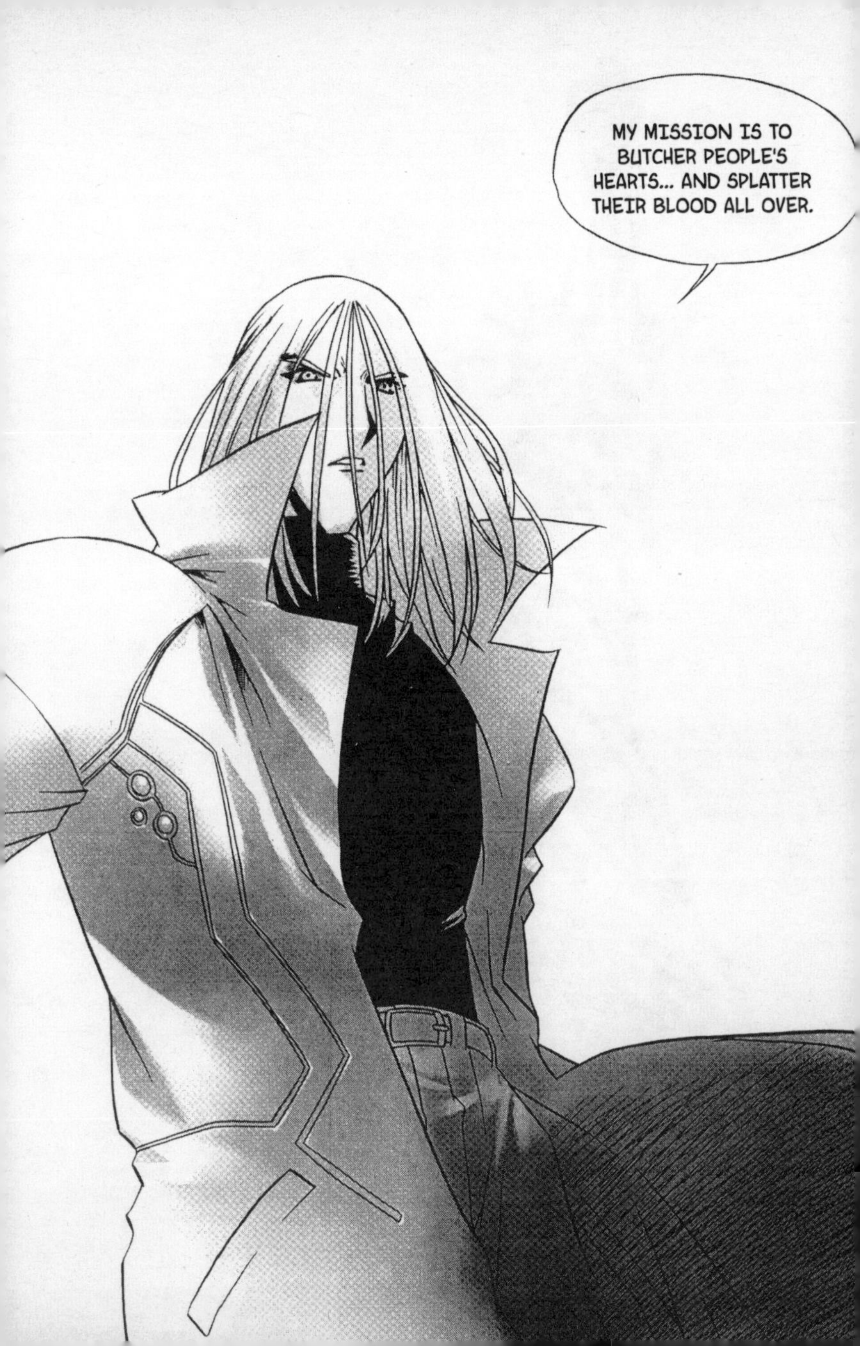
MY MISSION IS TO BUTCHER PEOPLE'S HEARTS... AND SPLATTER THEIR BLOOD ALL OVER.

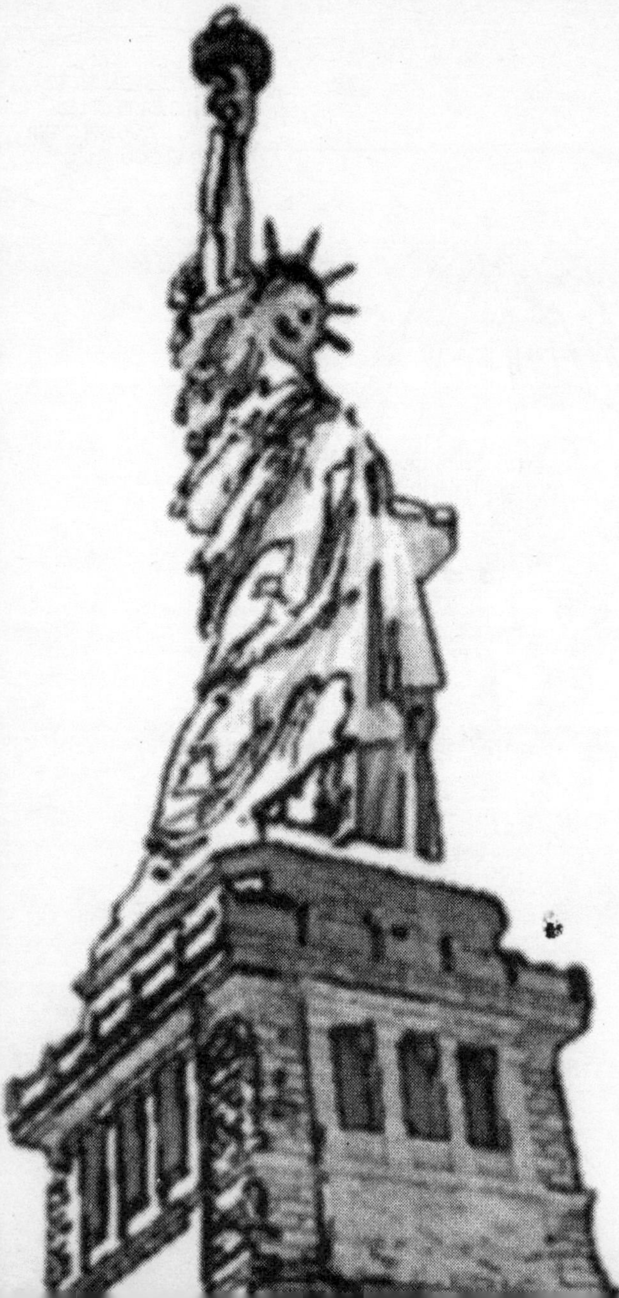

YOU PEIGENZ...
BEING THE WEAKLINGS THAT YOU ARE,
YOU DON'T EVEN HAVE THE RIGHT TO
CLAIM THAT YOU'LL PROTECT
THE STATUE OF THE GODDESS.

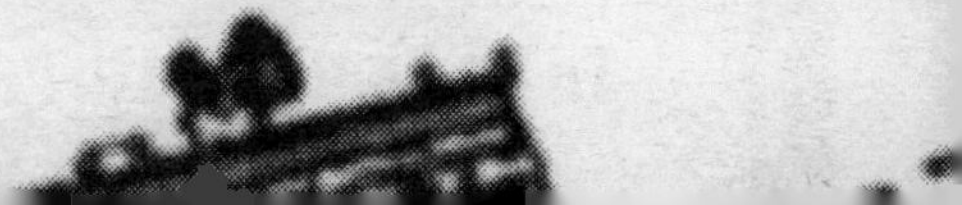

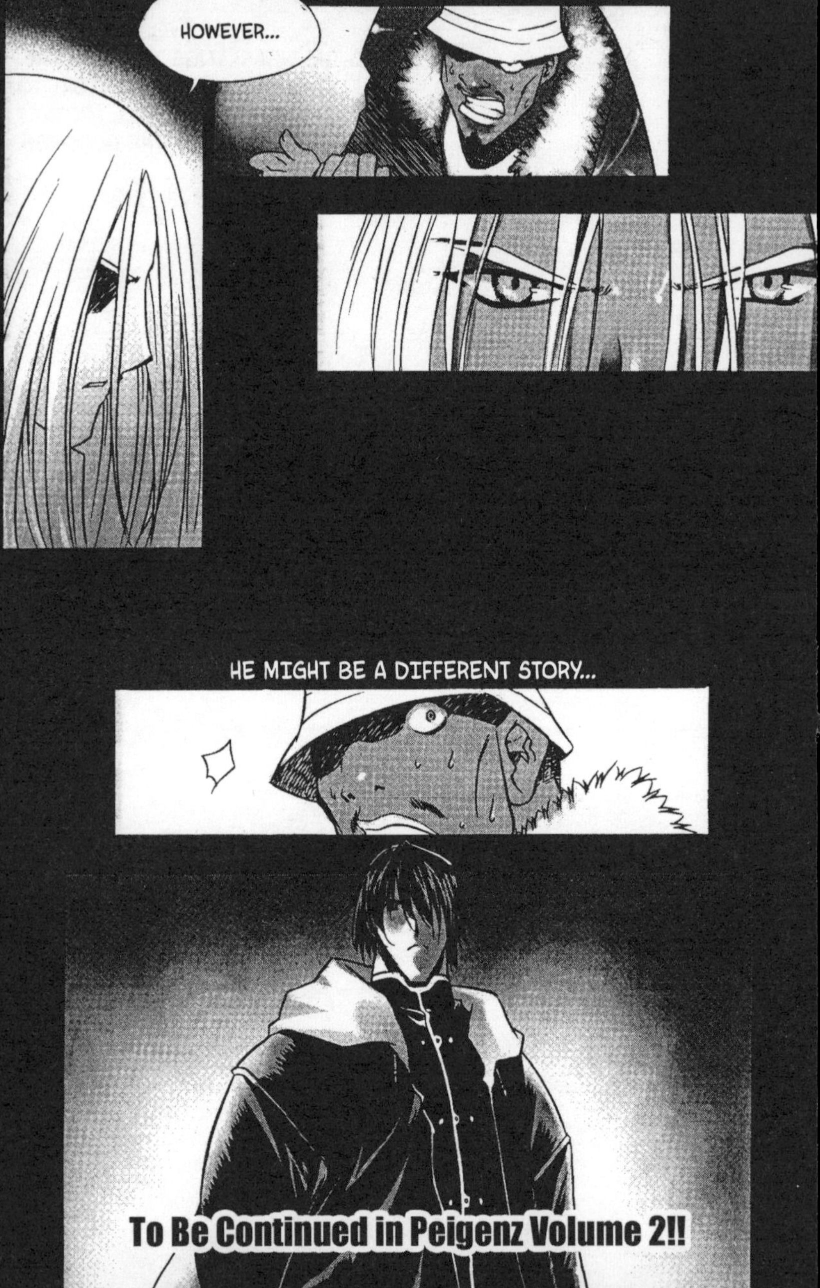
HOWEVER...
HE MIGHT BE A DIFFERENT STORY...
To Be Continued in Peigenz Volume 2!!

comics ONE www.ComicsOne.com

Infinity Studios
www.infinitystudioz.com

Péigenz 1

Art by Park Sung Woo
Story by Suh Gwong Hyun

English Version First Print
July 2004

Produced by

Comics One
www.comicsone.com

&

Infinity Studios
www.infinitystudioz.com

48531 Warm Springs, Blvd. #408
Fremont, CA 94539

6331 Fairmount Ave. Suite #1
El Cerrito, CA 94530

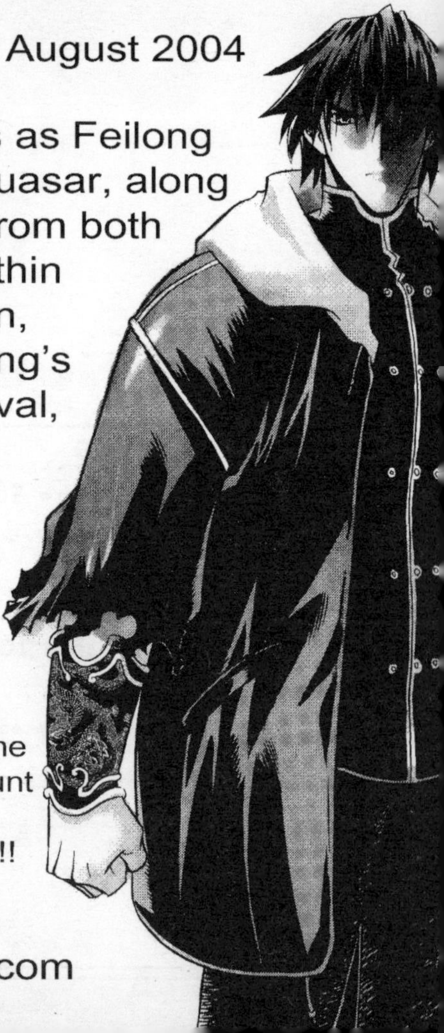

Péigenz

まにいD─ド
MANIAC ROAD

SHINSUKE KURIHASHI

©SHINSUKE KURIHASHI

This is a comedy about three sisters who in their attemtps to run an old run dow electronics store in the backstreets of Akihabara, they hire the resourceful Takezo This young man quickly refashions the store into the perfect shopping ground fo Japanese "otaku" (those who absolutely crave manga and Japanese animation). Wit its finger on the pulse of the modern-day otaku, this hip comedy will hilariously an stylishly thrust you into the eclectic world of Japanese pop culture.

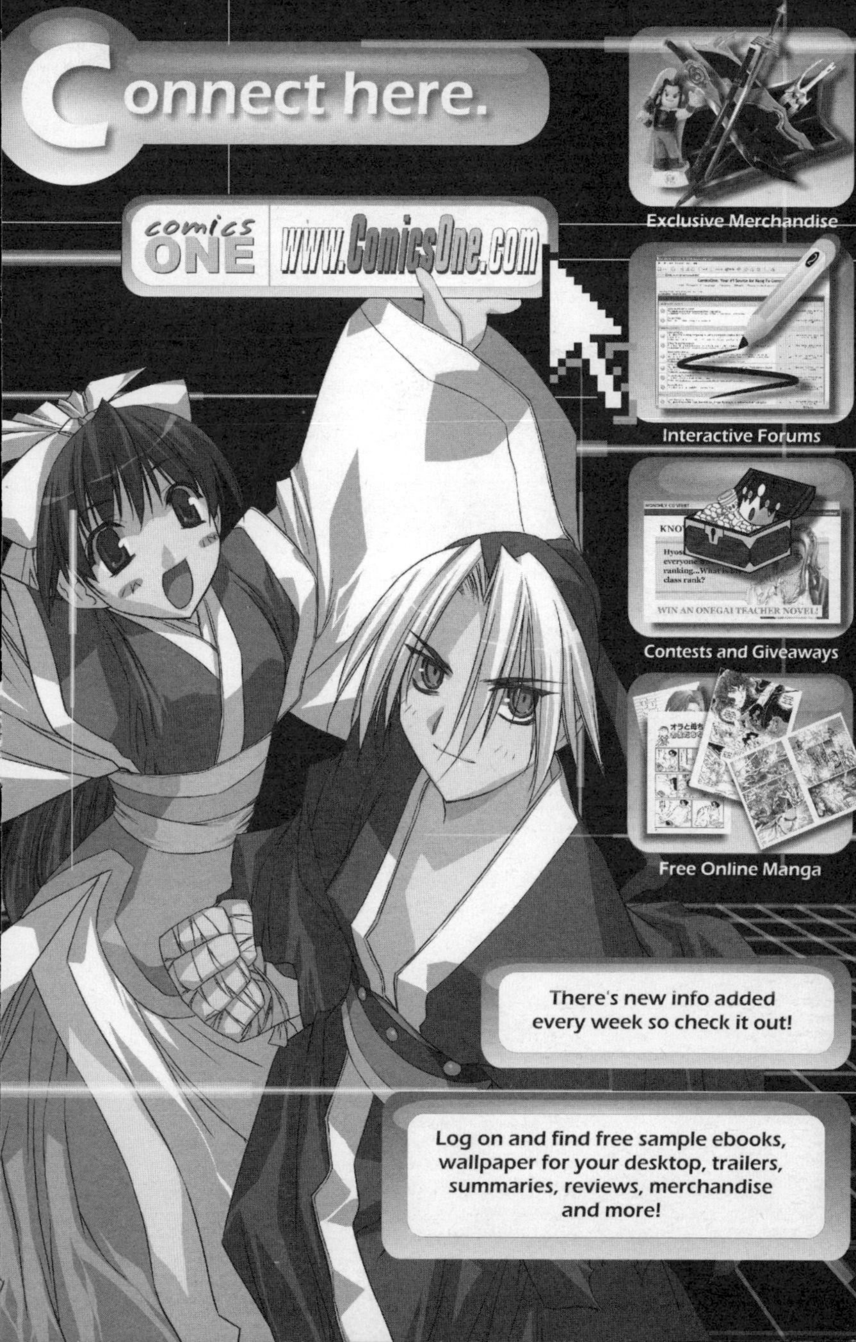
Connect here.
comics ONE
www.ComicsOne.com
Exclusive Merchandise
Interactive Forums
WIN AN ONEGAI TEACHER NOVEL!
Contests and Giveaways
Free Online Manga
There's new info added every week so check it out!
Log on and find free sample ebooks, wallpaper for your desktop, trailers, summaries, reviews, merchandise and more!